The Rules of Success

This book is about the rules of long-term professional success. The international study on which this book is based suggests that success is, above all, one thing: the quest for a combination of happiness and satisfaction, coupled with economic independence. However, the data also suggest that the definition of success varies significantly from person to person. And furthermore, it seems like success is not an objective quality, but at least partly it results from a process of comparison with a peer group – which means in turn that the selection of your peer group is crucial for your perceived level of success in life. The author argues that, in fact, certain success factors do exist and that they are fewer in number than one might think. But above all, if we look thoroughly at the lives of truly successful people, it soon becomes apparent that success primarily has to do with overcoming setbacks, failure and crisis. This ability to effectively process adversity is also known as resilience. Because of its criticality for success this concept is discussed in greater depth using the FiRE model (Factors improving Resilience Effectiveness) as a structure. This concept has been developed by the author through many years of research. It differs from existing models due to its holistic approach including analysing different disciplines of science such as biology, medicine, brain research, epigenetics, sociology, psycho-neuro-immunology etc.

Karsten Drath is an entrepreneur, coach, author and speaker. He is a managing partner of Leadership Choices, one of the leading providers of executive development in Europe.

The Rules of Success

How Managers Can Overcome
Setbacks and Grow

Karsten Drath

Routledge
Taylor & Francis Group

LONDON AND NEW YORK

First published 2019
by Routledge
2 Park Square, Milton Park, Abingdon, Oxon OX14 4RN

and by Routledge
711 Third Avenue, New York, NY 10017

Routledge is an imprint of the Taylor & Francis Group, an informa business

British Library Cataloguing-in-Publication Data
A catalogue record for this book is available from the British Library

Library of Congress Cataloging-in-Publication Data
Names: Drath, Karsten, author.
Title: The rules of success: how managers can overcome setbacks and grow / Karsten Drath.
Description: Abingdon, Oxon; New York, NY: Routledge, 2018. | Includes bibliographical references.
Identifiers: LCCN 2018006797 | ISBN 9780815395669 (hardback) | ISBN 9780815395676 (pbk.)
Subjects: LCSH: Executives—Psychology. | Management—Psychological aspects. | Resilience (Personality trait) | Success in business.
Classification: LCC HD38.2 .D73 2018 | DDC 658.4/09—dc23
LC record available at https://lccn.loc.gov/2018006797

ISBN: 978-0-8153-9566-9 (hbk)
ISBN: 978-0-8153-9567-6 (pbk)
ISBN: 978-1-351-18330-7 (ebk)

Typeset in Times New Roman
by codeMantra

Printed and bound by CPI Group (UK) Ltd, Croydon, CR0 4YY

For our children, who are spreading their wings
in search of happiness and success in life.

Contents

Illustrations

Figures

Tables

Foreword

I was delighted when Karsten reached out to me asking whether I would be interested in writing a foreword for his latest book on the topic of success. I have known Karsten through my work at the Center for Creative Leadership for more than five years and his previous book on resilience has been integrated into much of the work that we do at the Center and his work has touched many lives. Karsten is a no-nonsense kind of guy. He bases his writing on empirical research and delivers key messages without any sugar coating. So I was intrigued to hear what he would have to say in his new book called *The Rules of Success*.

Striving for success is an innate part of human life. We have evolved as a species as a result of our instincts for survival and our quest to become better and stronger. Many of the key inflexion points in our evolution have been instigated by individuals and teams that have been driven by an obsessive determination to achieve the unachievable and to think the unimaginable. Our evolution as a species has been dependent upon our ability to overcome adversities at an individual level, at a group level, at a national level and at a societal level.

As a business leader, I look for people that are driven by success in whatever shape, form or meaning that may have. As Karsten illustrates in this book, to be successful, one needs to be able to overcome adversity. Some people are more effective than others at this and getting a better understanding of the characteristics of successful individuals may help leaders to identify and pull together teams that will drive impact throughout their respective organisations.

As a father of two children, a husband to my wife, the youngest of six siblings, the son of immigrant parents, a leader of an organisation and a member of society, success has many different faces in my life.

My childhood was typical for the son of immigrants who moved to the United Kingdom in the early 70s, either fleeing from rogue nations or simply in search of a better life. I have many happy memories of my childhood and was raised in a caring, loving environment where both my parents tried hard to shield us from the financial hardships that we faced as a family endeavouring to settle into a new world with very little means. Living in a community where everyone seemed to be facing the same challenges and had the same resources available to them, I recall from an early age being intrigued about why some families seemed to do better than others, who was driving a bigger or newer car, who lived on the streets with semi-detached houses with front doors that did not reach straight out onto the pavement, as many of the terraced houses did. As a child, for me success was measured by comparing material belongings and was linked to social status. As a child, being successful meant having more.

I also realised from an early age, that having more meant working harder. There were no freebies in my childhood, no distant wealthy relatives that might leave an inheritance, no exotic holidays, no "once in a lifetime" presents under the Christmas tree. What I did have though, was a warm, loving, caring family, lots of laughter and freedom to explore. Until my teens, this was enough and it was only as I began to see the world through the lens of a wide-eyed teenager who wanted to conquer the world that I realised that it would take superhuman efforts to break away from the underprivileged social economic status that I had been born into. Being successful, whatever that meant, was my key to a new life.

In the early days of my newly found quest for success, I relied on working harder. I started playing tennis and working harder translated into spending more time on the practice courts. I was very competitive, had a hunger to win that I could sense was much stronger than most of the other kids I was practising with. Most of whom had private coaching lessons and a tennis court in their backyards. Driven by the injustice of the "haves" and "have nots", I knew that I had to work harder, be more focused, be stronger. I had to level the playing field. To be successful, I had to be competitive.

As I moved into the early stages of my professional life, the primary objective of working hard and being competitive was to move up the career ladder. I had decided at quite an early stage in my career that I wanted to gain experiences in different settings, different industries and in different roles. It was almost as if I was addicted to the thrill of proving that I could take on any challenge that was thrown at me. By this time, working long hours and with a high degree of intensity was normal. I found it difficult to switch off and was obsessed with delivering business results at any cost. I made many personal sacrifices and found myself attracted to organisations that were highly performance-driven. This served me well. How many organisations do not want people that are hard-working and obsessed with delivering business results? I was moving up the career ladder and I was successful.

Having just turned 50, I feel I have entered a new phase in my life. My children are both healthy, I have achieved a level of financial stability that allows me to reflect more on what I want to do and why I want to do it. For sure, I still have a strong competitive streak and a strong work ethic.

But for me, success is no longer measured by wealth and status. As I search for a deeper meaning in my own life, the concept of success has new parameters. Whilst as a business leader I am determined to drive business results, success is more about the way in which I deliver these results. Living the life I want to live with the values I believe in and the convictions that I have. Success is becoming more about the impact I can have on the world and how I can help others around me. I have nothing left to prove to anyone, except those people that I love and cherish.

This book is a great resource for your personal reflection on what success means to you.

Hamish Madan
Vice President, Managing Director,
Center for Creative Leadership, Brussels

Preface

This book is about the rules of success. The Oxford Dictionary, still deemed to be the authority on the English language today, defines success as the positive outcome of an effort or the attainment of fame, wealth, or social status. However, the international study conducted for this book suggests that this definition varies drastically both from person to person and also from one phase of life to another. So, how can success, or long-term professional success, to put it more precisely, be measured and made tangible? This quickly gives rise to the question: successful compared to whom? In summary, our study suggests that success is, above all, one thing: the quest for an equilibrium of happiness and satisfaction, coupled with a level of economic independence which is in line with a peer group. The link to the peer group seems to be essential because, as social animals, we feel successful only in comparison to others. Success, to most people that we have talked to, is in the end an agent for social status but also eventually life satisfaction.

What looks easy at first sight becomes a bit more complex and relative as we start zooming into the topic. As they say, wealth comes from having much or needing little. How can this kind of success be achieved? Is there just one magic recipe, known to only a few, composed of various ingredients that guarantee success? Is it only because of hard work? Or your genius? Maybe successful people are just lucky or somehow know how to design a successful career by making the right choices? Maybe they just happen to know the right people! What role does your gender or social background play? Or does even your genetic code or your personality play a role, and if so, which? Perhaps it is the other way around, and success is not determined by what positive characteristics you have, but rather by which negative personality attributes you lack. Or is it perhaps your ability to lead others? The answer is: all these aspects play a role but sometimes to a surprising extent. And this is yet not the full story. Success is not only seen in comparison to others but also according to the rules of a particular environment or context. This means that one person may be extremely successful as an entrepreneur, but may still end up failing to climb up the corporate ladder. On the contrary, a very successful senior executive in a consulting firm who has excelled in climbing up the hierarchy over the years may find himself on the brink of bankruptcy when changing careers and embarking on a start-up endeavour.

If we study successful people, it soon becomes apparent that success is not only relative, it also looks different from the outside than it feels on the inside. What looks like smooth sailing for the general public, for the individual very often means a lot of setbacks, disappointments and failures which need to be overcome. Above all, this quality seems to be the most important one: in our work as executive coaches, we find that success primarily has to do with the ability to overcome adversity. However, this brings us to the next question. Assuming this is true, which skills or strategies enable people to overcome difficult situations, and more importantly, which of them can be taken on board?

In this book, I advance the hypothesis that these contributory factors to success do, in fact, exist and that, if we focus on those we can actually influence, they are fewer in number than one might think. Some of them may come as a surprise to you. The good news is that the majority of skills behind these contributory factors to success can be acquired, as I will demonstrate by means of a number of different studies and practical models.

I hope you will find this book to be an inspiring read.

Karsten Drath
Heidelberg, November 2017

Acknowledgements

Book-writing is a team sport even if it does not look like it. This book would not have been possible without the support of a number of people, whom I would like to take this occasion to thank. First and foremost, there is my family. My wife Carolin as well as Kara, Tabea, Hannah and Samuel. And also Nournours, our dog, who is my running mate. They are the foundation of everything I do and give my life a whole lot of meaning. Furthermore, I would like to thank my team Petra Dehn and Nadège Prack who always keep the operations running while I am in my "writing cave". Also thanks to Lars Maertins and Celline Cullum who have been crucial in editing the manuscript. Further, I would like to thank Rolf Pfeiffer and Uwe Achterholt, my fellow managing partners at Leadership Choices, who again covered my back without grumbling. The same is true for my colleague Thomas Plingen who has taken over the lead of the resilience team within our company and is keeping everything together. And last but not least, I would like to thank friends and colleagues like Harri Morgenthaler, Stefanie Arnold and Volker Schuler for their companionship. Exchanging ideas with you is very important for me.

About the author

Karsten Drath is an entrepreneur, coach, author and keynote speaker. He is one of the managing partners of Leadership Choices. He has a passion for learning and for personal growth. In his life he has been a carpenter, engineer, economist, business consultant, manager, entrepreneur, coach and psychotherapist. After working for 16 years as a manager in global industrial corporations and business consulting companies, today he works internationally as a sought-after expert in the field of executive and organisational resilience. He lives near Heidelberg with his patchwork family.

Contact: karsten.drath@leadership-choices.com

About Leadership Choices

Leadership Choices is one of the leading providers of executive development in Europe. As a professional services firm with partners in six countries, Leadership Choices specialises in supporting executives, their teams and their entire organisations to be more effective in handling today's challenging market environments. The team of Leadership Choices is composed of former high-profile managers in international positions, who have made a conscious decision to become trained and certified executive coaches.

 leadership choices

1 What exactly is success?

What is the secret of long-term professional success? Is your professional success merely a matter of good fortune, destiny, a logical consequence of your social background, the result of outstanding intellectual abilities and hard work, or is it possibly even pre-programmed genetically? What can we learn in this respect from successful managers and entrepreneurs, and how can this be put into practice? And what is actually the price to be paid for being successful? What are the factors that hinder and impede success? This book addresses precisely these kinds of questions and provides answers that were drawn from various areas of research and complemented by our experience in working with several hundred managers. The results of a study carried out on over 200 managers, entrepreneurs and employees from various English- and German-speaking countries (see Figure 1.0.1) have also been incorporated into this book. The study participants, who were recruited from a wide range of sectors, were asked questions related to success and failure, and about how they had dealt with their own setbacks.

Anyone wishing to explore the rules of success must first of all determine what success and, more specifically, what professional success is. This might, at first glance, seem easy. But, if we take a closer look, a different impression arises. Success might, for instance, be described as the achievement of goals or the sum of right decisions taken. Does this already capture its essence?

Figure 1.0.1 Overview survey: career level and socialisation.
Source: Survey by Karsten Drath Dec 2015–Jan 2016.

And above all: Are these definitions universally applicable? In the field of psychology, success is broken down into objective and subjective aspects:

- Objective aspects are recognisable to outside observers and are based on social norms and expectations. They include money, influence and status.
- By contrast, subjective aspects of success are geared more towards the individual's values and convictions, including, for instance, self-fulfilment and the purpose or meaning behind their actions.

In the research undertaken for this book, the participants were asked to choose their own personal top 10 criteria for professional success from a list of 26 objective and subjective success factors. The results were very interesting and clear differences could be observed depending on the participant's career level. In order to simplify things, I have broken down the individual evaluations into the following clusters:

- Objective factors: status, power, money
- Subjective factors: development, balance, time
- Subjective factors: meaning, creativity, growth.

What is noticeable about the objective factors (see Figure 1.0.2) is that the importance of standing out from the crowd was evidently related to a manager's career level. It, therefore, seems that once the need for status has been

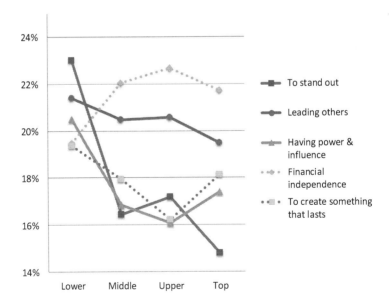

Figure 1.0.2 Objective factors: status, power, money.
Source: Survey by Karsten Drath Dec 2015–Jan 2016.

satisfied, this aspect quickly fades into the background. The same is true for wielding power and influence.

However, the aspect of being financially independent gains in importance. It grows steadily, the further someone advances in their career. Even among top managers, it is still considered to be the most important criterion, along with being happy.

Leading other people plays a consistently important role at all levels. At the upper management levels, the factor of promoting other people is also considered to be important, as we shall see.

To create something enduring is still important for managers at the lower end of the career ladder. The main focus here is probably not the company as a whole, but something more modest like a small team. As a manager's career progresses, the importance of this aspect declines, only to increase again in top management. This might be explained by the need for managers to advance through the different levels, where for many years they are expected to merely execute orders until they are finally able to become movers and shakers.

When it comes to the subjective criteria for success regarding meaning, creativity and growth (see Figure 1.0.3), it is noticeable that the idealistic goal of doing good is regarded as much more important at the lower end of the career ladder than at the top.

Another aspect becomes apparent too: namely that the abstract dimension of finding your calling and meaning diminishes as a manager's career

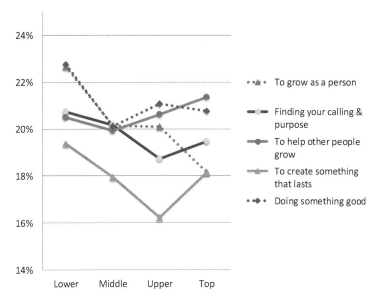

Figure 1.0.3 Subjective factors: meaning, creativity, growth.
Source: Survey by Karsten Drath Dec 2015–Jan 2016.

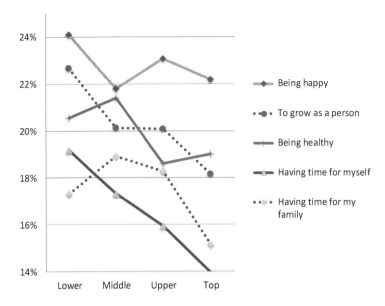

Figure 1.0.4 Subjective factors: development, balance, time.
Source: Survey by Karsten Drath Dec 2015–Jan 2016.

advances, whilst the concrete dimension of promoting other people becomes increasingly important.

The aspect of personal growth declines as a manager moves up the career ladder. This might have to do with the fact that high-profile managers tend to see themselves as "being in their prime", whilst managers who are at the start of their careers still very much feel the need to improve their skills.

With regard to subjective factors concerning development, balance and time (see Figure 1.0.4), the distinct impression arises that there is a growing focus on these aspects in the course of a manager's career.

Both the importance of being healthy and aspects such as having time for yourself or time for the family sometimes diminish markedly in relation to a person's career level.

I already mentioned the waning significance of the aspects of personal growth. It is only the abstract wish of being happy that never ceases to be important.

From this we might conclude that, in the course of a person's career, happiness is increasingly sought in connection with promoting other people, financial independence and creating something enduring, while at the beginning of their careers managers will tend to equate happiness with standing out from the crowd, personal growth and doing good.

It was also established that there is a fundamental shift in managers' expectations regarding work–life balance as they advance towards top management.

This may be because their children are grown up and are more independent, and they no longer have to spend as much time at home. However, it is more likely that it is those people, for whom getting the work–life balance right is not a priority, who choose a career in management in the first place.

We can generally conclude that getting the right combination of subjective and objective success criteria is beneficial for executives from all levels when it comes to achieving professional success. Professional success evidently has to do with the simultaneous achievement of personal and social goals. Yet how high the benchmark is set very much depends on your career level and what phase of life you are in. By nature, social goals are relative, in other words they are oriented towards other people. As the proverb goes: "Being rich means either having a lot, or needing little." Therefore, how much material wealth is needed and how high living standards should be for an individual to see herself as successful in relation to her peer group depend on a variety of factors. For one thing, it is decisive which peer group she chooses to be in. And by this we mean the group of people who are in a similar life situation which she wishes to belong to. It is an inherent part of being a social being that leads us humans to want to be part of a peer group. In the evolution of humankind, this has literally been vital and still is today, albeit from a social point of view.

EXAMPLE

While the relevant peer group for students will be fellow students, it will initially be other job starters for professionals, followed by colleagues and other managers later on. Neighbours and friends may also constitute a peer group. Millionaires compare themselves to other affluent people, film stars to other celebrities, and CEOs to other managing directors.

Apart from the peer group itself, the position one believes oneself to be in or would like to be in, relative to this constructed social group, is also important. Are you striving to be in a group, but don't yet see yourself there? Or are you part of a group and do you want to remain part of it? Or do you want to rise above the group? The reason we strive for such a position is undoubtedly based on our individual personality traits. Other aspects include, for instance, the local environment we are moving in. What is regarded as a higher living standard in the North Hessian or Lower Franconian provinces is not even considered to be the lower average in cities such as Frankfurt, Munich and Hamburg and their suburbs. So, let us take note that the supposedly objective aspects of success are, in fact, non-existent, since they are geared towards the social and regional environment in which we move.

From this perspective, individual and subjective aspects, such as satisfaction and self-realisation, can be seen as much more objective parameters. Yet, here too, the respective peer group plays a role. So, depending on the peer group, comparing himself with his colleagues might turn a slightly overweight but sporty manager, who is generally happy with his body, into a complete sports nut or into a panting steam engine.

Perhaps we would all feel much more successful and be happier if we compared ourselves less to other people. However, measuring the self against others is a modus operandi of the human mind, and in some ways it can be helpful, too. The inspiration you feel about someone else's achievements can increase your motivation to improve your own life. The recognition that your abilities are a notch above someone else's can deliver a boost to your self-esteem. But comparisons can be harmful when they leave you feeling chronically inferior or depressed. Seeing that the path to improvement is attainable is key. You're better off comparing yourself to someone a rung or two above you than to someone at the very top of the ladder. Loretta Breuning, author of *Habits of a Happy Brain*, recommends engaging in "conscious downward comparison". For instance, Breuning says, compare yourself to your ancestors. "You don't have to drink water full of microbes. You don't have to tolerate violence on a daily basis. It'll remind you that despite some frustrations, you have a fabulous life."

Sonja Lyubormirsky, a psychologist at the University of California, Riverside and the author of *The How of Happiness*, notes that "people who are happy use themselves for internal evaluation." It's not that they don't notice upward comparisons, she says, but they don't let such comparisons affect their self-esteem and they stay focused on their own improvement. "A happy runner compares himself to his last run, not to others who are faster."

The participants in our study were also asked which characteristics and skills were needed to achieve long-lasting success in their career. From 30 factors, they were to choose the top 10 which, in their opinion, formed the basis of a successful career. Figure 1.0.5 shows the attributes and skills which, in the eyes of these top managers, play a central role. Since not all of the factors can be clearly distinguished from one another, e.g. *convincing appearance* from *inspiring others*, only the top 15 factors are shown here.

As was to be expected, interpersonal aspects such as empathy, listening to others, making a convincing appearance and inspiring others were considered to be very important by the interviewees. Equally evident was the fact that having specialist knowledge and being intelligent were among the most highly rated attributes.

What was perhaps less evident, by contrast, was the fact that attributes such as the *need to lead* and the *ability to assert oneself* were not regarded as an essential requirement for being a successful manager.

As I will attempt to show in the following chapters by means of a number of examples, professional success has much more to do with being able to successfully and constructively master personal setbacks and crises.

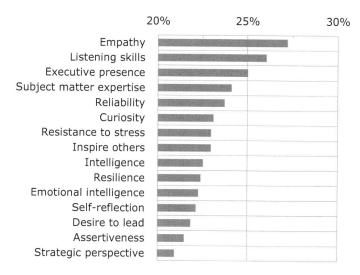

Figure 1.0.5 Essential qualities and skills required for long-lasting professional success.
Source: Survey by Karsten Drath Dec 2015–Jan 2016.

However, this is already evident at this stage, as resilience and self-reflection are rated by the study participants as being among the top attributes of success.

1.1 Success looks different on the inside than it does on the outside

Think of highly successful people: Who spontaneously comes to mind? Perhaps it is the names of well-known managers, entrepreneurs or politicians that crop up first. Perhaps you think of celebrity sportsmen or stars from the music, television or film industries.

Seen from the outside through the eyes of the media, success usually appears to be rather simple and straightforward (see Figure 1.1.1).

This is because we have the tendency to draw conclusions about someone's past based on their current level of success. We somehow assume that it was always clear that a certain person was destined for success or not. This phenomenon is known in the field of psychology as the *recency effect*, that is, current events, such as a person's level of popularity, shape our expectations and recollections of events that lie further back, for instance at the start of a career. In our work as executive coaches, we have worked with many thousands of managers who can clearly be regarded as being successful. And I can assure you that behind closed doors, an individual's own view of their personal success across the board is a very different one. The external perception of these people, who are considered

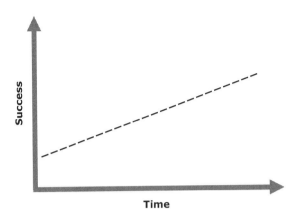

Figure 1.1.1 Individual success perceived from the outside.

to "have made it", does not correspond to their own perception. It is usually current crises, obstacles or setbacks or ones that have already been mastered that predominate, and that either threaten their success or call it into question.

EXAMPLE

Jack Ma, whose actual name is Ma Yun, was to become the founder of Alibaba. With a net worth of USD 47.5 billion, he is today one of the wealthiest persons in Asia. However, he was not always that successful. Before the rise of the internet he applied for 30 different jobs and got rejected by them all. This included a career as a policeman and a job at KFC. In interviews he frequently reports that "twenty-four people went for the job. Twenty-three were accepted. I was the only guy who got rejected." In addition, he applied ten times for Harvard and got rejected every single time. In 1994, Ma heard about the internet and he went to the US one year later. During his first encounter with an internet browser he searched for the word "beer". Although he found information related to beer from many countries, he was surprised to find none from China. The same was true for general information about China. So, he and a friend created a website related to China. He launched the website at 9:40 AM and by 12:30 PM he had received emails from some Chinese wishing to know about him. Supposedly, this is when Ma realised the potential of the internet. In April 1995, Ma, his wife and a friend raised USD 20,000 and started their first company: *China Yellow Pages*. Within three years, his company had made 5,000,000 Chinese Yuan which was equivalent to USD 800,000. The rest is history.

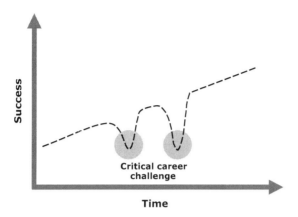

Figure 1.1.2 Individual success in terms of one's own self-perception.

The managers do not take their success for granted or even as God-given, but rather see it as something that could be jeopardised from one day to the next. Most of them have experienced numerous setbacks and critical career situations which certainly had the potential to put an abrupt end to their streak of success (see Figure 1.1.2).

EXAMPLE

James Dyson founded Dyson Ltd, a British technology company, in 1987. He reports that he and his team had built a total of 5126 prototypes of the world-famous bagless vacuum cleaner during their start-up phase. None of them would work. However, prototype number 5127 finally did.

1.2 Success means overcoming critical career situations

According to research conducted by the Center for Creative Leadership, CCL in short, a global provider of leadership development programmes, around two-thirds of all managers in Western, industrialised nations experience a crisis, a downturn or at least a dark period at some point in their careers, which they are happy to conceal later in the accounts given. At best, they are given a sideways promotion, but in most cases they are downgraded, lose power and influence – and, not uncommonly, their jobs too.

During the research undertaken for this book, I asked nearly 100 managers about their experiences with critical career situations of this nature, that is, about developments that had had the potential to jeopardise, damage or end their professional development, for instance through dismissal, annulment, stagnation or degradation, as a result of restructuring, staff cuts, severe conflicts, political constellations, the loss of a mentor or mobbing. The results confirmed and even reinforced CCL's assumptions. Of those questioned, as many as 95% had personally experienced such situations or felt threatened by them. On average, the managers interviewed had themselves experienced 2.8 of these critical situations. And they assumed that nearly 60% of the managers in their immediate environment, i.e. in their peer group, had also experienced critical career situations.

There are many reasons why managers will experience setbacks or unexpectedly reach a critical point in their careers. In most cases, the reasons have to do with ever-faster changes in many companies, which increasingly lead to new constellations of teams, colleagues, superiors, friends and fiends – events which an individual has no control over. Mentors leave the company, a division is restructured or merged with another one, a topic is suddenly no longer considered to be strategic, the new boss wants to place her own candidate, a manager's existing personal network becomes less important after that manager is promoted to a position in a different function and so forth.

The facts speak a clear language: more than two-thirds of all managers are affected by this. Long-term professional success, therefore, clearly has a lot to do with handling such critical situations well and not allowing oneself to be unsettled, embittered or led astray by them.

Some fail, though only superficially, in these unavoidable developments on the playing field. The reasons for a professional crisis are often, at least partially, to be found in the characteristics and conduct of the respective manager. As part of their personality, these managers have developed thought and behaviour patterns which cause them to go off the rails. Their self-management is not sufficient to adequately control this pattern. Instead, the opposite is frequently true and, under stress and pressure, they succumb to and are guided by these patterns. In the chapter on executive derailers I will address this in more detail.

During the research for this book, one of the things I asked managers was: Who, in their opinion, was responsible for their critical career situations? Who was to blame for this crisis? Was it solely the misanthropic or devious boss? Or is there also a part they can ascribe to themselves? The results revealed a high level of self-awareness among those questioned. High-ranking executives thought that 50–70% of the responsibility for such situations lay with themselves, while executives from lower and middle management only estimated their own share of responsibility to be 10–50%. Nobody thought that they bore no responsibility for their career crisis. As mentioned before, long-term professional success has primarily to do with handling your own career crises well. Yet if a substantial share of the responsibility for these crises lies with oneself, then it will only be possible for a manager to overcome a crisis if he is able to learn from his own experiences and mistakes. And this, in turn, requires self-reflection. Observing managers who have experienced long-term success reveals which characteristics might be useful for this.

Bibliography

Breuning, Loretta; Habits of a Happy Brain; Adams Media, Avon, USA, 2015.

Dotlich, David L.; Cairo, Peter C.; Why CEOs Fail; Wiley & Sons, Hoboken, USA, 2003.

Drath, Karsten; Spielregeln des Erfolgs: Wie Fuehrungskraefte an Rueckschlaegen wachsen; Haufe, Freiburg, Germany, 2016.

Lyubormirsky, Sonja; The How of Happiness; Piatkus, London, UK, 2010.

Webber, Rebecca; The Comparison Trap; Psychology Today, New York City, USA, 2017.

2 The foundations of success

What are the ingredients for long-lasting professional success? What do people have in common who have made it to the top? Some of these factors are in our area of influence, while others are not. Let's take a look at what can be seen as the foundations of long-lasting professional success. As such, these factors are mostly out of our control. However, they do play an important role when it comes to achieving success in one's career.

2.1 Can anyone make it to the top?

What role does the parental home actually play in terms of success? Are the children of successful and wealthy parents more likely to be successful and affluent themselves? Together with *Manager Magazin*, the private German business school WHU carried out a high-profile executive board study, published in 2015. Under the direction of Utz Schaeffer and Marko Reimer, the publicly available data of 633 managers, all of whom were executive board members of major companies, were compiled and complemented by an additional questionnaire on the managers' career paths. The aim was to test the findings of Michael Hartmann, a sociologist specialising in elite research. He stated and simultaneously criticised the fact that, for decades, four of every five top managers in Germany came from the elite top 3.5% of society, i.e. the German moneyed aristocracy. Schaeffer and Reimer's study showed, however, that nearly 80% of German executive board members did not actually come from the upper class (see Figure 2.1.1).

In concrete terms, around 14% of the top managers came from working-class families, that is, their parents were factory workers, for instance, as in the case of Siemens CEO Joe Kaeser, or farmers, as with Juergen Fitschen, Co-CEO of Deutsche Bank. They worked their way to the top, sometimes even without having a university degree, as in the case of Werner Wenning, the former CEO and current Chairman of the Supervisory Board at Bayer. 29% of the executive board members came from the middle class. This includes former VW Chairman of the executive board, Martin Winterkorn, and former CEO and current Chairman of the BMW Supervisory Board,

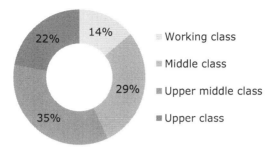

Figure 2.1.1 Social background of top managers.
Source: WHU Vorstandsstudie 2015; Prof. Utz Schaeffer and Dr. Marko Reimer.

Norbert Reithofer. The largest proportion of the German business elite (35%) came, in fact, from upper-middle-class parental homes, including for instance, Carsten Spohr, today's CEO at Lufthansa, whose father managed a construction company, or Margarete Haase, today's CFO at Deutz and Manager of the Year 2011. Her parents were wealthy meat manufacturers. What was most astonishing though was that only 22% of Germany's executive board members actually came from the upper class. This is just under half the share determined by Hartmann in 2002. It now seems equally possible for managers from all social levels to climb to the executive board level.

Why is this the case? What has led to this change? The authors of the study attribute the increasing permeability of management levels to greater pressure to perform and to be efficient, which is driven by the progressive consequences of globalisation and the acceleration of the business world, with the accompanying crises and uncertainties these bring. This, in turn, has reduced the importance of social background. Much-vaunted customs, in other words the ability to move easily on the social parquet and in the boardroom, are giving way to the importance of performance capability and the ability to be someone the workforce can identify with. We can safely assume that this trend will continue. Also, the children of top managers do not generally seek to follow in their parents' footsteps. Instead, they tend to be put off by the intense commitment and abundant sacrifices that are needed. According to Schaeffer's and Reimer's appraisal, this will continue to push the trend towards the lower social classes. However, it is also true that managers from the lower social strata have to work much harder and longer to reach the boardroom level (see Figure 2.1.2).

On average, working-class managers needed 12.6 years for this career path, whereas executives from upper-class backgrounds only took half the time – 6.3 years. This is often because working-class managers' school education does not progress evenly and, therefore, simply takes more time.

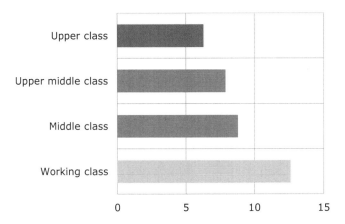

Figure 2.1.2 Number of years needed to reach the boardroom level.
Source: WHU Vorstandsstudie 2015; Prof. Utz Schaeffer and Dr. Marko Reimer.

EXAMPLE

This was the case for Ruediger Grube, the former CEO of Deutsche Bahn. His parents were farmers from northern Germany, who divorced when Grube was five years old. Grube went to a lower-level secondary school and then completed his intermediate school-leaving certificate against his mother's will. He was forced to repeat ninth grade because he had to help on the farm. He later completed an apprenticeship as an aircraft manufacturer at *Hamburger Flugzeugbau*, a Hamburg-based aircraft company belonging to the MBB group. Due to his commitment as an apprentice, he attracted the attention of the managing director who offered to pay for his university studies, which would otherwise have been completely unaffordable. He went on to obtain a doctorate and held various positions at MBB, DASA and Daimler. The rest is history.

Taking the bumpy road to the top is evidently a good lesson. Managers from lower social classes tend to show more perseverance, determination and resilience, as well as the ability not to be brought down by setbacks and other adversities. Furthermore, many are very extrovert, i.e. they find it easy and even enjoy becoming acquainted with unfamiliar people, which is of major importance in the business world. A high level of discipline and self-motivation are also needed, all character traits that most probably are already discernible in childhood and youth. Thus, 38% of the executives questioned stated that money was always scarce at home. 91% indicated that they worked alongside school and studies to earn money. Nearly 58% displayed a willingness to lead and inspire people early on, for instance as a class representative, a skill that is gaining importance in today's business world. The unanimous opinion of the executives questioned was that management has become more demanding these days. It is only possible to survive in today's competitive world if you can get your workforce to do more than work by the book or wait for instructions from above. After decades of process optimisation, restructuring and numerous rounds of redundancies, the employees' levels of motivation and independent thinking are becoming increasingly important for the company's long-term success in an uncertain market environment. Yet in order to facilitate this you must be able to get through to your employees on the emotional level.

2.2 The importance of your upbringing

As we have seen, everybody can in fact make it to the top, irrespective of what social strata they come from. However, if you come from a lower social class, your path is longer, harder and simply requires more persistence and resilience from you. Is there also a correlation between your upbringing and the amount of money you earn once you have made it to the top?

In a recent study, Daniel Laurison, a professor at Swarthmore College in Pennsylvania, and Sam Friedman of the London School of Economics, have found that equally high-qualified employees in London were paid less based on their social background. According to the study, professionals working in law, accounting and finance, whose parents did manual jobs or were unemployed, earned 20% less on average than their colleagues from upper-middle-class backgrounds (see Figure 2.2.1).

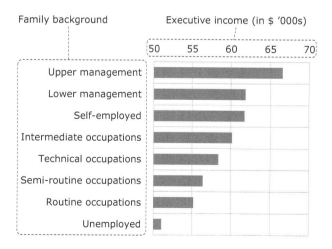

Figure 2.2.1 Impact of family background on income.
Source: Laurison and Friedman (2016).

EXAMPLE

Like many people at her law firm, which is headquartered in London, Claudine Adeyemi was a teenager when she decided to become a lawyer. But unlike her peers, she was homeless when she sat her A-levels at a state school, living in temporary bed and breakfast accommodation as a result of her mother's death and falling out with her father. Adeyemi reflects: "A lot of people I went to university with were of completely different backgrounds to me. I did not make many friends because I did not fit in very well." Many of her lawyer colleagues, she adds, made friends at university who later became their clients. "I don't have that." With regards to her career outlook she says, "I probably have to work three times as hard as other people, but I will embrace who I am. I hope it can be my unique selling point."

Although the aforementioned study focuses on the UK, it is complemented by research from Stanford University conducted in 2015. The key finding here was that the amount of money a manager makes can be roughly predicted by the wages his or her parents earned. The study found that children born into families which were in the top 10% of earners, typically made three times as much as the children of families who belonged to the bottom 10% of earners.

On the other hand, it was found that investment managers from low-income backgrounds consistently achieve better fund performance than colleagues from more wealthy backgrounds, according to a study conducted in 2016 in the USA by the National Bureau of Economic Research. The rationale is simple: because of the little support individuals from less-privileged backgrounds were getting in their career, only the most skilled and dedicated ones made it to actually managing a fund and showing the world their full potential.

EXAMPLE

Gerhard Schroeder never got to know his father either. He was raised in a working-class family regarded as "asocial". His mother was dependent on state support. Schroeder initially completed an apprenticeship as a retail merchant and then spent several years pursuing his intermediate and advanced secondary school education via the second-chance education path before going on to study law. Thirty-two years later he became Germany's seventh chancellor. He was popular with the media and able to move on the global diplomatic stage with the natural ease of a world leader.

This is further proof that our economic system is flawed and often unjust. Not all people receive similar levels of support. However, this is yet another reason why resilience is key when reaching for the top. And, while the statistics make a statement about the big picture, there are always individuals who beat the odds and inspire us to try the impossible.

2.3 Succeeding against the odds

There are plenty of examples that show how succeeding against the odds is clearly possible. We call this social mobility. It is the essence of the American dream: from dishwasher to millionaire. You set yourself a goal and work diligently and with tenacity towards it. You manage the setbacks you encounter along the way, focus on your long-term vision and resist temptations that may bring you off your course. In general, this is seen by many motivational authors and speakers as a sure way to success. However, modern research suggests that you can overdo it. If you fight too hard against a system which is not supporting you there is a price to pay. This is especially true when you don't take good care of yourself along the way. Gene Brody is a professor in paediatrics at the University of Georgia. In 2016, he and his team published a study that suggests that black adolescents from disadvantaged backgrounds, who have "a relentless determination to succeed", show a higher risk of developing diabetes later in life than control groups. The study looked at African American communities and focused in particular on people who had outgrown their peer groups either academically, professionally or financially. The personality trait that describes this kind of willingness to succeed is often referred to as grit or hardiness. It is seen as desirable by many. Common sense would suggest that climbing up the social ladder will eventually result in improved health, simply because a person who has a well-paid job is able to afford health insurance. However, many different studies suggest that quite the opposite is true. If people fight hard over a long period of time to improve their social status in a system that is not giving them the same opportunities as everybody else, their health will actually deteriorate.

The effect has become known as *John Henryism*. The term was coined by a young researcher named Sherman James in the 1980s after he met a man called John Henry Martin. Martin was born in 1907 into a poor working-class family. Throughout his life he had worked tirelessly to escape the system, and when he turned 40, he had finally managed to own 75 hectares of farmland. But in his next decade he began to suffer from hypertension, arthritis and a severe case of peptic ulcer which required the removal of nearly half his stomach.

After studying this case, James developed the so-called *John Henryism scale* to measure the high-effort coping of underprivileged people confronted with socioeconomic adversity. The questionnaire contained statements such as: "If things do not go the way I want, this makes me work even harder" or "I always had the feeling that I could make everything I wanted out of my life".

Meanwhile it has been found that *John Henryism* does not only apply to black people. Mahasin Mujahid, an assistant professor for public health at Berkeley, was able to show in a study published in 2016 that disadvantaged minorities in Finland are also more prone to having heart attacks if they score highly on the John Henryism scale. Why might this be? The theory which is shared by most researchers suggests that fighting relentlessly against an unfair system over many years increases the chronic stress level in the body, resulting for instance in inflammatory responses, impairment of the immune system and a tendency to suffer from cardiovascular diseases.

As I will describe in Section 6.3, *Resilient or tough?* there is a limit to toughness. If you exclusively focus on being tough then it is just a question of time before something becomes tougher than you. This applies here, too.

Being tough or hardy can be seen as a combination of a high level of self-discipline and low self-awareness (see Figure 2.3.1). You are determined to climb up the social ladder like John Henry Martin even if everybody else is trying to hold you down. However, you are so focused on reaching your goal that somehow you forget to reflect upon your own needs and take good care of yourself. Resilience, by contrast, is a combination of concentrated self-discipline and pronounced self-awareness. This means not only being diligent in working your way up, but also making sure that you are not feeling angry and stressed out all the time.

Research shows that simple practices like regularly talking about your emotions to others, especially when confronted with severe adversity, are actually very effective in reducing your likelihood of developing inflammatory reactions in the body or an impaired immune system.

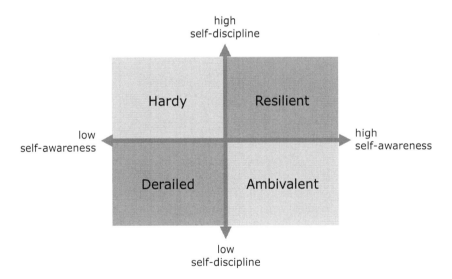

Figure 2.3.1 Resilience combines self-discipline with self-awareness.

When human body cells reproduce the expression of certain gene sequences, this is influenced by our lifestyle and, more specifically, our stress levels. A high level of chronic stress, caused by fighting social adversity over many years for instance, leads to the expression of gene sequences that favour inflammatory processes and reduce the immune system's effectiveness. These sequences are called CTRA (Conserved Transcriptional Response to Adversity). In 2015, Steve Cole from the University of California, Los Angeles, showed that elderly people, who frequently shared their emotions with others, had lower CTRA levels than those who kept everything to themselves, as a result perhaps of suffering from social isolation. The phenomenon could not be explained by other factors such as age, gender, ethnic origin or weight. This fascinating area of research is called *epigenetics*. While it is still rather new and many correlations have not yet been fully understood, different findings suggest that an increased level of self-awareness and self-care may have the potential to counterbalance the effect of prolonged negative stress. Hence, in order to truly succeed against the odds, meaning climbing up the social ladder and staying healthy at the same time, you not only need dedication and self-discipline but also the conscious practice of resilience, as opposed to merely "toughing it out".

2.4 The gender gap

Talking about the foundations of success in life, we also have to ask the question: What role does gender play in this? In the past I have always shied away from that question because I wanted to avoid triggering an emotionally loaded gender discussion. However, as the father of girls who will soon be entering the professional world, this question has finally become very relevant even for me.

Today, only 32 out of 500 companies on the *Fortune 500* index are run by women. While this is an all-time high since the ranking was first established in 1955, it is still only 6.4%. Frontrunners like *Facebook's* COO Sheryl Sandberg and *PepsiCo's* CEO Indra Nooyi clearly show that it is possible today for women to make it to the top, be it in the world of business or the world of politics, as female icons like the German chancellor Angela Merkel or Christine Lagarde, who heads the International Monetary Fund, demonstrate. However, the chances of success between the genders are not yet evenly distributed.

This is a pity, not only from a humanistic point of view but also from a purely economic standpoint. In 2017, Credit Suisse, not necessarily an institution known for its feminist tendencies, conducted a large study, which empirically showed that companies perform better over the years if at least one board member is female (see Figure 2.4.1). The bank's research arm has created a database that tracks the gender mix of some 28,000 executives in board positions and below at 3000 companies in 40 countries around the world on an ongoing basis. This is probably the largest database of its

Figure 2.4.1 Link between financial performance and executive gender mix.
Source: Credit Suisse Gender 3000.

kind. The report then compared these data to the companies' financial results. The findings are striking: companies with more female executives have
higher returns on equity, higher valuations, better stock performance and
higher payouts of dividends.

Although the correlation is very strong, it does not make a statement
about whether companies are in fact performing better because they have
more women in executive positions or because better companies simply employ more female top managers. Anyhow, it seems to make good business
sense to improve these numbers.

But what is special about female career success? How do they make it
to the top? In a recent piece of research conducted by the professional services company Korn Ferry in 2017, 57 female CEOs were studied to de-
code their recipe for success. To a degree, the study confirmed the obvious:
much like men, 40% of female executives started their careers coming from
a more technical or scientific background, while 20% came from business
or economics. A large degree, 40%, had other backgrounds. Interestingly,
not one female executive had a background in HR which today is still the
most female-dominated business area. However, women worked harder
and longer than their male peers to get to the same positions. The female
CEOs worked in a higher number of roles, functions, companies and industries than men running companies of a comparable size, which gave them a
broader experience base and a more diverse set of skills. Just like their male
counterparts, the female executives scored high in personality traits such

as courage, resilience and tolerance for ambiguity. Many female careers entailed critical career situations because the executives readily embarked upon crisis management mandates with a high probability of failure – and they survived. The learnings from these tough times proved invaluable for many during their later career steps. However, about two-thirds of the female CEOs never realised their potential to get into their top position until someone else gave them a gentle push. In these cases, a mentor or executive sponsor proved to be crucial for their career success.

But some of the study's findings were also less obvious. The scores for humility were much higher in women than in men. Compared to their male counterparts, female executives felt less in complete control regarding the destiny of an organisation and were more appreciative of the contribution of others. More than two-thirds of the studied CEOs were more driven by a sense of purpose and community than by merely gaining power and influence. The fact that what they did was connected to creating something which they perceived as deeply fulfilling and meaningful helped them to overcome the proverbial glass ceiling in their organisations. So, female top executives seem to score higher than men in some of the traits which are connected with effective leadership in a world which is becoming increasingly complex, ambiguous and fast moving. Aspects like humility and collaboration as well as a focus on purpose, values and culture are in fact connected with the longevity and the sustainable market performance of an organisation. Could this in fact explain why companies with more female executives outperform the corporations which are led by only men?

2.5 The role of warm relationships

Let's get to another foundation of success. One of the most exciting and insightful studies of human development is the so-called Grant study which began in 1938. Well, to be precise, it is actually a study about male development. Over a duration of 75 years it has followed 268 male Harvard undergraduates (women were not allowed at Harvard back then), measuring a large range of psychological, anthropological and physical factors to find out what contributes to a happy and successful life. Many of the study participants had successful careers, one of them being the former US President John F. Kennedy.

In his book *Triumphs of Experience* George Vaillant, who directed the study for more than three decades, describes his key findings. According to this team's research, the quality of relationships during childhood, adolescence and adult life was strongly correlated to success and happiness in life. As an example, the peak salaries of the 58 study participants who had the highest values for "warm relationships" in their adult lives, were on average $141,000 higher than the income of the 31 men who had the lowest scores in the same domain. That is a lot of money as I am sure you will agree. This means that having found the right partner in life is one of the strongest predictors of sustainable wealth and success. For the sake of illustration, the former group was also three times more likely to have achieved professional success worthy of inclusion in *Who's Who*. Also, a strong link to childhood relationships could be found. Study participants who reported "warm" childhood relationships with their mothers still earned an average of $87,000 more a year than men whose mothers were described as uncaring. This correlation is pretty impressive considering the number of decades that pass between adolescence and when the peak salary is reached, which is typically between the ages of 55 and 60. While the data obviously have a strong gender bias due to the design of the original study, it can safely be assumed that the importance of warm and caring relationships for long-lasting professional success is not substantially different for women.

2.6 The old question: nature or nurture?

Let's take a look at an even deeper level. What does long-term success actually have to do with a manager's personality, i.e. with their basic behavioural preferences? Is success even logged in a genetic code? What might at first appear absurd, is not, in actual fact. A study conducted on twins in 2012 revealed that whether or not a certain person will ever occupy a leadership position can be determined to a level of about 25% by the expression of the genotype RS4950. But it is not our genes alone that make us who we are. An individual's personality is determined to a level of about 50% by their genetic predisposition and also by the formative stage of their life, i.e. their early childhood experiences during the first seven to eight years of their life.

This connection between personality and behaviour patterns in certain situations has also been established in personality psychology. This is a branch of psychology that is concerned with describing and distinguishing individual psychological characteristics and complex personality traits, also known simply as *traits*. Such a trait can describe and predict certain aspects of a person's behaviour that remain constant over time in a certain category of situations. The personality trait *extraversion*, for example, serves to describe and predict behavioural aspects such as sociability, emotional warmth, dynamics and readiness to trust in situations involving interacting and communicating with other people.

Are there traits, i.e. personality characteristics that are stable over time, on the basis of which one can predict a manager's success? In a study conducted by Truity Psychometrics on 25,759 participants, the correlations between personality type and various career aspects, such as average wage and number of employees, were examined. The Myers-Briggs Type Indicator (MBTI) was the underlying method used in this case. To this end, a test subject completes a questionnaire and is given his MBTI type as the result. It consists of four main classes, each of which may include one of two values:

- Extraversion (E) vs. introversion (I)
- Intuition (N) vs. sensing (S)

- Feeling (F) vs. thinking (T)
- Judging (J) vs. perceiving (P).

The study revealed that the combination of personality traits E, T and J was clearly predominant when it comes to who earns the most and who manages the largest number of employees. Very simply put, this allows us to identify the following personality traits as indicators of professional success:

- E: sociable, likes working with others
- T: rational, focus on facts, figures and data
- J: structured, creative, organised.

However, due to its high degree of error proneness, the MBTI methodology is viewed very critically in the field of psychological research. Nevertheless, instruments that are considered to be much more robust and reliable in their findings have produced very similar results. They include personality instruments based on the Big Five method (the big five personality factors).

The history of the Big Five is very interesting. The British writer and polymath Sir Francis Galton, a cousin of Charles Darwin, introduced the so-called lexical hypothesis in the late nineteenth century, which states that all significant human personality traits must be colloquially represented by adjectives of a given language. He also laid the groundwork for the development of factor analysis, a statistical method that can reduce a large amount of empirical data to a few relevant factors. However, he could not verify or prove either of these in the absence of powerful computers. This was achieved more than half a century later by scientists such as Louis Leon Thurstone, an engineer and psychologist at the University of Chicago who further developed factor analysis, and Gordon W. Allport, a professor of social psychology at Harvard. Taking up Galton's lexical hypothesis, Allport used Thurstone's findings on factor analysis and the first emerging computers to develop five essential personality factors from the more than 18,000 adjectives that describe a person's nature, later to be referred to as the "Big Five".

The "last mile" then finally was made by Paul Costa and Robert McCrae of the National Institute of Health in Bethesda. They developed the NEO Five Factor Inventory (NEO-FFI) based on Allport's findings. The designations for the individual factors, however, rather remind a non-psychologist of psychiatry, which is why Pierce and Jane Howard developed a more business-like variant with the instrument "Workplace Big Five", in which, for example, the name of the first dimension is no longer "neuroticism" but "the need for stability". Which manager would like to hear that he is neurotic?

Due to the large number of validation studies that were carried out to corroborate these instruments, these surveys are seen as the gold standard of personality psychology today. Here too, the test subject completes a questionnaire and is given scale values on five main scales as a result. These are described as follows:

- Need for stability (N)
- Extraversion (E)
- Openness to experience (O)
- Agreeableness (A)
- Conscientiousness (C).

Numerous studies, including a longitudinal study by the American professor in Management Theory, Timothy Judge, from 1999, confirmed that high values for extraversion (E+) and conscientiousness (C+) correlated strongly with salary and with success in a person's career. The same applies for low values on the scales of a need for stability (N–) and agreeableness (A–). Greatly simplified, this means that people who have very successful careers will tend to have the following personality traits:

- E+: sociable, likes working with others
- C+: structured, creative, organised
- N–: emotionally stable, more stress-resistant
- A–: resistant to conflict, asserts their own interests.

As you can see, the results of the different methods used are very similar. However, this does not mean that those who do not possess these character traits should give up. For one thing, this only reveals statistical correlations. Certain personality traits are de facto more commonly found among managers than others. This does not mean that one cannot be a successful manager or make a career if one does not have one of these traits. Secondly, there is a logical error in all investigative approaches, such as those presented here. Examining a sample reveals that there is an x% increased probability that, for instance, extrovert people are managers. Well, this is not really news for us. Here is a little mind game regarding this: Replace the term "extrovert" by "masculine", for instance. Most managers these days still tend to be men. Does this mean that a woman cannot be a successful manager? No, of course not. She might possibly have to work harder and be more determined than her male colleague though. Furthermore, we still don't know what other personality traits are inherent in the totality of all successful managers. Here is an example to illustrate this.

In this respect, individual career ambitions should not be influenced by statistical frequencies. So, are people actually born with certain personality traits that are needed to become successful managers? Are these perhaps even a fixed component of their personal make-up? Well, perhaps partly, but this still does not say anything about the individuals themselves. In principle, any healthy and well-educated person can pursue a career if they are willing to push themselves. The examples given in Chapter 3 illustrate this.

EXAMPLE

Let us assume that the aim is to investigate the frequency of yellow cars on German roads. Sooner or later we will realise that the majority of yellow vehicles are, in fact, mail vans. Most probably, more than 80% of all yellow vehicles in Germany are mail vans. What does this say about the remaining 20%? That's right: absolutely nothing. It was just as "easy" for these cars to become yellow, without necessarily having to deliver letters and packages, as it was for the mail vans.

2.7 The importance of impulse control

One particular personality trait which is linked to sustainable success in life is impulse control, also referred to as the tolerance for delayed gratification. Back in the late 1960s, Austrian-born personality psychologist Walter Mischel started his behavioural experiments at Stanford University. In one-on-one sessions, members of his team gave children something sweet, for instance a marshmallow or a biscuit. They explained to each child that they would now leave the room and that the child could choose to either eat the sweet straight away or, if they waited until the team member came back into the room, they would be given a second sweet. The children did not know how long they would have to wait for the team member to return. Typically, they would have to endure this difficult situation for about 10 minutes until the tester came back into the room. The first follow-up tests on those children who participated in the original test took place 10 years later. Mischel astonishingly found a clear correlation between the length of time those children could resist the sweet and their school performance and ability to cope with life. On average, those children who had demonstrated good control of their impulses had much better grades and higher school-leaving qualifications. Subsequent studies also showed there to be correlations with professional success and even with physical fitness.

In 2011, around 40 years after the original experiments, Mischel carried out further follow-up tests with the help of the imaging techniques in brain research that were by then available. By doing so, he was able to demonstrate that significant differences in two brain structures were dependent upon how long the person had, as a child, been able to withstand the temptation of eating the marshmallow straight away. These structures were the prefrontal cortex, which is responsible for methodical thinking and action, and the so-called "addiction centre". The ability to control inner impulses and to be disciplined is evidently of central importance for a person's general ability to be successful in life.

2.8 The role of your IQ

Is there a link between our intelligence, as commonly measured by IQ tests, and long-lasting career success? Let's recap. The intelligent quotient (IQ) is measured in standardised tests like the Stanford-Binet test. The average IQ score is 100. Anything above a score of 140 is considered a high IQ. Between 0.25% and 1.0% of the population are estimated to fall into this category. Common wisdom would in fact assume that a high IQ translates into more financial, academic or political success. In one of his famous tweets, even US President Donald Trump has claimed to have an IQ that is "one of the highest", suggesting that his wealth was somehow linked to his intelligence. Let's look at the findings of a fascinating piece of research: the so-called Terman study. This longest-running longitudinal study in history started back in 1921, when Stanford psychologist Lewis Terman began to investigate the life and career progression of children with a high or very high IQ. He selected roughly 1500 children between the ages of 8 and 12 years. This study population had an average IQ of 150. 80 of the study participants even had scores of over 170. Over the next decades, Terman continued to track the children through their adolescence. Among the original participants of the study were personalities like the educational psychologist Lee Cronbach, "I Love Lucy" writer Jess Oppenheimer, child psychologist Robert Sears, scientist Ancel Keys, and over 50 others who afterwards became faculty members at colleges and universities. After Terman's death in 1956, other psychologists decided to carry on the research, which is still running today. One of the researchers who carried on Terman's research after his death was Melita Oden. He decided to compare the 100 most successful individuals to the 100 least successful ones. While both groups essentially had the same IQ levels, the least successful ones only earned slightly more than the average income at the time and had higher rates of alcoholism and divorce than the most successful ones, whose earnings were significantly above average. When looking at his research even Terman himself had found earlier that "intelligence and achievement were far from perfectly correlated". Oden's findings only confirmed this. But how could this disparity be explained? By digging deeper into the data, Oden found that the two groups differed significantly in the prevalence of certain personality traits. The most successful ones exhibited personality characteristics such as self-confidence, prudence, forethought, willpower, perseverance and the desire to excel. These findings are also confirmed by other studies which I mentioned in Section 2.6, *The old question: nature or nurture?*

So, what does this tell us? While IQ can reliably predict a person's academic success, personality traits and other aspects remain the more determining factors for their overall achievement in life. Or, in other words, while intelligence might be seen as an indicator for the potential for success in life, it is the character traits and other factors which determine how much of this potential will actually be realised in a person's lifetime.

Also, the aforementioned Grant study found that intelligence does not contribute to a successful career above a certain level. No significant difference in maximum income could be found when comparing study participants who had IQs in the 110–115 range to those with IQs higher than 150.

Is there a link between intelligence and life satisfaction then? Yes, there is. However, it is not the most intelligent that are the happiest in life. In fact, some studies suggest that children with exceptionally high IQs may be more prone to depression and social isolation than less intelligent ones.

To sum it up, there is no reason to be frustrated if your IQ should not be one of the highest. It will not stop you from making it big if you make this your top priority and consider the other factors described in this book.

2.9 Is it only luck?

Generally, people do not easily accept luck as a reason for their success as it hurts their ego and self-determination. In our competitive world, nobody wants to see luck behind their success. If executives say that they were lucky enough in their career it is often interpreted as if they did not succeed through their own talent. In reality, luck or the right opportunity at the right time in fact plays a very important role, even if you work hard. In our experience in working with very successful managers the three elements of luck, determination and bouncing back from setbacks contributed equally to their success.

The author and investment banking expert Michael Lewis, who wrote books like *Moneyball,* mentions that luck is the difference between a successful person and an unsuccessful person who is equally talented and has the same level of confidence and commitment. As a result, it is important to be thankful for the opportunities life has to offer, not to mention the experience we gain through the lessons we learn.

Or as the Roman philosopher Seneca put it: "Luck is what happens when preparation meets opportunity."

While luck in life is by its nature unpredictable, it coincides with the will to take a risk and the ability to overcome crises. It is not enough to just meet the right people or to be given a unique chance to excel, it is also about giving it a try and leaving the security of the known and comforting behind you. It is about not being disillusioned easily if things don't pan out as originally planned.

EXAMPLE

While the German Alex Atzberger was at Harvard in 2005, he wrote a paper that argued that a small, unknown company named *Salesforce. com* was soon going to take away substantial market shares from the dominant market leader for enterprise software, *SAP*. He argued that *SAP* was overlooking an upcoming technology trend which would

(Continued)

change the dynamics of the entire software industry. Today, we call this *cloud computing,* but that name had not been invented back then. In contrast to big SAP, small Salesforce.com focused exclusively on cloud computing, which enables phenomena like exponential growth because of its focus, standardisation and ease of use. The professor of Atzberger at that time was Clay Christensen, author of *The Innovator's Dilemma.* He was impressed by this point of view and since he knew the then Co-CEO of SAP Jim Hagemann Snabe, he sent it to him to read. Not long thereafter SAP recruiters started calling Atzberger. However, he was not interested at first because he wanted to join a dynamic start-up environment. After some time though, he realised the possibility and impact a role at SAP might bring and he decided to join. But that was not the only time that luck hit. For the next two years, not much happened. During the Independence Day celebrations in 2007, Atzberger was working alone in the SAP office near Philadelphia. His co-workers were all celebrating with their families, but since he was alone he decided to work instead. So did Bill McDermott, who had been recently appointed as head of sales to SAP's executive board. McDermott roamed the empty offices searching for some PowerPoint support and came across Atzberger. He asked him to help him with his upcoming presentation to the board. Atzberger invested the whole weekend and thought he would never hear from McDermott again. A couple of days later though, McDermott called him and said, "Alex, I want all my future presentations to the board to be done by you." After this, his career took off. He was sent to Asia to develop growth plans for SAP's business in Japan and China and became chief of staff for McDermott who had meanwhile become CEO. Today, Atzberger is the president of Ariba, one of SAP's biggest cloud acquisitions, focusing on the procurement function. The paper which he had written back in 2005 had proven true and he is now at the helm of making SAP a market leader also in the cloud computing business.

Bibliography

Brody, Gene H. et al.; Resilience in Adolescence, Health, and Psychosocial Outcomes; Pediatrics, American Academy of Pediatrics, Itasca, USA, 2016.

Cherry, Kendra; Are People with High IQs More Successful? A Modern Look at Terman's Study of the Gifted; verywell.com, USA, 2017.

Chetty, Raj et al.; Mobility Report Cards: The Role of Colleges in Intergenerational Mobility; http://www.equality-of-opportunity.org; July 2017.

Chuprinin, Oleg et al.; Family Descent as a Signal of Managerial Quality: Evidence from Mutual Funds; The National Bureau of Economic Research, Cambridge, USA, 2016.

Cole, Steve W.; Loneliness, Eudaimonia, and the Human Conserved Transcriptional Response to Adversity; PubMed.gov, Washington, DC, USA, 2015.

Credit Suisse Gender 3000; The CS Gender 3000: The Reward for Change, Credit Suisse AG, September 2016.

De Neve, Jan-Emmanuel et al.; Born to Lead? A Twin Design and Genetic Association Study of Leadership Role Occupancy; PMC, Bethesda, USA, 2012.

Drath, Karsten; Spielregeln des Erfolgs: Wie Fuehrungskraefte an Rueckschlaegen wachsen, Haufe, Freiburg, Germany, 2016.

Hamblin, James; Why Succeeding against the Odds Can Make You Sick; The New York Times, New York City, USA, 2017.

Judge, Timothy A. et al.; The Big Five Personality Traits, General Mental Ability, and Career Success across the Life Span; Personnel Psychology, Wiley, Hoboken, USA, 1999.

Laurison, Daniel; Friedman, Sam; The Class Pay Gap in Higher Professional and Managerial Occupations; American Sociological Review, SAGE journals, Thousand Oaks, USA, 2016.

McGregor, Jena; More Women at the Top, Higher Returns; The New York Times, New York City, USA, 2014.

Mujahid, Mahasin S.; Socioeconomic Position, John Henryism, and Incidence of Acute Myocardial Infarction in Finnish Men; Social Science & Medicine, Elsevier, Amsterdam, The Netherlands, 2016.

Owens, Molly; Personality Type & Career Achievement, Does Your Type Predict How Far You'll Climb?; Truity Psychometrics LLC, San Francisco, USA, 2015.

Reimer, Marko; Schaeffer, Utz; WHU Vorstandsstudie; WHU, Vallendar, Germany, 2015.

Rovnik, Naomi; How Social Class Can Affect Your Pay, Professionals from Elite Backgrounds Earn More than Peers from Working-Class Families; Financial Times, London, UK, 2017.

Stevenson, Jane Edison; Orr, Evelyn; We Interviewed 57 Female CEOs to Find out How More Women Can Get to the Top; Harvard Business Review, Boston, USA, 2017.

Stevenson, Jane E. et al.; CEO Pipeline Project; Korn Ferry, Los Angeles, USA, 2017.

Stossel, Scott; What Makes Us Happy, Revisited; A New Look at the Famous Harvard Study of What Makes People Thrive; The Atlantic, Washington, USA, 2013.

Terman, L.; Oden, M.; Genetic Studies of Genius. Vol. V. The Gifted at Mid-life: Thirty-five Years' Follow-up of the Superior Child; Stanford University Press, Stanford, USA, 1959.

Vaillant, George E.; Triumphs of Experience: The Men of the Harvard Grant Study; Harvard University Press, Boston, USA, 2015.

3 How success works

As we have seen, a lot of factors contribute to long-lasting professional success which are in fact not, or not entirely, under our control. However, many aspects like the level of dedication, the level of education and the career choices we make are entirely under our control. Let's take a closer look at what can be learned from this.

3.1 The patterns behind successful careers

EXAMPLE

Over the past 30 years, hardly anyone has changed the face of German industry more than Heinrich von Pierer. After joining Siemens in 1969, he worked his way up to the executive board in the space of 20 years. In 1992, he was appointed Chairman of the Managing Board. He was Angela Merkel's chief economic advisor and held numerous other prominent positions. Between 1993 and 2006, for instance, he was Chairman of the influential Asia-Pacific Committee (APA) of German business. Von Pierer was elected to Siemens' Supervisory Board in 2005. In 2007, he was forced to resign from his post, following a case of bribery which shook the entire company. Heinrich von Pierer's credo of success and work ethics can be summed up in one formula, which he coined during his time as Merkel's advisor: "Knowledge of the customers' needs plus inspiration, multiplied over a long period of time, plus transpiration, equals market success." Today, von Pierer lectures to students and is an independent consultant. In an interview with the journalist Carsten Knop, he states that he is frequently asked by seminar participants: "How do you become an executive board member?" His advice: initially, by having a decent education. This includes quickly completing a course of study and having some experience abroad. Then, one should become proficient in English. One should not be overly ambitious or too self-confident.

He thought absolutely nothing of a career approached according to the motto: "Right, so where's the piano?" You might be successful once by using your elbows to get ahead, but probably not the second time around. Whatever job you are doing right now, you have to do it well. But, in addition to hard work, a portion of good fortune is needed too. You should also be able to view many of your character traits critically. And nobody should despair if they are not a member of the executive board. It is still possible to have a very fulfilling professional life below this level.

Steve Jobs was another person who brought about lasting changes to a number of businesses. Together with Steve Wozniak, he founded Apple in 1976 and facilitated the advance of personal computers, graphical user interfaces, smartphones, legal music downloads, MP3 players and much more. As a result of internal power struggles, Jobs was forced to leave Apple in 1985 and founded two other companies in quick succession, NeXT and Pixar. In 1996, Apple finally acquired NeXT in order to gain access to the technology developed by it. This initially led to Jobs working as a consultant for Apple only to then, once again, be appointed as its CEO within a very short space of time. Pixar was the first company to release a fully digital animated cinema film, *Toy Story*. Other blockbusters were to follow. When the company went public, Jobs became a billionaire. In 2004, Jobs was diagnosed with cancer, but recovered. In 2005, he gave a world-famous speech in front of graduates of Stanford Business School, in which he talked about his career and about success:

> I'm sure that none of this would have ever happened if I hadn't been fired by Apple. It was awful-tasting medicine, but I guess the patient needed it. Sometimes life is going to hit you on the head with a brick. Don't lose faith. I'm convinced that the only thing that kept me going was that I loved what I did. You have to got to find what you love. [...] Your work is going to fill a large part of your life and the only way to be truly satisfied is to do what you believe is great work. And the only way to do great work is to love what you do. If you haven't found it yet, keep looking. And don't settle. As with all matters of the heart, you will know when you find it. And like any great relationship, it just gets better and better as the years roll on. So, keep looking. Don't settle.

In 2008, Jobs succumbed to cancer a second time. After a prolonged absence from all public appearances, he returned once more to the public stage in 2009 for a product presentation. In 2011, after a long drawn-out battle, he eventually died of cancer, aged 56.

For more than five years, Gillian Zoe Segal, a New York author, has interviewed many successful celebrities in the USA, among them the financial investor Warren Buffett, one of the world's richest people, as well as Michael Bloomberg, founder of Bloomberg financial data services and former mayor of New York City. In her interviews with them, she was particularly interested in what lay behind the facade of their success stories, what pitfalls had to be avoided, what hurdles overcome. In her intriguing book *Getting There*, she points to seven critical factors which her 30 interview partners had in common.

They know and take into consideration their "circle of competence". They know their strengths and weaknesses and take these into account when choosing a profession and shaping their career. So, apart from a healthy amount of self-confidence, self-reflection and a small amount of modesty we need to recognise that we are not equally good at all things. Segal's interviewees had recognised the skills that set them apart from others. At times this was a very wearisome process. They also compensated for their own weaknesses or the qualities they were missing through a good team.

They make use of their passion and have stamina. According to Segal's interviewees, being successful has a lot to do with dedicating yourself completely to one thing, inspiring people, overcoming obstacles, swallowing rejections and failures, and dealing with your own fears and insecurities. To have the energy to keep this going for many years, you need stamina and you have to be dedicated to what you are doing. Seen from the outside, this might look like an obsession because it means always doing your best, not just going by the book. Striving for money alone or trying to fulfil social conventions or other people's wishes is not a good source of motivation for long-term success.

Their career paths are flexible. Success has less to do with unwaveringly pursuing some internal master plan, than with taking advantage of the more or less subtle opportunities life has to offer. Having too rigid ideas about your own career path might lead you to miss unique opportunities. In hindsight, Michael Bloomberg only founded his financial data company because he was sacked from the investment bank Salomon Brothers.

They create their own opportunities. None of the interviewees hung around waiting to be discovered by someone. They did not pursue conventional career paths, but forged their own. They sometimes even adopted rather unconventional methods to create opportunities by taking conscious risks and by being willing to make large sacrifices in order to be seen by superiors, business partners and customers, so that they could get into business.

They call everything into question. Segal's interviewees all shared the quality of not sticking to conventions and established structures, but ignoring them. Just because something has always been done that way does not mean that it is the best way to do things. Thus, Gary Hirshberg, the inventor of the first organic food shops in the 1970s, took a total of nine years to be successful with his concept. Initially, the market simply was not ready for organic food. So, he first had to spend a lot of time preparing the ground for what was later to become a huge industrial sector.

They don't let themselves be deterred by fear of failure. Many of the interviewees were raised in rather poor or difficult circumstances. This resulted in them becoming independent early on and recognising that you can't do anything without money. So, early on in their lives, they started doing vacation and evening jobs and worked hard to support their families. Many sold products or services door-to-door and had to face rejection and resistance at a young age. Others were subjected to traumatic experiences, such as the Vietnam war, in their youth. Experiences such as these shaped their lives. They gave them another perspective on life. They instilled in them a more relaxed attitude towards taking risks and accepting their vulnerability, and took away the fear of failing in their professional lives.

They are resilient. This seems to be the most important quality of all. All the successful people Segal interviewed over the years had had to deal with a number of severe setbacks. They had lost their jobs, gone bankrupt, been dropped last-minute by investors etc. And yet they had somehow always managed to get back on their feet. The interviews showed clearly that, to a large extent, success is about getting up more often than you are knocked down by life.

This list of characteristics of successful people and their careers is, of course, not complete, and rather US-influenced, but it is a good starting point to question your own motivation and mindset. As we have seen, luck plays a key role too, of course, in other words the state of being "in the right place at the right time". However, an individual must also be able to grasp an opportunity when it arises. The emotional support people get from their partner and family also plays an important role when it comes to dealing with setbacks. The more a manager has advanced in his or her career, the more the whole family has to carry this commitment too, as the price to be paid is considerable.

3.2 Becoming comfortable with the unknown

Sir Ken Robinson, a British art professor and author, has aptly described the importance of mental agility for success in life in a highly acclaimed 2007 TED talk. He claims that children who enrol into school today, will, after completing schooling, education and studies, encounter a professional world that will have changed numerous times before they will retire in about 65 years.

The background is the ever-increasing speed of fundamental changes due to technology and other factors, and the associated increase in uncertainty, complexity and unclear situations. Concealed behind all the dynamic and sometimes rather chaotic developments in society and the economy, many people still hope to find a predictable order that can help them to cope. After all, human beings are always seeking to understand and handle the environment. But it is precisely this which is becoming increasingly difficult to do, as a glance at the last 70 years shows. Following the end of World War II, the world was divided into a two-front system, known as the "Cold War". There were two main geopolitical camps: the USA and the USSR, with their respective allies, who aligned themselves – politically, militarily and economically – towards their respective hegemonic power. The enemy images on both sides were clear, making it relatively easy to predict future developments. Following the collapse of the USSR, the two-front system has developed into a four-front system.

This phenomenon is often described in the literature by the acronym VUCA (see Table 3.2.1). Where does this term come from? At the US Army War College in Carlisle, Pennsylvania, future generals are trained in strategy and warfare. There, at the end of the 1990s, an acronym was coined to reflect an increasingly complex geopolitical world order: VUCA. The abbreviation stands for volatility, uncertainty, complexity and ambiguity and was initially used mainly by the college lecturers there. Following the terrorist

Table 3.2.1   The meaning of VUCA

Volatility	Refers to the increasing frequency, speed and scope of changes taking place
Uncertainty	Describes the increasing unpredictability of events
Complexity	Refers to the increasing number of linkages and dependencies, which makes topics difficult to comprehend
Ambiguity	Describes the ambiguity of the facts of the situation that increases the likelihood of misinterpretations and making wrong decisions

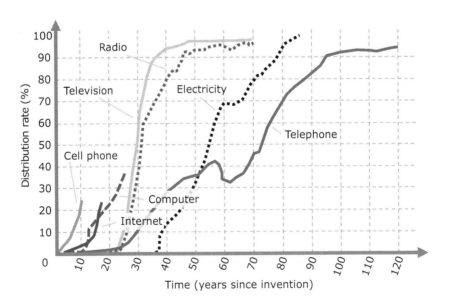

Figure 3.2.1 Spread of technological innovations.
Source: Peter Brimelow, The Silent Boom, Forbes, 1997.

attacks of 9/11, the new term was ultimately also adopted by management pioneers, who recognised the increasing complexity, not only in the military and power-political realm, but also in the development of the globalised economy.

The VUCA phenomenon did in fact have a considerable impact on how companies are managed today. Through the rise of new business models, mega-trends such as globalisation and digitalisation are increasingly leading to fundamental changes in the market environment that have the potential to marginalise established companies within no time at all. Figure 3.2.1 illustrates this by means of the time span needed by groundbreaking innovations to spread in the Western industrialised nations. Whilst the spread of the telephone took 120 years, the television only needed 35 years in order to achieve the same level of market penetration. Mobile telephones achieved the same in less than 20 years.

EXAMPLE

In 2013, during the press conference announcing the sale of Nokia's mobile phone branch to Microsoft, Nokia CEO Stephen Elop ended his speech by saying: "We didn't do anything wrong, but somehow, we lost." When he said that, some claim to have seen tears in his eyes. I personally doubt that, since he was also pretty relaxed about laying off half of Nokia's employees during this transaction. Maybe his package of €19 million has helped him to overcome his pain. Anyway, one year later he was also fired from Microsoft.

Since producing their first mobile phone in 1987, Nokia has been a respectable company, which over many years even defined and dominated the entire industry. Who of Generation X will not remember the legendary Nokia 6210, which had a battery life that lasted for even an intense business week and which was robust enough to survive being dropped from a height of two metres? Don't even think of trying this with an iPhone or Samsung today.

Sure, success is good for your self-confidence and it may make you bold and look big. However, sometimes it also entails a certain sense of entitlement. At one point Nokia was known in the industry for its arrogance, which prevented it from learning from the outside world: "We are Nokia; we have all the engineering knowhow in-house!"

At that point Nokia confused "knowing" with "learning".

However, in today's fast-moving world, it is now longer about "knowing". Market dynamics, technology and regulations change so quickly

(Continued)

that knowledge about how things used to work is increasingly marginalised in importance. At times it can even be counterproductive. In fact, in fast-changing times "learning" too is not an option anymore. It no longer separates the good from the average companies, it has become a question of mere survival. If you are not leaving your comfort zone to try out something new, to feel clumsy, lose performance or even fail, then you are most certainly setting yourself up for failure in the long run. This is true for companies as well as it is for their leaders.

The point is that you don't have to do it. You can continue doing what made you successful in the first place. You can even become really good at it, just like Nokia. However, while you are still optimising yourself, the competition is changing the rules of the game and then change becomes increasingly hard. If you are forced to change then you are in an uphill battle.

This development leads to a reduced focus on long-term strategies and to a short-sighted management approach, where the next crisis is already seen to be lurking around the next corner. In such a volatile and insecure environment, marked by increasing restructuring and market adjustments, managing employees takes on a new meaning for a company's competitiveness. In future, those managers will be most successful who secure the trust of their employees and bind them emotionally to themselves and to the company's goals.

EXAMPLE

A glance at the statistics reveals the extent of this change. Standard & Poor's is an international rating agency that manages the S&P500 stock index. This index is among the most important in the world. According to a study by the consulting firm Innosight, the length of stay of companies in this index in 1990 was 20 years, while in 1965 it was still at 33 years. According to Innosight's forecast, it will drop to 14 years by 2026. This means that around 50% of the companies listed in the S&P500 today will no longer be in the index in 10 years' time, as they will have been replaced by other rising stars.

Richard Sennett is an American professor of sociology who today teaches at the London School of Economics. In his book *The Culture of the New Capitalism* Sennett describes how, over a long period of time, companies initially appear to be stable, predictable systems that are both an iron cage and a home to their employees. Security and a livelihood have been provided for many decades in exchange for discipline, subordination to hierarchies and the provision of services. Since the end of the last century, this rigid order has given way to a growing flexibility, marked by a decline in stability and predictability.

The reason for this, in Sennett's view, is the altered role of the capital market. After World War II, the world economy was governed by the Bretton Woods system, which coupled the exchange rates of the world's leading economies via a band of exchange rates to the US dollar, which in turn had a fixed exchange rate to the gold standard. This system gave the participating economies stability, but it ultimately failed in 1973 as a consequence of the USA's current account surpluses. The dollar could no longer be sufficiently safeguarded by the gold standard. After the collapse of the global monetary system, vast amounts of capital became available worldwide, which sought short-term interest rates. As a result of progressive globalisation and the new possibilities offered by the emerging communication technologies, this 'impatient' capital flowed worldwide into corporate bonds, with the aim of making short-term profits from the rising share prices. The consequence was a more intense global networking of financial interests. Revenues were now hardly expected to come from dividends, which meant that it was no longer the stability of companies that seemed desirable, but maximising their share prices to generate greater financial returns. Since this development, the capital market system, along with the associated evaluation by financial analysts, determines the quarterly performance of listed companies. This short-term competition for the favour of investors and analysts leads to widespread irrational behaviour on the markets, allowing a company's share prices to rise, for example, if it cuts back on R&D staff or restructures for no apparent reason. This type of behaviour, which is incomprehensible from an entrepreneurial point of view, allows the share price, and thus the market value of a company, to rise, which effectively prevents a company from being taken over.

Companies that do not bow to this logic are undervalued in this new financial system and consequently end up being bought up by other companies that stick to the rules of the game. Therefore, in order for a company to retain its share price and ensure its long-term attractiveness as an investment object, the company must undergo constant change by the management. A change of strategy, restructuring, acquisitions, portfolio adjustments and downsizing, coupled with a good story for the market, have thus become an end in itself and a key feature of good corporate management. Long-term changes, such as the restructuring of a company as a result of a major change of strategy, are hardly possible anymore. The consequences of these worldwide developments, coupled with ongoing globalisation and the increasing spread of modern communications technologies, shape the everyday work of managers today. High time and performance pressure, unconditional mobility, long working hours, permanent reachability, a constant feeling of uncertainty and a neglect of private life are the consequences of this.

But the VUCA phenomenon also affects the way careers are shaped. Our entire education system is geared to conveying knowledge. During the 12 to 13 years we spend in school, plus about 5 years of university studies and initial training, we mainly learn detailed knowledge which can, if necessary, be easily looked up or which will, in any case, be completely obsolete in 5 to 10 years' time. What are missing are the practice-based transmission of relevant experiences, and the ability to learn independently and to understand complex relationships. It is this ability, in particular, which is of central long-term importance when it comes to adapting to an ever more frequently changing market and leadership environment.

If you compare the post-war generation with current teenagers, it can indeed be found that the half-life of knowledge has decreased dramatically over the last 70 years. One reason for this is the fact that growth in technology works on the basis of network laws and thus exponentially, while people tend to postulate mostly linear relationships when predicting future developments. Against this background, it would be much more important to foster the joy of learning itself as opposed to the mere learning of facts.

In the management literature, this continuous learning skill is also known as mental agility. In our work with managers we repeatedly encounter situations in which the manager's previously acquired tools are no longer sufficient or suitable to tackle the new challenges that come with the new career step. Instead, these previous strengths sometimes even end up being a weakness. While specialist expertise and the capacity to act might previously have been important to underpin a manager's credibility, they might well be a hindrance in the next step up the ladder where more empowerment – i.e. the delegation of responsibility – and fewer details are required to be able to tackle the dramatic rise in responsibility. The further a manager progresses up the hierarchy, the more his performance depends on others – a further complexity which needs to be learned. Figure 3.2.2 gives further examples of new skills which need to be acquired and mastered when progressing up the hierarchy.

Learning new things or skills entails leaving the comfort zone, and thereby questioning one's own experience. It means making mistakes due to lack of experience, feeling incompetent for a while – and, of course, it also includes the possibility of failure. Anyone who has ever tried to learn Mandarin or Tango Argentino surely knows what that means.

EXAMPLE

The American management guru Peter Drucker made it a habit every three years to proclaim a topic which he wanted to study in his spare time. This way he acquired a broad knowledge of many disciplines over the years that had to do not only with "his" theme of leadership, but also with more exotic fields of knowledge such as "mushrooms" or "Baltic States". This way, he sought new inspiration for his lectures and trained his mental agility.

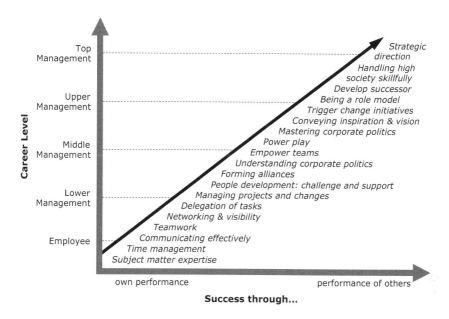

Figure 3.2.2 Examples of learning agility in the course of a manager's career.

3.3 Characteristics of successful managers

In preparation for their acclaimed book *Great by Choice*, Jim Collins – an American management expert and former professor for entrepreneurship at Stanford University – and his colleague, Morten T. Hansen – professor for management at the business schools Berkeley, Harvard and INSEAD – investigated a number of companies which performed outstandingly, that is, at least 10 times better than comparable companies in the same sector. They asked themselves: Are these companies managed differently? Which leadership factors increase companies' efficiency, thus enabling them to be more adaptable and competitive in a globalised economy, with dynamics that are progressively harder to predict? What distinguishes the top management of companies that are outstandingly successful from others that have developed less favourably? The following criteria were set up to identify the relevant companies:

- newly founded companies that have not yet had time to establish themselves on the market;
- companies that were successful, even though their framework conditions were volatile, unstable and complex, and could not be influenced by them;
- companies that, over a period of at least 15 years, showed a more positive development than the stock market as a whole and their respective sectors.

Table 3.3.1   Successful companies examined within the scope of a study conducted by Collins and Hansen

Companies	Sector	Time frame	Performance vs. market	Performance vs. sector
Amgen	Biotechnology	1980–2002	24-fold	77-fold
Biomet	Medical engineering	1977–2002	18-fold	11-fold
Intel	Information technology	1968–2002	21-fold	46-fold
Microsoft	Software	1975–2002	56-fold	119-fold
Progressive Insurance	Insurance	1965–2002	15-fold	11-fold
Southwest Airlines	Airline	1967–2002	63-fold	550-fold
Stryker	Medical engineering	1977–2002	28-fold	11-fold

From an initial list of over 20,000 companies, Collins and Hansen finally selected seven companies according to these criteria. These companies were then compared with the whole market and with companies in the same industry. This study involved examining innumerable documents from the respective corporate histories as well as conducting interviews in order to identify common patterns relating to management style, decision-making, risk tolerance, innovation etc. from a total of 6000 years of corporate history (see Table 3.3.1).

Collins and Hansen's study found that the company bosses of the most successful companies were by no means particularly courageous and venturesome visionaries. In actual fact, they were no more venturesome, bold or visionary, nor any more creative, than their comparable counterparts. And it wasn't that they were just more fortunate than their less successful colleagues either. In fact, fortune and misfortune tended to be pretty much on a par among all the companies investigated.

However, the most successful company bosses were more disciplined in the pursuit of their goals and tended to take a more empirical and cautious approach. Both researchers found that the top managers of the analysed companies that were the most successful stood out from the others because of the following characteristics (see Figure 3.3.1).

Accepting the circumstances: Successful managers are aware that they are exposed to permanent uncertainty and that they are neither able to control nor precisely predict major incidents happening in the world around them.

Locus of control: The thought that coincidental occurrences and other factors beyond their control could have an impact on the achievement of their goals never crossed the minds of the most successful managers.

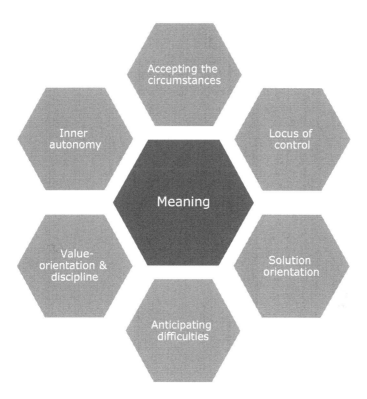

Figure 3.3.1 Characteristics and convictions of persistently successful managers.

They always saw the responsibility for both the fate of the company and their own destiny as being in their own hands.

Solution orientation: The toughest managers were prepared, in spite of all the adversities, to put all their strengths into focussing on their goals. They had an unbending will to achieve this, which – in the majority of cases – also led to success.

Anticipating difficulties: The managers of the top seven companies had one attribute in common: they continued to grow in both economically bad and also economically favourable times, and to see sudden, unexpected changes, crises and threats as normal or even probable. Due to their almost paranoid alertness, they were better prepared to deal with sudden changes in their environment than other managers.

Value-orientation & discipline: The managers with the best company performance distinguished themselves by a strong set of values and the intention to bring their own actions into balance with their values. This discipline served them as an inner compass, ensuring that they did not drift off course, even in the face of very uncertain surrounding factors.

Inner autonomy: The top seven managers all had a high level of inner autonomy when it came to assessing the present situation and deriving possible solutions from it. In doing so they neither based themselves on predominant opinions, nor did they primarily orient themselves to what other people did or didn't do. By relying on their own fact- and experience-based assessment of the situation, they were able to make bold, creative decisions. They were also willing to completely call these unconventional solution strategies into question if their assessment of the situation required this. This often rather non-conformist approach, which deviated considerably from the conventional course of action, frequently earned them harsh criticism, yet this did not make them change their minds.

Meaning: The most successful managers felt themselves to be committed to a higher purpose, and they invested all their energy and ambition into accomplishing a mission or into benefitting the company or society, with this never being solely for their own benefit. Their conviction that their efforts also served a higher purpose shielded them against the consequences of difficulties they had to face.

The long-term success of top managers is, therefore, not merely an accident, but can very frequently be attributed to certain factors. Of course, a company's success does not solely depend on the people running it at the top. After all, the actual work is performed by the hundreds or even thousands of executives and employees within the company's hierarchy. However, in top management, far-reaching directional courses are charted and decisions taken, whose soundness is frequently only recognised years later. Avoiding serious mistakes in decision-making and getting employees on board are, therefore, in themselves already major steps towards success. This is confirmed by the insights of a number of well-known managerial personalities.

3.4 The magic recipe

What evidence, if any, is there supporting the existence of a magic recipe for long-lasting career success? What career choices contribute to success and which are detrimental? In 2016, the social media platform LinkedIn, today the most influential online network in the business world, used a big-data approach to answer this question. A research team around Guy Berger looked at the careers of 459,000 members globally in the time from 1990 to 2010. Of these about 64,000, roughly 14%, made it to the top of organisations. The team was looking for factors which contributed to this impressive career success. What they found is surprising. The classical factors *educational background, gender, work experience* and *career transitions* only correlated about 14% with career success.

Here are some other factors that actually play an even greater role.

Generalist over expert: Working across several job functions, such as manufacturing, marketing or finance, provides a well-rounded understanding of business operations that is needed to become successful as an executive. In the LinkedIn study, each additional job function was found to be worth the equivalent of three years of work experience.

Stay in your industry: While working across functions correlates positively with career success, changing industries has a slightly negative impact upon moving up the corporate ladder. This is most probably due to time lost by climbing up the learning curve yet another time and in establishing new relationships and networks.

Education matters but it has to come from the right school: Conventional wisdom would suggest that formal education is important. While this was found to be true by the study, other aspects like the brand strength of a university played an important role, too. To illustrate this: while completing an MBA at a normal university yielded an equivalent of five years of relevant work experience, the same MBA degree coming from one of the top schools was found to boost careers with the equivalent of thirteen years of work experience.

Location matters: The study found that for those who work internationally, being in New York City increased the chances of becoming an executive, while being employed in Houston or Washington, D.C., decreased them. Globally, Mumbai and Singapore served as career accelerators, while São Paulo and Madrid had the most negative effects. Most probably this is due to the higher concentration of company headquarters in those regions. Another important factor is the nature of the industries that are prevalent in these cities, e.g. the financial services industry tends to be more hierarchical than the high-tech industry, which is why it is very important to be in New York when you want to make a career in the financial sector.

Gender (still) matters: As I described in Section 2.4, *The gender gap,* it is not to our total surprise that the LinkedIn research team found that men still have a slight advantage in making it to the top of the house. Men with the same qualifications and who were similar in terms of the other factors mentioned here needed an average of 3.5 years of work experience less than comparable women to reach the executive level.

To illustrate the study findings, imagine a person who is male, has an undergraduate degree from a top international school and a non-MBA Master's, lives in London, and has worked in two different job functions for two companies in two industries. According to the research team his probability of becoming an executive is 15% (see Table 3.4.1).

Table 3.4.1 Career decisions

Career decision	Probability of becoming an executive
Four job functions rather than two	+8%
Only one industry instead of two	+3%
Worked for four companies rather than two	+4%
Undergraduate degree from a top 10 US school rather than a top international school	+3%
MBA from a top 5 US program rather than a non-MBA Master's	+21%
Moved from London to New York City	+4%
Ten more years of work experience	+15%

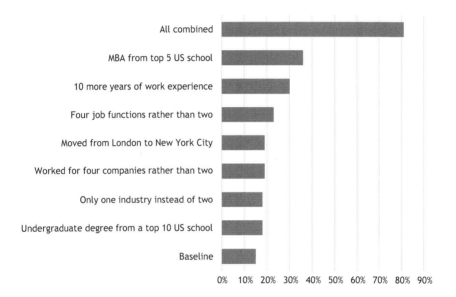

Figure 3.4.1 Career decisions and their impact on success.

Had this person made all of the choices highlighted in Table 3.4.1, his probability of becoming an executive would have increased from 15% to a total of 81%. Figure 3.4.1 illustrates the findings.

3.5 Four aspects for the right path to the top

One professional who is particularly well-acquainted with the careers of successful managers is a headhunter. It is not uncommon for this type of consultant to accompany managers over several decades in their careers. If you ask representatives of this profession for universal advice, you will

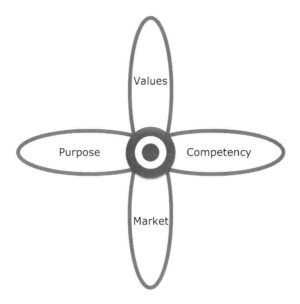

Figure 3.5.1 Aspects of long-term professional success.

usually be given the rather vague response: "It all depends..." This vagueness is not a result of their unwillingness to offer advice, but rather because it really does depend on a number of factors. Each person and their career just function differently. But, as it is so often the case, here too there are universally applicable insights which will help you to rethink your own career plans. These are part of our career coaching methodology. The basic underlying questions are what you want for yourself, what you are able to do, what gives you meaning and what is needed by the market. Long-term professional success is most likely to be achieved if as many as possible of the following four aspects are addressed (illustrated in Figure 3.5.1).

Values

Are you creative and do you continuously come up with new ideas? Or would you prefer to just stick to and implement plans? Are you a risk-taker and welcome change or do you appreciate certainty and plannability? It is important that you do what suits you, what is really important to you and what you love doing. Trying to find the activity that really inspires you can be a tedious affair, which may take several years and occasionally come to a dead end, to only later turn out to be a good thing. Yet, successful careers show that inspiration for a cause is of fundamental significance. What are the things that are most important to you in your life?

EXAMPLE

Someone who cares about people's growth might find a deeper meaning in good leadership, i.e. in promoting and challenging people, and in supporting them in their personal development. By contrast, someone for whom individuality, aesthetics and dynamics take priority, might find working for a sports car manufacturer very fulfilling and extremely meaningful.

Competence

Each of us has strengths and weaknesses that are part of our personal make-up. We could choose to work so long on eliminating our weaknesses until they are all gone. However, it might be more effective if we were instead to focus on reinforcing our strengths. If you prefer to work with people, rather than numbers, then it would perhaps be better for you to work in the HR department, rather than in accounting. If you prefer to be alone and undisturbed in developing plans and concepts, then perhaps the field of research and development is more suitable for you than the sales sector. Whatever you choose to do should correspond to your area of competence. But first you have to find this out. What is your area of competence? What are your strengths and what are your weaknesses?

EXAMPLE

Let us assume that you have a phenomenal memory of people. If you work in IT support, this will be of little use to you. By contrast, in sales you could considerably raise your market value, since here it is very useful to know the name of your interlocutor, and personal details about his or her colleagues and boss.

Market

Irrespective of the individual skills you may have, it is important to ascertain whether there is a market for them, and to find and then tap into it. Irrespective of whether you are working for a medium-sized or large corporation, whether you are an employee or entrepreneur, there are abundant niches everywhere which you can exploit, using your creativity and natural wit. Where can you make optimal use of what is important to you and what you are good at?

For example, I studied engineering because having a meaningful job was always very important to me and because renewable energies seemed extremely worthwhile to me. I also wanted to do development work, which is both meaningful and comes with the guarantee of never-ending demand on the market, since – at least for the next generations – there is very likely to be an abundance of underdeveloped or ravaged countries. It soon became clear that thermodynamics and fluid mechanics did not feature among my natural competencies. I was also quickly bored by engineering work, as my values also included working with people and always learning and creating something new, while I find technical details rather tedious. But I still needed to have this experience in order to be able to draw conclusions from it. The versatile work of a business consultant, by contrast, was a much better match for my skills. Further career steps in the consulting business revealed my affinity for working with people and interacting with customers. But I had to experience several critical career situations in my life before all four aspects of long-term successful careers merged almost perfectly into one. Working as a businessman, coach, author and speaker together constitute the perfect combination for me, but this would have been unimaginable to me ten years ago.

Meaning

In order to be professionally successful in the long run, to face obstacles and overcome setbacks, it is important to see whatever you do as a contribution to something greater, a higher goal that appears good and desirable to you. This meaningfulness is not always apparent at first sight. It needs to be found and developed. The opposite is true if a phase in your career turns out to be without meaning or if its meaning gradually fades away.

EXAMPLE

Many employees and managers working in the private banking sector once found it very meaningful to advise people on how to invest their money well and safely. Today however, bankers are incentivised to sell financial products to people who do not really need them. Many suffer greatly because of this situation.

The loss of meaning saps energy and reduces resilience in the long run. It is therefore worthwhile trying to identify the social value provided by your actions. In your opinion, what is meaningful and what is not? Admittedly, the attempt to combine all four aspects with one another might resemble the quest for the Holy Grail. Even worse, it is often only possible in hindsight to recognise that a certain career decision was perhaps not the best one.

Critical career situations are, therefore, not merely setbacks and crises. Rather, they are decision-making points that enable us to make adjustments along the way to allow our career path to become a better reflection of who we really are. This might even entail leaving the well-trodden paths of the corporate world in order to launch a whole new career.

3.6 Choosing your environment: manager or entrepreneur?

Whether senior vice president, managing director or executive board member, part of the salary you obtain in a company, irrespective of its size, is paid as a result of associating your own name and title with a more or less well-known brand, and thus with its social significance as well as its associated role authority. This is also known as status.

And yet another particularity of having a permanent position is that, for many, it comes with the advantages a large company can offer: a certain degree of consistency, plannability and, by extension, security. What is the price of this? You have to abide by the company's rules, which always entails a certain amount of external control and thus also of arbitrariness. Furthermore, the path up the different rungs on the career ladder is long, tough and very uncertain.

If you choose to be self-employed, things are different, but there are risks here too. Entrepreneurs choose between the risk of failure or remaining meaningless their whole life long. They also choose to work around the clock for many years in order to build something out of nothing. The prize beckoning them is the small chance of achieving great financial success and popularity, like Mark Zuckerberg (Facebook), Ralph Dommermuth (United internet) or the Samwer brothers (Rocket internet), and a large degree of self-determination and influence. There is no magic formula when it comes to this fundamental decision either. Not everyone has the same degree of willingness to take risks and put up with stress or the same capacity to manage a complex organisation and orchestrate it as they see fit. According to the logic of risk and reward, risky investments generate higher profits than their low-risk counterparts. The same evidently also goes for long-term successful careers. Here, too, taking higher risks is rewarded with greater monetary gains. The American business magazine Forbes published a list of the most successful people since 1987. It is no coincidence that among the top 10, only entrepreneurs are to be found with estimated assets between 47.5 billion dollars (tenth place) and 86 billion dollars (first place):

- Bill Gates, USA: Microsoft
- Warren Buffett, USA: Berkshire Hathaway
- Jeff Bezos, USA: amazon
- Amancio Ortega, Spain: Inditex, Zara
- Mark Zuckerberg, USA: Facebook
- Carlos Slim Helú, Mexico: Telmex, América Móvil

- Larry Ellison, USA: Oracle
- Charles G. Koch, USA: Koch Industries
- David H. Koch, USA: Koch Industries
- Michael Bloomberg, USA: Bloomberg.

The situation is no different in Germany. However, the list of the 500 richest Germans, listed annually in *Manager Magazin*, is largely dominated by entrepreneurial dynasties with an estimated family fortune of between 9.2 billion euros (tenth place) and 33 billion euros (first place):

- Family Reimann: Reckitt Benckiser, Coty, JAB Holding, Jacobs Douwe Egberts
- Stefan Quandt and Susanne Klatten: BMW, Altana, Delton, SGL Carbon
- Dieter Schwarz: Lidl, Kaufland
- Georg and Maria-Elisabeth Schaeffler: INA Schaeffler, Continental
- Families Albrecht and Heister: Aldi Sued, Muelheim
- Family Theo Albrecht Jr. and Babette Albrecht: Aldi Nord, Essen
- Family Otto: Otto Versand, ECE
- Klaus-Michael Kuehne: Kuehne+Nagel, Hapag-Lloyd
- Heinz Hermann Thiele: Knorr-Bremse, Vossloh
- Family Wuerth: Wuerth Group.

By comparison, the wages of executive board members of the listed companies appear rather modest. According to the DSW study, the average annual salary of executive board members of the 30 DAX companies in 2017 was 3.4 million euros. Their US colleagues earn significantly more – 17.1 million euros. With an average of around six years in their position as executive board members, this time at the pinnacle of their careers is not sufficient to earn anything close to the wealth accumulated by the most successful entrepreneurs.

But money, or wealth to be more precise, is not everything as they say. Power, creative freedom and popularity are not to be underestimated either and there is every hope of finding this in start-up companies. Reflecting the idea of being mystical creatures that stand for what is pure and good, successful start-ups these days are known as *unicorns*. Not profits, but the share value is taken as an evaluation criterion, as many of these companies do not make a profit, but are nevertheless seen as being very promising by the market and the media.

Here are some of the best-known and highest-valuated start-ups which currently make the hearts of investors beat faster:

- Uber (CEO: Dara Khosrowshahi): transportation services
- Didi Chuxing (CEO: Chéng Wéi): transportation services
- Xiaomi (CEO: Lei Jun): consumer electronics

- AirBnB (CEO: Brian Chesky): apartment rentals
- Palantir (CEO: Peter Thiel): enterprise software
- WeWork (CEO: Adam Neumann): workspace sharing
- Lufax (CEO: Greg Gibb): finance marketplace
- Meituan-Dianping (CEO: Wang Xing): group buying portal
- Pinterest (CEO: Ben Silbermann): image-based social network
- SpaceX (CEO: Elon Musk): space transport services company.

The crunch question is not, therefore, easy to answer. Last but not least, personality traits such as the *need for stability* also play a central role. But the influence of role models and the values lived and conveyed by them should not be underestimated either. Hence, a whole generation of managers was influenced by icons like Jack Welch, former CEO of General Electric. Today, the idols of many budding managers are instead called Mark Zuckerberg or Elon Musk. The understanding of success also differs between managers and entrepreneurs. The research I carried out for this book showed that the self-employed and entrepreneurs define success via criteria such as

- doing something meaningful, or
- creating something that is lasting,

while employed managers tend to see aspects such as

- financial independence and
- economic security

as success factors.

Yet, in addition to the basic career decisions discussed above, there is also another aspect which defines professional success today.

3.7 The role of good leadership

What is the role of good leadership, something which is considered rather a soft skill? There is evidence that good leadership and getting employees emotionally on board lead to success for a company and its leader in the long term. It was for this reason, too, that the Bertelsmann media group, one of the world's biggest media corporations based in Gueterloh, Germany, assessed its 220 subsidiaries according to the performance and quality of their managers. Its main focus was to determine the extent to which the employees were able to identify with their company's goals and with their management. The results were set against the company's profits. This clearly showed that good leadership is closely linked to high workforce identification and a good corporate result (see Figure 3.7.1). Obviously, long-term success can, in fact, be attributed to the managers' inner stance and conviction, and to their leadership style.

Figure 3.7.1 Relationship between management style, employee identification and sales revenues.
Source: Dr Franz Netta, VP HR Bertelsmann, 2007.

Another piece of recent research surfaced even more striking insights. In 2017, Michael Frese and Mona Mensmann from the University of Lueneburg, Germany, published a study which was conducted together with the World Bank, headquartered in Washington D.C. In 2013, the research team started studying 1500 small entrepreneurs in Togo, Western Africa. Their companies averaged a payroll of about three employees with annual earnings of a little over $2000. About one-third of them did something like accounting and only 5% had a budget for any given year.

Using a classical set-up, the 1500 companies were evenly divided into three randomly defined groups. The first group served as a control group. 500 entrepreneurs continued muddling along as usual; another group of 500 company owners received a traditional business administration training like they would get in any MBA. The third group of people received a psychologically based training that taught them basic leadership skills like setting goals, how to deal with criticism and setbacks, and how to develop more resilience.

Two and a half years later, the leaders who had received the leadership and resilience training had increased their sales by 17% and their profits by a roaring 30% compared to the control group, which had not been trained. Also, they had developed and launched more products than their two peer groups.

Even more interesting, however, was the fact that the group of entrepreneurs who had gone through the MBA-like business training barely showed any progress over the control group. While business knowledge did not hurt their progress, learning about leadership and resilience proved to be the true clincher when it comes to economic success.

3.8 The helping hand: a mentor

Do you have a mentor? Many successful people we work with report that they have been fortunate enough to have had great mentors who were willing to take a bet on them, providing them with meaningful opportunities for growth. However, even if a senior person is willing to support you, these relationships don't just work by themselves. A lot of factors have to fit like the chemistry, for example. It starts with having the courage to reach out to a senior executive and daring to ask them. Don't expect them to ask you. However, even if this is accomplished, it also requires the willingness of a more junior person to be open to the advice, support and new opportunities a more senior person is offering, and that they do not just see this opportunistically as a shortcut to advancement in one's career. It requires investing energy and commitment into such a relationship, making it interesting, for both sides to make time for it in their ever-busy schedules.

In our experience, having a mentor can be essential in many ways:

- **Expertise:** Ideally, you can consider your mentor as your role model and get inspired by his or her success. Knowing what professional skills are required for advancing in your career is one of the major benefits that you receive. You can then focus on the skills you are lacking, develop them over time and enhance your career.
- **Networking:** A mentor may have more professional and social contacts that may help in establishing your career. However, it requires a lot of trust in the mentee before these doors open up because it is always the reputation of the more senior person which is at stake.
- **Feedback:** By providing supportive and constructive feedback in areas like interpersonal skills, communication, technical knowledge, leadership skills and social relationships, a mentor can bring about drastic change in a mentee's career, helping him or her to avoid career traps based on some dysfunctional behaviour patterns or even career derailers.
- **Orientation:** A mentor can give you a better idea about the culture of your organisation and the unspoken and implied rules that often are more important than the official ones.
- **Balance:** Sometimes mentors develop into a kind of friend over time. As a result, they may also guide their protégées in their personal life. As we will see later in this book, it is really important to maintain a reasonable balance between your professional and personal life, and a good mentor will help you do that.
- **Emotional support:** If you are lucky, you can also share the frustrations and issues you are facing inside or outside your organisation. Often, a trusted person listening to you attentively is all that is needed. However, it is important to also share your successes with your mentor.

EXAMPLE

Back in 1994, Constanze Ulmer-Eilfort joined the law firm Baker Mc-Kenzie as an associate directly from law school. Nearly 18 years later, she became the company's first female managing partner in the German-speaking region. Today, Baker McKenzie is ranked as the second-largest international law firm in the world, with 77 offices in 47 countries.

Looking back, she reflects upon the importance of mentors for her career success: "I was fortunate enough to have a strong mentor, an older partner of our law firm. On my career path, whenever I had to make a decision or in the preparation for an upcoming partner election, he supported me, encouraged me and paved the way for me. For a woman in a male-dominated professional environment, such a mentor can be crucial."

3.9 Your approach to networking makes a difference

While mentors clearly play an important role for sustainable success in your professional life, what role, if any, does your network, i.e. the amount of personal relationships in general that you have, play for your success? Back in 2001, Hans-Georg Wolff and Klaus Moser, from the University of Erlangen in Germany, launched the first longitudinal study, with about 200 participants over a period of three consecutive years, to measure the link between the nature of your network and success measures like salary and career satisfaction. They showed that a larger personal network correlates with a higher salary, a higher growth rate of a person's salary over time as well as increased career satisfaction. Furthermore, the findings suggested that maintaining a strong network inside the organisation where you are employed is more effective for professional success than a network outside of the organisation.

The work of Ronald Burt from the University of Chicago Booth confirms these findings and adds another dimension to them: the structure of your personal network. For many years, Burt has studied the ways that personal networks create competitive advantages in careers. His findings even go a step further. He claims that no other factor is more important in predicting a person's career success than the nature of her network. However, he concludes that simply having a large network of people you know is not enough. The research team around him found evidence that the most effective networking strategy, in terms of professional success, is on the one hand to be an interface between different networking clusters that are not naturally related to one another. On the other hand, it seems to be advisable to leverage this interface position to actively foster the exchange of ideas and creation of new links between people within these otherwise unrelated network clusters. According to Burt, the ability to be a hub for this cross-pollination of ideas and the connection of different people increases the social value of an individual and his likelihood for success (see Figure 3.9.1). Hence, Burt differentiates between open and closed relationship networks.

If you are part of a closed network, you are exposed to people who already know each other, whereas in an open one, you serve as the link between people from different companies, societal groups or nationalities who do not know each other (see Figure 3.9.2). The more your network has an open structure, the more you are exposed to new ideas and ways of thinking and seeing the world. And the more you leverage these contacts by means of mutual introductions and the creation of synergies between members of different clusters, the better it is for your professional success over time. In

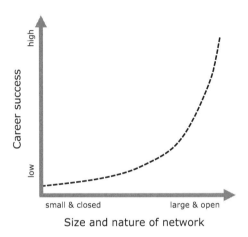

Figure 3.9.1 The link between career success and personal network.

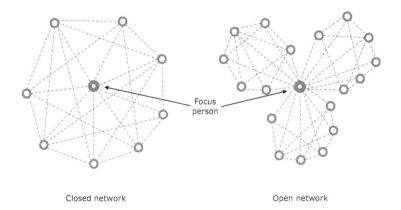

Figure 3.9.2 Closed vs. open personal relationship networks.

contrast, people who are part of a closed network like a clique, according to Burt, are exposed to the same ideas and mindset over and over again and so no synergies or cross-pollination can materialise.

Unarguably, the ability to network effectively is one of the most powerful tools that you can use to advance in your career and attain sustainable success in life. How about your network?

3.10 The formula of success

As we have seen so far, there are different ways of defining success. All in all, it is a combination of objective factors such as money and status, as well as subjective factors like time for family and personal growth. However, the exact proportions differ from person to person. It is this right mix which allows the individual to define his or her current position in life as successful. Furthermore, we have seen that the ingredients for achieving this equilibrium change over time.

We have also seen that there are certain factors that correlate with the likelihood of a person being successful in their life. Some of them are hard or impossible to influence. In Section 2.5, *The role of warm relationships,* we have seen the importance of being given loving attention by your parents during childhood for your future success. Just like the social class you happen to be born into and your gender, this happens to be outside of your control but it has powerful implications, as I showed in Section 2.2, *The importance of your upbringing.* As we have also seen in Section 2.6, *The old question: nature or nurture?* certain personality traits like sociability, stress-resistance, assertiveness, perseverance and impulse control play an important role, too. However, by definition your personality set-up, which is a function of your genetic code and your experiences during the first couple of years in life, is outside of your sphere of influence, too. As I showed in Section 2.8, *The role of your IQ,* your level of intelligence also plays a certain role for career success but the correlation is not strong. As long as a certain threshold value is given, more is not necessarily better, unless you want to excel in academia. However, also your IQ can't be changed just like that. Most certainly, also luck plays a major role as I have laid out in Section 2.9, *Is it only luck?* Being at the right place at the right place, doing the right thing is key for success as we have seen in the example of Alex Atzberger. As we all know, luck can – fortunately or unfortunately – not be forced. What can be influenced though, is the degree of preparation and mental readiness enabling the optimal response to lucky coincidences.

We then looked at the factors which correlate with sustainable success and which can in fact be influenced by you. Through Gillian Zoe Segal's interviews with highly successful people we have seen in Section 3.1, *The patterns behind successful careers,* that dedication, passion and stamina are important to create opportunities where others see none. However, it is at least as crucial to be aware of your circle of competence and to be ready to complement your weak spots by teaming up with others, which is a key leadership competence. Other aspects focused more on resilience. A high degree of agility was amongst these, combined with a tendency to question conventional wisdom and to think independently instead. According to Segal, key resilience aspects like high levels of frustration tolerance and perseverance were amongst the highest-ranking factors in order to master the inevitable *critical career situations*. More evidence regarding the importance of mental agility for professional well-being in a VUCA world was discussed in Section 3.2, *Becoming comfortable with the unknown*.

In Section 3.3, *Characteristics of successful managers,* I showed that the findings of Jim Collins and Morten T. Hansen confirm the importance of key resilience aspects as a condition for success. This also includes the acceptance of circumstances, focusing on solutions rather than on problems, and taking full responsibility for your own destiny. Of equal importance are the ability to anticipate difficulties, having a strong focus on values and meaning, and inner autonomy and self-discipline.

The LinkedIn research discussed in Section 3.4, *The magic recipe*, revealed that successful careers are also shaped by the choices we make, for instance regarding the type of education, career steps and locations we choose. The choices we make also contribute to the skills and experiences we acquire which are essential, too. Another type of choice we make are our relationships. It takes effort, focus and time to build these, a special kind of relationship being the one with a mentor, as I described in Section 3.8, *The helping hand: a mentor*. Also, the size and nature of your network play an important role for success as we have seen in Section 3.9, *Your approach to networking makes a difference*. Building and maintaining your personal contacts and capitalising on these relationships belong to the career choices we make.

The importance of a good set of individual competencies, values, meaning and market demands was discussed in Section 3.5, *Four aspects of the right path to the top*. Part of this cultural set is also about choosing the right type of career as we have seen in Section 3.6, *Choosing your environment: manager or entrepreneur?*

Finally, as we have seen in Section 3.7, *The role of good leadership,* long-term professional success correlates strongly with good leadership skills and a high degree of resilience.

However, there is also a dark side. If we want to understand professional success we must not forget to analyse what makes managers stumble. Different factors bring the career trajectories of high-potential managers to a grinding halt, especially when amplified by critical career situations. In Chapter 5, *The most dangerous career traps*, I will discuss these career derailers, which have the potential to cause some spectacular career fatalities.

These are the factors contributing to sustainable professional success, which everyone can actively influence, but how are they linked? Well, formulas might not be everyone's cup of tea, but they do at least get to the crux of the matter. When setting up such a formula it makes sense to focus only on the factors that are based on actual behaviour, i.e. on aspects that can be influenced. Based on the foregoing summarised findings of this book, I would like to contend that long-term professional success behaves in line with the following formula:

$$Success = \left(\frac{\left(Dedication + Skills + Choices \right) \times Cultural\ fit}{Derailers} \right)^{Resilience}$$

Let's recap the exact meaning of the individual terms.

Dedication: Being passionate about a cause is of fundamental importance. This is more than just motivation. What I mean is rigour, persistence and relentlessness in pursuing a project or business idea, for instance. It is the crazy amount of time and effort which you put into your work that eventually creates opportunities where others do not see any. Let's use a car as a metaphor. In this case the equivalent of *dedication* would be the engine.

Skills: Interpersonal and leadership skills are of crucial importance as are professional skills, and having the relevant experience and specialist knowledge. In the case of a car this would be the gearbox.

Choices: The type of education you have had and your career decisions, i.e. how long you stay in a particular function, company or industry, play an important role. Another aspect is the relationships you entertain. Going back to the car metaphor, this would be the steering.

Dedication + Skills + Choices: This term combines everything that pushes you forward and gives you direction.

Cultural fit: A Formula 1 race car will not be successful when it comes to a race through the desert like the rally Paris–Dakar. However, on a high-speed track, it is hard to beat. With the right team, a charismatic visionary might be a very successful entrepreneur. However, if he is employed as a manager in a large corporation, in which he has to try to work his way up through the career echelons, he is likely to fail. It is also important to find a match for your own values and for what your environment (e.g. the market or the company) needs.

Derailers: Certain destructive personality traits that surface under great pressure have the potential to bring careers to a grinding halt if they are not kept in check through adequate self-management. These derailers include excessive arrogance and distrust towards others. The more these derailers determine visible behaviour, the more likely they are to impede long-term success. It is a bit like a car with a huge engine and rear drive. If you are not careful in certain situations like on winding, slippery roads and do not slow down, you are most likely to find yourself in the ditch sooner or later.

Resilience: If you are not able to embrace change and withstand setbacks, failures and periods of crises, then your dedication, skills and choices won't get you very far. As we have seen in Section 1.2, *Success means overcoming critical career situations*, crises and critics will inevitably surface on the path to success. These hostile encounters have to be dealt with constructively. The more resilient you are, the more buffer capacity you have to absorb setbacks and the more likely you are to succeed. Staying with the car metaphor, think of resilience as the chassis which gives stability and as the suspension which buffers away the impacts of adverse road conditions.

Bibliography

Anonymous; Startup Companies Valued at One Billion U.S. Dollars or More by Venture-Capital Firms Worldwide, as of October 2017, by Valuation (in Billion U.S. Dollars); Statista, New York, USA, 2017.

Bennett, Nathan; Lemoine, G. James; What VUCA Really Means for You; Harvard Business School Publishing, Boston, USA, 2014.

Berger, Guy; How to Become an Executive; LinkedIn, Mountain View, USA, 2016.

Burt, R. S.; Structural Holes; Harvard University Press, Cambridge, USA, 1992.

Collins, Jim; Hansen, Morten T.; Great by Choice; Harper Business, New York City, USA, 2011.

Drath, Karsten; Resilient Leadership: Beyond Myths and Misunderstandings; Taylor & Francis, Abingdon-on-Thames, UK, 2016.

Goldsmith, Marshall; What Got You Here Won't Get You There: How Successful People Become Even More Successful; Profile Books, London, UK, 2008.

Jobs, Steve; Stanford Commencement Address; Stanford, USA, 2005.

Kail, Eric G.; Leading in a VUCA Environment; Harvard Business School Publishing, Boston, USA, 2010.

Kroll, Luisa; Dolan, Kerry A.; Forbes 2017 Billionaires List: Meet The Richest People On The Planet; Forbes, New York, USA, 2017.

Lewis, Michael; Moneyball: The Art Of Winning An Unfair Game; W. W. Norton, New York City, USA, 2003.

McCall, Morgan W.; Lombardo, Michael M.; Morrison, Ann M.; The Lessons of Experience, How Successful Executives Develop on the Job; Free Press, New York, USA, 1988.

Nesshoever, Christoph; Die reichsten Deutschen – Familie Reimann verdraengt BMW-Erben; Manager Magazin, Hamburg, Germany, 2017.

Netta, Franz; Partizipation, Gesundheit und wirtschaftlicher Erfolg, Neue Analysen und Erkenntnisse zum Gesundheitsmanagement; Helm Stirlin Institut, Heidelberg, 2007.

O'Connor, Roisin; People Who Read Books Live Longer Lives, Study Says; The Independent, London, UK, 2016.

Robinson, Ken; Do Schools Kill Creativity?; TED, www.ted.com, USA, 2007.

Schoenherr, Katja; Erfolg ist eine Frage der Energie, Unternehmen meistern Krisen, wenn die Mitarbeiter mitziehen. Nur wie?; Zeitverlag: Die Zeit, Hamburg, Germany, 2011.

Segal, Gillian Zoe; Getting There; Abrams, New York, USA, 2015.

Sennett, Richard; The Culture of the New Capitalism; Yale University Press, New Haven, USA, 2006.

Sonnenfeld, Jeffrey A.; Ward, Andrew J.; Firing Back: How Great Leaders Rebound after Career Disasters; Harvard Business School Publishing, Boston, USA, 2007.

Thorborg, Heiner; Kann man Unternehmertum trainieren? Ja, aber nicht mit BWL-Wissen; Manager Magazin, Hamburg, Germany, 2017.

Various; Studie zur Vergütung der Vorstände in den DAX- und MDAX-Unternehmen im Geschäftsjahr 2016; Deutsche Schutzvereinigung für Wertpapierbesitz e.V., Duesseldorf, Germany, 2017.

Verfuerth, Claus; Debnar-Daumler, Sebastian; Auf der Überholspur ausgebremst; Rundstedt, Duesseldorf, Germany, 2015.

Wolff, Hans-Georg; Moser, Klaus; Effects of Networking on Career Success: A Longitudinal Study; University of Erlangen-Nuremberg, Germany, 2008.

4 What makes managers stumble?

The previous chapters contained an overview of what success actually is and what influences successful careers. As we have seen, dealing successfully and constructively with critical career situations plays a central role here. But what factors actually cause successful managers to stumble in their careers?

4.1 Leadership starts with leading yourself

Professional success is not attainable without being able to lead yourself and others well. Both aspects primarily have to do with being familiar with your own strengths and weaknesses, and working on yourself. Accordingly, my research for this book revealed that self-reflection is one of the most important prerequisites for pursuing a successful career.

Being able to manage yourself and others is undoubtedly one of the most difficult tasks in professional life. The worst thing is that managers are frequently not sufficiently prepared for it. The predominant belief in our education system and even in elite business schools is that leadership, meaning the conscious use and control of emotions in a professional context, is not particularly relevant for corporate success and is at best subsumed under the term "soft skills". This belief costs many managers their health and, ultimately, even their lives, as I will endeavour to show. Most companies still do not take the topic of executive development seriously enough, especially at the top executive levels, where in many cases there are practically no options for further training. In a study entitled *Ascending to the C-Suite*, published by McKinsey in 2015, only 27% of 1195 board members questioned stated that their company had adequately prepared them for and supported them in their career step up to executive/board level.

To avoid any misunderstanding: I do not see managers as innocent victims of the "system". We all have a duty to continue to develop our own skills. This is not something that can be delegated to anyone else. Even though dependencies and decision-making dynamics in the company "system" often put many managers in rather awkward and unpleasant situations they would rather avoid, it is not enough to simply continue pursuing the everyday agenda in the face of these dynamics and to lose sight of your own development. A manager must be able to make unpopular decisions time and time again. There will always be situations in which they are not permitted to communicate anything even though this would be helpful to the employees, for instance in the case of impending restructuring measures.

And yet, in our experience, managers still have plenty of room for manoeuvre, which they often fail to fully exploit. Today's managers must really work towards becoming experts in the leadership of people and of themselves. This also means recognising themselves as the person they are – including their body, mind and soul – as their most important productive resource and getting themselves fit accordingly. It would never cross anyone's mind to run a marathon without any experience or training. But many managers do this every day, as they are usually quite unprepared when they first take on the job of managing themselves, their employees and their companies, and this is definitely a long-distance discipline.

There is another way in which aspects of the VUCA world play an important role in an executive's everyday life today, and more specifically in the IT sector and its growing influence over the past 20 years. Today, it is possible to make grave erroneous decisions in a much shorter period of time than would have been possible in the past.

EXAMPLE

The last financial crisis linked to US subprime mortgage loans could only occur as a result of financial products developed on the basis of a digitally networked economy.

Furthermore, the social media ensured that the mistakes made were disclosed in no time at all and led to negative public reactions, for instance in the form of shitstorms. The demands made on the professionality and moral integrity of managers have, therefore, clearly risen over recent decades. A successful manager has to be able and want to deal with such pressure. Yet managers are "only" humans, too. What are you supposed to do with the emotions triggered by this pressure?

4.2 Emotions in business

The prevailing opinion in the training of future executives is still that emotions, particularly destructive ones, do not belong on the executive floor. Executives must always convey tranquillity, serenity, optimism and aplomb. Excessive matter-of-factness is fine, but negative or even destructive emotions are not appropriate. Yet, this is not always that easy. Every human being, and this of course also includes executives, has an inner thought stream and feelings such as anger, doubt and fear. Our brains are simply made that way. They constantly try to predict and solve potential problems and to avoid possible dangers. In our work as coaches, we deal a lot with executives who not only have unwanted thoughts and emotions, but who also feel trapped by them like a fish on a hook. They either identify themselves with these thoughts and emotions or try to avoid situations that trigger them, such as new challenges.

When dealing with their own thoughts and behaviour patterns managers sometimes criticise themselves for having such negative emotions. Particularly tough managers ignore their negative emotions and try to actively desensitise themselves against situations that trigger those thoughts and feelings. In any case, destructive thoughts and feelings take up too much space with these managers. They divert cognitive energy away from other, probably more important topics. This is a common problem that is frequently reinforced through popular self-management strategies. We regularly encounter managers with recurring emotional difficulties, such as fear of decisions, fear of rejection, a constant focus on their own perceived weaknesses, or exaggerated envy, who have developed their own handmade techniques to get a grip on their problems, often unsuccessfully. There is plenty of available research illustrating how the attempt to ignore a thought or emotion reinforces it in the long-term. In one famous study conducted by a Harvard professor, Daniel Wegner, participants were asked to suppress any thoughts of a white bear. Of course, they had trouble doing this. Later, when the prohibited thought was lifted, this group unwillingly thought more frequently, longer and more intensively about the white bear than did the control group. Hence, the goal cannot be to suppress supposedly negative impulses. Instead, this energy needs to be sensibly channelled, which is also known as self-control. The ability to control oneself becomes essential, particularly under great emotional pressure, as in the critical career situations described above.

4.3　Insecure overachievers

Since the 1950s, McKinsey & Company, one of the world's leading strategy consulting firms, has been known to employ the best graduates from the best universities, and to use performance incentives and a very formative high-performance culture to shape these young, hungry "high potentials" according to their requirements. After these young consultants are pushed to the maximum by their international projects, most of them voluntarily leave the company on good terms after three years at the latest in order to take up leading positions in the industry and then to become potential customers of their former employer. Over the past few decades, this HR strategy and its accompanying high-performance culture were adopted in the field of professional services by the majority of international companies and they are now also entering many more traditional industrial and service-based companies.

The expression which best describes McKinsey's employee profile is the "insecure overachiever", who is to be found in many management positions today. This type of person is well-educated, intelligent, often good-looking, mobile and highly performance-motivated. However, the moment you look behind the shiny facade, which we of course regularly do in our work, you find people who are continuously plagued by the question "Am I good enough?"

Of course, there are many kinds of people walking through life with these or similar questions occupying their minds, but this group of persons compensates for these nagging inner doubts with permanent high performance and success, not having any other available mechanism for accepting themselves in their state of imperfection, which we all effectively share. This inner pressure is an enormous career engine and leads to a very specific way of life, which focuses on work alone. As long as insecure overachievers are successful, the flywheel continues to turn. Problems generally arise when they are no longer successful and when they run out of physical resources; then they feel like "driven people", like they are no longer in control of their inner world.

The situations in which this happens are typically marked by high pressure or insecurity. This account describes the typical effect of inner beliefs, which also constitute a risk factor, both for one's inner mental balance and for one's resilience. Beliefs are decisions with regard to one's life that people have made in their childhood and internalised. Long before an employee or manager has to prove himself in the "company system", he has developed success strategies in the "family system". A lot of managers don't like to think back to the time when, unlike now, they were small, weak and insecure, and feel like they are "on the couch" when the topic of their childhood crops up. And yet, it was already at this point in time that the course was set. As a child, each person already learns how best to handle the family system in order to be successful. Love and attention are the success criteria of a child. Beliefs are therefore strategies with which a child tries to obtain parental love and attention. In the corporate world, this is later known as "visibility" and "recognition". When devising its strategy, a child can of course only fall back on its childlike logic. This is characterised by magical thinking – that is to say the belief that the child's environment behaves as it does only in response to the child's behaviour. Examples of magical thinking are: "I have to be obedient, so that my brother gets healthy again", or "I have to work really hard at school, so that Mum and Dad don't argue so much anymore".

These childlike decisions become consolidated as coping strategies over the years, finding their equivalent in the brain in the form of neuronal stimulation patterns. This is why these strategies remain relevant into late adulthood, even though the family or professional system in which the person then manoeuvres is a completely different one.

Interestingly enough, in our work with managers we have noticed that the number of beliefs that these managers have internalised is limited. They can

Table 4.3.1 Musts and must nots

Musts	Must nots
I have to be perfect.	I must not show myself as I am.
I have to be quick.	I must not be different.
I need to please everyone.	I may not be successful.
I must be strong.	I must not be like everyone else.
I must make an effort.	I must not ask for help.
I must be careful.	I must not show my feelings.

usually be reduced to a certain number of musts (i.e. positively formulated beliefs) and must nots (i.e. negatively formulated beliefs) (Table 4.3.1).

Do any of these feel familiar to you?

These beliefs surface more frequently when a manager is not in his or her comfort zone – for example because he or she is encountering something new, unfamiliar, particularly thrilling or threatening. Since neuronal patterns cannot be deleted, an old belief cannot simply be erased. Instead, a new and more appropriate behaviour strategy has to be developed and practised.

It is important to understand that beliefs used to serve a positive purpose. Their intention was to protect us and guarantee access to positive affection. However, as we grow older and become adult professionals the side effects of our beliefs become more and more visible. Say you are running the belief, "If I am not good enough then I will not be loved". In fact, this is the evergreen of all beliefs. The benefits of this belief are most probably that you care for performance and that you like to deliver good work. Most probably you have had some sort of success in your career because of this belief and you enjoy a good reputation. The downside of this belief might be that you cannot enjoy your success because in the very moment you have achieved something it becomes normal. Also, you may feel the urge for external appreciation to the degree that it might become an actual dependency. When you are not feeling it, this may stress you out and you may actually feel threatened by the situation. In Section 7.7.2, *Transforming inner beliefs*, I will outline how these dysfunctional beliefs can be reshaped into something more productive.

4.4 Managers as victims

EXAMPLE

When, on 23 August 2013, Steve Ballmer proclaimed that he would resign as CEO of Microsoft before the end of the year, the software giant's share value bounced up 7% on the same day. This was a clear sign by investors that Monkeyboy, as Ballmer was also called for his extremely loud and flamboyant stage appearances, had obviously long passed his zenith as management figure of the Silicon Valley icon Microsoft – even though Ballmer had made a significant contribution. As Microsoft's first manager he had been one of the main protagonists in its success story since 1980. Getting this kind of feedback when you step down is painful. So painful that, after a brief interim period as an executive board member, Ballmer broke off all contact with Microsoft and chose to pursue basketball instead.

During my research for this book, I asked my interview partners about the negative emotional, cognitive and physical consequences that critical career situations had had on them. The results are illustrated in Figure 4.4.1.

For the purpose of simplicity, they can be subdivided into three segments:

- The most frequent emotion was fear and the feeling of being a victim.
- Symptoms of medium frequency ranged from sleeping disorders and despondency to increased irritability down to emotional numbness.
- The symptoms in the last segment occur rarely, since their consequences are much more serious and threatening. They range from thinking about disaster scenarios over heightened alcohol consumption to suicidal thoughts.

If one compares these symptoms with the characteristic course of unfolding mental exhaustion, also colloquially known as burnout, then striking resemblances can be seen in the symptoms and their sequence, as shown

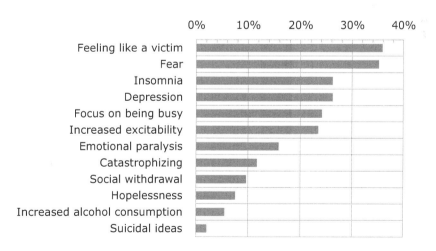

Figure 4.4.1 Consequences of critical career situations.
Source: Survey by Karsten Drath Dec 2015–Jan 2016.

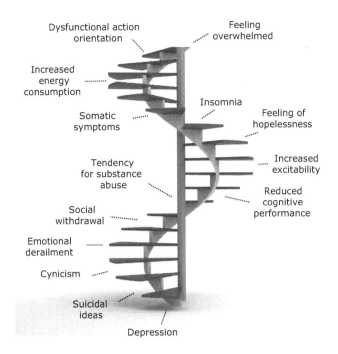

Dysfunctional action orientation

Feeling overwhelmed

Increased energy consumption

Insomnia

Somatic symptoms

Feeling of hopelessness

Tendency for substance abuse

Increased excitability

Reduced cognitive performance

Social withdrawal

Emotional derailment

Cynicism

Suicidal ideas

Depression

Figure 4.4.2 Individual effects of critical career situations.
Source: Fotolia, Selensergen.

clearly in the staircase illustration (Figure 4.4.2). It must also be borne in mind that the magnitude of the consequences of a particular critical career situation not only depends on the gravity and frequency of the symptoms, but also on how long they last.

43% of the managers questioned stated that the consequences of the severe setbacks, for them personally, lasted several weeks. With 28% of the study participants, the repercussions went on for six months. At least 12% of those affected maintained the symptoms over a period of one year, in nearly 7% of the cases even over several years. The frequency of suicidal thoughts among those managers, who experienced long-term repercussions from their critical career situations, was nearly 10%.

How can these figures be explained? What played a key role was the manager's sense of being a victim of the circumstances and having no choice but to suffer. This is, of course, a distorted view of reality, as there are always options. Yet, in the context of difficult career situations, this victim mentality is almost always present. When this is the case, it is extremely difficult to get a manager to think more constructively.

The background is a phenomenon known as secondary morbid gain in the field of medicine. Imagine a child has a cold and a high temperature. Normally both parents work, but now one of them has to stay at home to look after the child. The child is given hot soup in bed and stories are read to it. It is allowed to eat ice-cream and watch television as much as it wants. The symptoms of the illness are unpleasant but the loving attention it gets from its parents and the luxury of suspended rules are superb. The child enjoys this so much that the illness is subconsciously prolonged for another two days in order to enjoy this secondary morbid gain a bit longer. But what morbid gain can the manager draw from his or her victim mentality? There are various aspects:

- **Blame:** As long as the manager is in martyr mode he cannot be blamed, because he was pushed into his misery by others. Good and evil are clearly defined.
- **Entitlement:** She is emotionally in the right and morally superior to her adversary. She is entitled to solidarity and support from other people.
- **Responsibility:** He is not responsible for the events because he could not have done anything in that situation. His hands were tied.
- **Sympathy:** If one is subjected to something unpleasant, one can expect to get support and sympathy from others.
- **Carte blanche:** Someone who has lost a lot is more likely to get away with misconduct and negligence, since allowances must be made for them.

So, there are a number of good reasons for critically examining ourselves when we perceive ourselves in the role of the victim. But this is easier said than done, as our brains are so bombarded with adrenaline and noradrenaline during these stressful situations that, from a cognitive point of view, we revert back to our most primitive instincts. This is due to rather unhelpful thought patterns which we need to recognise and correct.

4.5 Watch out, thinking trap!

At the beginning of 2017, I was on my way to a prestigious leadership symposium held by a large car manufacturer. For the following two days, I was supposed to be one of the experts facilitating workshops for the 80 or so participating managers. The topic of my workshop was called "Resilience and Leadership" and I was very much looking forward to it. I had just completed the manuscript of my new book called *The Art of Self-Leadership*. It was my eighth book on the topic and I really think of myself as an expert when it comes to dealing with adversity and hardships – at least in theory. As it was early February there had been a very cold period with snow and ice in the past few days. However, this very morning sudden rain had turned the steps in front of my house into an ice rink and despite my wife's warning the blessings of gravity hit me by surprise and I fell hard on my back. The pain was remarkable but I quickly got back on my feet and since I was running late I somehow got my luggage and myself into the car and drove to the venue of the event without much further ado. At this moment, I was not thinking very much. There was only one voice in my head, saying, "You have to get there somehow and you must not be late." I don't recall exactly how I got out of the car since I could barely walk. When I arrived at the conference the organisers looked at me with deep concern in their faces, indicating that I looked exactly as bad as I felt. They asked me if I wanted to cancel the workshops. I briefly considered it, but it just did not feel right. From previous experience, I knew that a bruised rib is a painful but a relatively hazard-free medical condition. However, I was also aware that a broken rib feels exactly the same way but with a substantially higher degree of risk associated with it, due to possible punctures of your intestines. Not a very funny thought. I recall that I heard two voices in my head. Number one felt like it was coming from an older part of my brain as it was very loud and was going something like:

- Don't be a wimp. You can't let the client down!
- They will hate you and will certainly not come back to you!

However, there was also another, yet much weaker voice which was probably coming from a more rational part of my neocortex. It was mumbling something like:

- You are a flipping resilience expert. You have to be a role model for showing your boundaries. Don't repeat your past mistakes!

Needless to say, I delivered the workshop of the first day with the help of a lot of painkillers and my usual endurance. Somehow, I survived it but I really felt that the participants had only gotten about 50% of my normal performance. However, in contrast to say ten years ago, I did not feel guilty for that. I had given it my best. Also, I had made it transparent to the managers that there had been an accident and that I might have to stop the workshop should my condition go south. Nevertheless, I felt somehow stupid for toughing it out.

In our workshops on resilient leadership my colleagues and I talk about the difference of being truly resilient as opposed to being just hard on yourself, which we will see in Section 6.3, *Resilient or tough?* The difference here is self-awareness. When you are just disciplined without listening to your own needs this makes you tough. This applies to many managers we work with, including my former self. The problem with exclusively focusing on toughness and denying your vulnerability is that one fine day something will come along that is tougher than you. And then this hits you by surprise and you are very likely to have no strategies to cope with this. In contrast, being self-aware means listening to your own needs and accepting your own vulnerability. However, you are still on your own when you make your decision whether to continue or not. This is what we call *ambivalence*. And while both options may not feel great, at least you are making a conscious decision as opposed to just acting out some unconscious drivers – like "I will be rejected if I don't show everybody how committed I am!" – which date way back to your childhood days.

On the morning of the next day I felt much better. The pain was OK and also my mirror image resembled more the memory of my own face on a good day. This time the workshop went much smoother with great participant interaction and good feedback. I was grateful and felt a great degree of relief. Everything was geared up for a happy end and I was sure this would be a nice story on resilience to tell in my workshops to come. But "it ain't over till it's over", as they say. So, I travelled on to the next town and the next hotel to run yet another workshop on resilience the next day. What an irony! I still felt as if I had been run over by a truck. And then things turned really sour. In the middle of the night I woke up with the most intense pain in my back and my chest. Luckily, I had never encountered anything as painful as that before. This time there was no doubt that it was a bit more serious. One hour later I was hospitalised and my X-ray showed a nice fracture in my ribs. I had to cancel the workshop and this time I did not feel any ambivalence. There were no longer two voices in my head trying to influence my actions. The only voice I heard was my own screaming "uhhhh" and "arggghh" whenever I made a wrong move or just took a breath a tiny bit too deep. In a bizarre way, the strong physical pain was a relief for my decision process with regards to going on or giving in. It basically relieved me of having to make the decision. I had to stay another three days in hospital until the medication and my body started to cooperate and I could walk straight again. A lot of quality time for reflection.

When executives experience difficult, even traumatic situations, such as severe health conditions or political struggles, depending on their personality structures they may be particularly susceptible to so-called thinking traps. These are dysfunctional cognitive patterns that can frequently be observed when a person is subjected to great pressure. The following are the most common thinking traps.

Thinking in disaster scenarios

The person concerned turns the solvable problem into an insurmountable crisis by means of distortion and exaggeration.

EXAMPLE

"I will lose my job and not find a new one. We will have to sell the house. I won't be able to pay for my children's studies, and so they will end up despising me. I will be a nobody and sooner or later my wife will leave me."

Generalisation

To standardise the undifferentiated view of the problem, as – without exception – this situation was always that way and will always remain that way, without any chance of improvement.

EXAMPLE

"I'm simply not born to be a manager. Right from the start, I was the wrong choice for the job, I just did not realise this. The truth is I don't have what it takes. It takes a different type of person to do the job."

Maximising the negative, minimising the positive

Once old self-doubts have been triggered during a career crisis, they tend to take control. All of a sudden, previous successes fade into the background and only failures are remembered.

EXAMPLE

"Failed again! My father was right after all that nothing decent would ever become of me. Last year's salary increase, the high-potential programme and the extraordinary praise I received from my boss two years ago mean nothing now. As we can see now, all that was worthless. The truth is, I'm not up to it."

Reading thoughts

People with a chip on their shoulder tend, irrationally, to take everything personally.

EXAMPLE

"My associates are so nice to me. And my colleagues whisper and laugh behind my back in the coffee corner. Even my secretary gives me knowing looks. No doubt, everyone already knows that I've been fired. Who knows, perhaps they're even behind it and ran me down to my boss."

Emotional reasoning

Under great pressure, emotions and cognitive thinking become blurred. Our actions and decisions tend to be more irrational, i.e. based on emotions.

EXAMPLE

"My boss fired me. There is no rational reason for this. He just doesn't like me. I always knew it. I hate him. He has no good qualities. I'm sure that in reality he's a psychopath and has some kind of personality disorder."

External locus of control

In the victim role it is difficult or even impossible to realistically gauge one's own responsibility for events and the options available for moving forward out of one's misery.

EXAMPLE

"This is all because of the strategy that the new board member introduced. It is complete nonsense, from beginning to end, and simply cannot work. I had no other choice but to oppose it. If they had been a bit savvier up there, I would have been appointed board member and then everything would have been fine."

Are you familiar with any or even all of these thinking traps? Don't worry, you're in good company. Nevertheless, the potential for damage to be done by these cognitive distortions and generalisations is immense, as it makes a situation that is already difficult unbearable. Thinking traps are poison for the mind; they can lead us into seemingly hopeless situations. The good news is: if a manager does manage to get himself out of this emotional swamp, like the Baron of Münchhausen did, then critical career situations are usually processed well and lead to personal growth. Hence, nearly 63% of the study participants reported having consistently higher performance levels after overcoming a job crisis. Only 13% reported having a worse performance.

4.6 Managers as martyrs

These expressions are commonly used by managers: "My neck is on the line" and "I have skin in the game". These rather martial-like sayings reflect the fact that many managers identify so strongly with their professional lives that they can no longer distinguish between their job and their life outside this role. These decision-makers almost always perceive any threat to their career as a threat to their very existence. Sometimes this identification has tragic consequences. Since companies these days are becoming increasingly transparent and the media ever faster, some of those events – though by no means all – which would probably have been dealt with more discreetly 15 years ago, go public. This includes the fate of some managers, which I would like to dwell on to illustrate how identifying too closely with one's role as a manager can be life-threatening.

The case of Carsten Schloter, the charismatic and busy CEO of Swisscom, who committed suicide in 2013, is one of the more recent cases of a CEO suicide in the German-speaking realm. Seen merely as an isolated case, it appears extreme and very tragic. However, if we take a look at the developments of the past few years, a worrying trend can be observed among managers who evidently do not have enough resilience to withstand the increasing pressure. When confronted with tragic events like Carsten Schloter's suicide, rationally minded people often ask themselves: "Why did he kill himself?" The example of Schloter shows that there is never just one reason or one culprit, but a whole range of factors which, combined, undermine a manager's resilience and may eventually lead to a catastrophe, be it suicide, burnout, substance abuse or something else. Schloter was seen as charismatic, extremely hard-working, mobile and innovative. He dedicated his life to his profession and his performance. He was tough on himself, in excellent physical condition and always available. He was an exemplary manager, like many others too. But there was also another side to him. His wife and children had lived separately from him for many years already, and accounts of conflicts with the chairman of the board of directors made the rounds. In recent interviews he had admitted having difficulties finding a work–life balance and occasionally feeling driven and desperate. He was obviously not alone in having these feelings, as Table 4.6.1 shows. However, some of his manager colleagues managed to catch themselves just in time, for instance by taking time off and not allowing things to go to the extreme. Nevertheless, in all of the cases mentioned, the negative consequences on the company are clearly visible from the outside, e.g. the drop in the share price.

Another recent and equally tragic incident happened in Germany. Heinz-Joachim Neubuerger, former CFO of Siemens, enjoyed an excellent reputation throughout his career. In 1989, he had switched to Siemens from his position as head of investor relations at the investment bank JP Morgan, and he was appointed CFO nine years later. The bribery affair which came to light in November 2006 and its long-lasting and messy reappraisal were to unknowingly have major repercussions on his life. Even though he was regarded as Heinrich von Pierer's potential successor, he was forced to resign from office after the affair became public. Yet the shock did not end there. In 2008, the company asserted claims for damages against 11 managing board members, among then Neubuerger. Several possibilities for

Table 4.6.1 Top managers mentioned in the press in previous years because they committed suicide (selection, not definitive)

Name	Function	Incident (according to the press)	Country	Year
Martin Senn	Ex-CEO Zurich	Suicide at the age of 59 years	CH	2016
Heinz-Joachim Neubürger	CFO Siemens	Suicide at the age of 62 years	D	2015
William Broeksmit	Board candidate Deutsche Bank	Suicide at the age of 58 years	UK	2014
Karl Slym	CEO Tata Motors	Suicide at the age of 51 years	IND	2014
Otto Beisheim	Owner Metro Group	Suicide at the age of 89 years	D	2013
Carsten Schloter	CEO Swisscom	Suicide at the age of 49 years	CH	2013
Pierre Wauthier	CFO Zurich Group	Suicide at the age of 53 years	CH	2013
Adrian Kohler	CEO Ricola	Suicide at the age of 53 years	CH	2011
Adolf Merckle	Owner of Ratiopharm, among other companies	Suicide at the age of 74 years	D	2009
Alex Widmer	CEO Julius Bär	Suicide at the age of 52 years	CH	2008

finding an out-of-court settlement were not seized in the following years. It was only in 2014 that Siemens and Neubuerger managed to reach an amicable agreement. At the beginning of 2015, around nine years after one of the largest corruption scandals of German economic history came to light, he committed suicide.

The list in Table 4.6.1 is by no means complete and only comprises the cases mentioned in the media in German- and English-speaking countries over recent years.

Critical career situations can have serious and even life-threatening consequences. From a psychological perspective, processing critical career situations is comparable with dealing with grief or trauma. Various models have been developed over the past few decades which could help to raise understanding of the emotional, cognitive and physical reactions.

4.7 Grieving managers

Until then, life had been in the fast lane. Everyday life under pressure, where working days were rarely less than 12 hours long and where one appointment followed the next. And then? An emergency stop! Standstill. At first there is shock, quickly followed by an unfathomable void and a sense of meaninglessness. Later, often only self-pity, helplessness and rage remain. These or similar words are the ones used by many executives to describe the moment they are informed about their dismissal, one of the worst kinds of critical career situation.

EXAMPLE

For Léo Apotheker, former CEO of the software giant SAP, it was a phone call he received one Saturday evening in February 2010, after coming out of the cinema with his wife. Hasso Plattner, founder of the company and today's chairman of the board of directors, first discussed trivial matters with him before ending with the sentence that Apotheker's contract as CEO would not be renewed. Apotheker had worked his way up the company over a period of 20 years. For nine months he had been at the head of the board of managers after the previous widely respected manager, Henning Kagermann, had resigned. He had been given an aggressive mandate by the supervisory board and, in implementing it, turned the entire client base and also some of the employees against himself. In response to the collapse of Lehman Brothers, he pushed through a stringent cost-cutting package and, at the same time, increased the fee for the customers' service package. Both moves were made rather callously and without much sensitivity. Now he was fired, for the first time in his career. It was not to be the last time, but this one time will undoubtedly remain imprinted on his memory. After being dismissed, he needed three to four months to digest the shock. He expressed this to the journalist Carsten Knop in an interview. Hours after his dismissal was made public, he had received 3500 emails in which colleagues thanked him and tried to cheer him up. However, most of his colleagues and employees heaved a sigh of relief and did so openly. He withdrew into the circle of his friends and family to try to find himself again. He had many conversations to try to rid himself of his resentment. He analysed the situation and what had happened.

In hindsight, it is questionable whether he came to the right conclusions. In November 2010, much to many people's surprise, he was appointed CEO of the hardware giant Hewlett-Packard. His predecessor had come a cropper because of an affair and the company needed some tranquillity and clarity at the top to drive forward its new direction. Here too, Apotheker managed to turn the markets, customers and employees against him within an extremely short space of time. His plans to split the corporate group led to a 45% decline in the company's share value. Not even a year after taking on the new position, he was sacked a second time. This time he received a settlement of 7 million US dollars.

Top managers, such as Léo Apotheker, are used to turning the big wheels, leading negotiations at the highest level and constantly jet-setting around the globe. Their job is their life and serves, at the same time, as an external source to feed their own egos and sense of self-worth. They relish their influence and high standing and receive remuneration that is disproportionately high. It is obvious to everyone that they play in the premier league. But then suddenly they fall into the abyss and the fall is fast and extremely painful. As a result of the unwanted loss of their position most executives are thrown into a severe personal crisis. Cut off from the circles of power, of confidential information and critical crisis meetings, they suddenly become aware that their feeling of being irreplaceable was an illusion. Whilst they recently still attributed nearly every success story to their own performance, the new situation calls their entire self-concept into question. It is easier said than done to not retreat into your shell after experiencing such a situation but instead to see the career downturn as an opportunity for personal and professional growth. And this is exactly where resilience, or inner resistance, comes into play. The more resilient a manager is, the better he or she has learned not to regard such upheavals as a devaluation of themselves as an individual, but rather as an interesting learning experience that is just part of the "big business" game. This game is not amusing, as it is an adult game, but it still works according to the principles of a game. It has rules, even if they are not written down; there are game pieces that have their own interests; there are event cards that throw one's own plans overboard; and there are winners and losers, who are often "thrown out" by the roll of a die.

If one examines the course of decisive career changes, it becomes clear that the individual processing steps resemble the different stages of loss, as Elisabeth Kuebler-Ross described it. The Swiss-American psychiatrist dedicated her professional life to dealing with the dying, with grief and with the processing of grief. In her book *Questions and Answers on Death and Dying*, she drew worldwide attention to herself back in 1971, particularly because of her model of the five stages of loss, which she developed after innumerable conversations held with the dying. She has been granted 23 honorary degrees by various universities and colleges and 70 national and international awards for her life's work. In 1999, the news magazine *TIME* named her among the "100 greatest scientists and thinkers of the 20th century".

Figure 4.7.1 shows the typical course of processing critical career situations, using the five stages of loss model with managers who had been dismissed. If this illustration reminds you of the change curve diagram frequently used in business, this is no coincidence. Kuebler-Ross' model served as a model for this.

The summarised findings listed next originate from our work with managers in comparable situations. They are also based on the study *Auf der Überholspur ausgebremst*, published in 2014, a collaborative effort carried out together with the University Fresenius, the *HPO Research Group*, and the talent consultancy *von Rundstedt*.

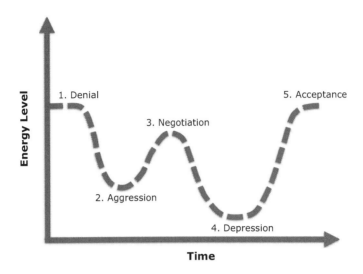

Figure 4.7.1 The five stages of grief according to Elisabeth Kuebler-Ross.

Stage 1: Denial. A manager has successfully worked his way up to his position over the years and can proudly look back on previous successes. But recently, things have not been going so smoothly. The atmosphere is increasingly tense, he is no longer receiving the customary support from superiors, and colleagues are suddenly distancing themselves from him. The more secure a manager feels, the less he relates these harbingers to himself. Instead, he will tend to see any faulty behaviour as stemming from his counterparts and see himself as irreplaceable. Of course, nobody admits this openly. Experienced executives, who have experienced comparable upheavals and can, therefore, draw parallels and see similarities, usually recognise these signals earlier than others.

Stage 2: Aggression. Then all of a sudden comes the blow which knocks everything apart: his dismissal. This is a tremendous shock for the manager as, with the loss of his job, one of the central pillars of his life concept falls away too. Not being part of the "system" would have been inconceivable up to that point in time. The feeling of helplessness and of not being able to actively influence the situation is new to him and triggers anger and frustration. It becomes very difficult for him to think clearly and act prudently. This is further exacerbated by a sense of shame and the worry of not being able to maintain his customary living standard, as there is a reputation and a facade to keep up. Like most ousted managers, the manager concerned will tend to blame himself for not having interpreted the signs properly or taken countermeasures in time. One is always wiser with hindsight. Once the initial shock has been overcome, administrative processes ensure that the pain does not remain vague but becomes palpable. What was previously on paper, becomes more and more a reality when the office keys, key cards and business car are reclaimed and the manager becomes more and more cut off from customers, colleagues and employees. Thoughts like "Who undermined me?" or "Whom can I still trust?" often nag the departing manager.

Stage 3: Negotiation. In this stage the initial numbness and accompanying aggression gradually begin to subside. Bolstered by his customary professionalism and firm belief in success, the manager emotionally works his way back up to the top and tries to regain control. His response is: forge ahead. His ego might have taken a severe bruising, and yet, nevertheless, the manager enthusiastically goes on the search for a new and equivalent position with discipline and with the tried-and-tested strategies he knows from the past. There is an enormous need to put the current pain and shame behind him. The manager is still convinced that this is only a short downward spell and that he will quickly regain his former status. After all, he does have an impeccable network, doesn't he? He does not allow the thought that this lean period might last a bit longer to cross his mind. The search for a new challenge is often characterised by zealous optimism. Yet, all too often, expectations are disappointed. In spite of all the efforts, the idea of "making a quick comeback" frequently turns out to be an illusion, partly fed by the manager's conviction that previous successes are inseparably linked to his own personality and partly by a misjudgement of the labour market, which usually does not have anything nearly as attractive or promising to offer at that level.

Stage 4: Depression. In this stage, the manager is thrown back into a complexity of roles and his old self-doubts, believed to be long-forgotten. This complexity of roles is shaped by many interdependent areas of life, including the individual's family, hobbies and social involvement. It forms the basis of a person's sense of self-worth and identity. The more numerous the areas are, out of which this complexity of roles is shaped, the more the loss of one of these areas – such as one's job – can be emotionally compensated for by the others. In the case of high-ranking managers, their career has, for most of their professional life, dominated and even pushed aside the other areas of life. Social contacts were often lost along the way. Other identity-shaping roles, such as the parental role or role of a best friend as a long-time companion, are increasingly pushed aside until the individual and his position ultimately merge into one.

In addition, the old, familiar self-doubts that were present in childhood, which one had always sought to conceal through career, success and reputation, come creeping back. The ensuing depression is all the more intense, the less of a role complexity there is and the stronger these self-doubts are. The old saying starts to ring true: "As soon as a fish is out of the water, it starts to smell." Time is passing, and against the manager. Meanwhile, already half a year has passed without a new mandate. At some point he starts to consider taking on a lower-level position, but even this is not so easy.

Stage 5: Acceptance. Denial, aggression and depression have left their mark. They will accompany the manager for a long time to come. The manager still feels shame and insult when he thinks back to the preceding fall. What hurts most is the manner in which the dismissal occurred, after all that he had done for the company.

However, gradually the manager begins to realise that, in spite of all the annoyance, this difficult situation, which he would love to have been spared, still has a positive side. After some time has passed, he starts to feel less and less burdened by external expectations. New spaces open up, allowing him to thoroughly explore his own goals and values. The question of "What is it I actually want?" surfaces and is initially not that easy to answer. However, it is worthwhile giving this some thought, as this gives rise to new perspectives and opportunities.

It takes quite some time to be able to integrate your own failings into your self-image. But it is worth it. The manager will be more self-critical, think differently and question himself more as a result. He will have become tougher and more serene. By focusing on his own personal goals and values, he will ultimately manage to constructively overcome the upheaval and get off to a flying start in a new position. He has subjected his skills, values and perceptions to a critical assessment and now sees himself in a new and more realistic light. His self-image no longer depends so heavily on having a key role or position. Instead of being driven by the need to tackle each task, the focus is now on having fun on the job. In conjunction with this, the new professional position is often more closely linked to that manager's own personal direction and brings a greater sense of satisfaction with it.

4.8 All's well that ends well?

In the aforementioned study *Auf der Überholspur ausgebremst*, three-quarters of all top managers interviewed stated that, in hindsight, they enjoyed more freedom and more creative space in their new position. More than 80% claimed to have more freedom than previously. Their personal relationships improved too (nearly 90%). All study participants stated that they had at least as much *joie de vivre* as before the upheaval, if not more. The findings of this study are undoubtedly most informative and console the managers who are affected. Yet they should be treated with caution, as only those managers who had succeeded in achieving a new direction took part in the study. In actual fact, many top managers find it very difficult to cope with the kind of job loss outlined previously, despite all their experience, education and intelligence.

Back in 2007, the American economic scientist Jeffrey A. Sonnenfeld published the results of an analysis of 450 CEOs from listed companies who had lost their jobs. Only 35% of them returned to a position as chairman of the board of managers. 22% of them subsequently took on a consulting position. However, for a large portion of the managers (some 43%) their dismissal was the de facto end of their management career. The greater the fall from grace, the more devastating the consequences of a critical career situation will be for a manager. If we then bear in mind that managers tend to assume a large part of the responsibility (up to 50%) for the occurrence of the critical career situation themselves, as the study I carried out in preparation for this book shows, it soon becomes clear which fields of action need to be addressed.

Bibliography

Borysenko, Joan; Fried: Why You Burn Out and How to Revive; Hay House, Carlsbad, USA, 2011.

Casserley, Tim; Megginson, David; Learning from Burnout: Developing Sustainable Leaders and Avoiding Career Derailment; Butterworth-Heinemann, Oxford, UK, 2009.

Chandran, Rajiv et al.; Ascending to the C-Suite; McKinsey & Company, www.mckinsey.com, April 2015.

Drath, Karsten; Resilient Leadership: Beyond Myths and Misunderstandings; Taylor & Francis, Abingdon-on-Thames, UK, 2016.

Drath, Karsten; Spielregeln des Erfolgs: Wie Fuehrungskraefte an Rueckschlaegen wachsen; Haufe, Freiburg, Germany, 2016.

Dunsch, Juergen; Nach Suiziden: Die Schweiz bewegt eine Serie tragischer Manager-Schicksale; Frankfurter Allgemeine Zeitung, Frankfurt/Main, Germany, 2013.

Freye, Saskia; Fuehrungswechsel, Die Wirtschaftselite und das End der Deutschland AG; Campus, Frankfurt/Main, Germany, 2009.

Grabe, Martin; Zeitkrankheit Burnout, Warum Menschen ausbrennen und was man dagegen tun kann; Francke, Marburg a.d. Lahn, Germany, 2005.

Haendeler, Erik; Die Geschichte der Zukunft, Sozialverhalten heute und der Wohlstand von morgen; Brendow, Moers, Germany, 2005.

Heinemann, Helen; Warum Burnout nicht vom Job kommt, Die wahren Ursachen der Volkskrankheit Nr. 1; Adeo, Asslar, Germany, 2012.

Illig, Tobias; Jammern ist gut fuers Unternehmen, Resignative Reife; manager Seminare, Bonn, Germany, 2012.

Johnson, Barry; Polarity Management: Identifying and Managing Unsolvable Problems; HRD Press, Amherst, USA, 1992.

Kowalsky, Marc; Carsten Schloter (†), Was den deutschen Topmanager in den Tod trieb; Axel Springer: Die Welt, Hamburg, Germany, 2013.

Kowitz, Dorit; Pletter, Roman; Teuwsen, Peer; Manager unter Druck, Wieder nahmen sich zwei Topmanager das Leben: Das Leben der Chefs wird haerter; Zeitverlag: Die Zeit, Hamburg, Germany, 2014.

Kuebler-Ross, Elisabeth; Questions and Answers on Death and Dying; Simon & Schuster, New York City, USA, 1972.

Kwoh, Leslie; When the CEO Burns Out, Job Fatigue Catches up to Some Executives amid Mounting Expectations; No More Forced Smiles; Wall Street Journal (Dow Jones), New York, USA, 2013.

Lawrence, Kirk; Developing Leaders in a VUCA Environment; UNC Executive Development, Chapel Hill, USA, 2013.

Mahlmann, Regina; Unternehmen in der Psychofalle, Wege hinein. Wege hinaus; Business Village, Goettingen, Germany, 2012.

Mitchell, Sandra; Komplexitaeten, Warum wir erst anfangen, die Welt zu verstehen; Suhrkamp, Frankfurt/Main, Germany, 2008.

Mourlane, Denis; Resilienz, Die unentdeckte Faehigkeit der wirklich Erfolgreichen; Business Village, Goettingen, Germany, 2013.

Nagel, Gerhard; Chefs am Limit, 5 Coaching-Wege aus Burnout und Jobkrisen; Hanser, Muenchen, Germany, 2010.

Obholzer, Anton; Zagier Roberts, Vega; The Unconscious at Work: Individual and Organizational Stress in the Human Services; Routledge, Chichester, UK, 1994.

Petrie, Nick; Future Trends in Leadership Development, A White Paper; Center for Creative Leadership, Colorado Springs, USA, 2011.

Petrie, Nick; Wake Up!, The Surprising Truth about What Drives Stress and How Leaders Build Resilience; Center for Creative Leadership, Greensboro, USA, 2013.

Reeves, Martin et al.; The Most Adaptive Companies 2012: Winning in an Age of Turbulence; Boston Consulting Group, New York, USA, 2012.

Schmid, Michael; Management by Psycho; NZZ: Format, Zuerich, Switzerland, 2013.

Snowden, David J.; Boone, Mary E.; A Leader's Framework for Decision Making, Wise Executives Tailor Their Approach to Fit the Complexity of the Circumstances They Face; Harvard Business School Publishing, Boston, USA, 2007.

Thadeusz, Frank; Raubtiere ohne Kette; Spiegel, Hamburg, Germany, 2013.

Verfuerth, Claus; Debnar-Daumler, Sebastian; Auf der Überholspur ausgebremst; Rundstedt, Duesseldorf, Germany, 2015.

Winerman, Lea; Suppressing the 'White Bears': Meditation, Mindfulness and Other Tools Can Help Us Avoid Unwanted Thoughts, Says Social Psychologist Daniel Wegner; American Psychological Association, http://www.apa.org, USA, October 2011.

Wuepper, Gesche; France Télécom, Ex-Chef muss sich fuer Selbstmorde verantworten; Axel Springer: Die Welt, Hamburg, Germany, 2012.

5   The most dangerous career traps

In their highly commendable book *Why CEOs Fail*, based on thousands of cases they analysed, David Dotlich, a former top manager at Honeywell, and Peter Cairo, a lecturer at Columbia University, listed the most common reasons for top managers failing in their careers. In their book they refer to the work of university professor Robert Hogan, who is internationally recognised as a pioneer in the area of personality typing of managers, as well as to the research conducted at the Center for Creative Leadership (CCL), which has been involved in research into good leadership since 1970.

Dotlich and Cairo were interested in the question of why around two-thirds of all managers in Western industrialised nations experience a critical career situation in the course of their careers, be it that they are fired, disempowered or receive a sideways promotion. They found out that many managers are not able to set up and develop an efficient team. Everything

Figure 5.0.1   Skills lacked by unsuccessful managers.
Source: Dotlich and Cairo, *Why CEOs Fail*, 2003.

that inhibited them from building a team also hampered their performance as a manager, since a high-ranking manager can only exert a controlling influence over a company through her executive team. Many managers are unable to bring people together, get them to commit to common goals and set an example with their own behaviour (see Figure 5.0.1). They are, in a way, too focused on themselves, always wanting to stay in control. In their work with managers, Dotlich and Cairo identified 11 traits that could jeopardise careers, including arrogance, a tendency to over-dramatise or an inclination towards passive-aggressive behaviour. However, these career derailers, as Dotlich and Cairo call them, only typically become real career traps if they occur too frequently.

Executive derailers are traits that are deeply embedded in a person, forming part of their personality. These traits typically appear when a person is under a lot of pressure, i.e. when they can no longer use learned behaviour to conceal them. In such cases, these managers literally lose control of their own behaviour. These findings were also confirmed by a study conducted by the American leadership development consultant, Jack Zenger, and his colleague, Joseph Folkman, an American organisation psychologist. The study was published in the *Harvard Business Review* in 2009. Zenger and Folkman analysed the results of 360-degree feedback given on more than 11,000 managers and compared this feedback on the managers' behaviour patterns to the managers' actual career success, particularly of those who had been fired or downgraded. The first four most frequently criticised behaviour patterns were directly linked to the set-up and development of a functioning team (see Figure 5.0.2).

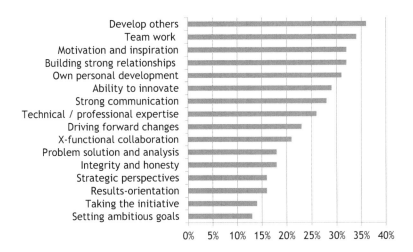

Figure 5.0.2 Traits that are most likely to make managers fail.
Source: Zenger and Folkman, *Harvard Business Review*, 2009.

In stressful situations, most people manifest negative traits. The personality psychologist Robert Hogan calls them risk factors. These are character traits that under normal circumstances might well be considered strengths. Yet if stress leads to these character traits being enhanced, then they can actually increase the risk of professional failure. If a manager is overworked, stressed, anxious or otherwise unsettled, these risk factors may appear and undermine their efficiency and the quality of their relations with customers, colleagues and employees. Employees and colleagues are generally familiar with their manager's behavioural shortcomings. Some will tolerate these traits – usually out of fear of negative repercussions for them personally – or turn a blind eye due to a misconceived idea of loyalty. Others may perceive these negative traits, but frequently won't give feedback for fear of jeopardising their own careers. This often increases the divide between self- and outside perception even further. It is not, therefore, surprising if managers themselves are hardly aware of their own behavioural weaknesses.

5.1 The blind spot

> ### EXAMPLE
>
> Indra Nooyi has been the CEO of PepsiCo since 2006. In the course of her career, the manager from Calcutta, India, has developed a reputation for being "pretty honest and outspoken", as she told Wall Street Journal Europe. So, you sit in a meeting and someone presents a five-year plan, and a typical Nooyi comment in such a situation would be, "That's crap. This is never going to happen!" Others who might have had the same thought would probably have expressed this in a much gentler way, as in: "That is very interesting. But perhaps you can try and think about this slightly differently." Only when one of her colleagues found the courage to address her about this, did she become aware of the impact her behaviour had on others, namely that colleagues and employees feared her and were not, therefore, telling her the whole truth or giving her their full trust. This was undoubtedly an unpleasant remark to hear but it gave her the opportunity to reflect on her behaviour and to weigh up the pros and cons of her somewhat brash approach.

Research has, in fact, shown that managers develop certain risk factors in their behaviour early on in life, with their parents, peers, relatives and others. These behaviour patterns become so automated that they largely take place subconsciously.

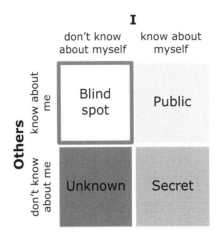

Figure 5.1.1 The Johari window (derived from the first names Joseph and Harry).
Source: Joseph Luft and Harry Ingham, 1955.

Joseph Luft and Harry Ingham, two American social psychologists, coined the term blind spot as early as 1955 to describe this phenomenon (see Figure 5.1.1), where, for instance, the manager does not know or perceive his own behaviour, even though his entourage is very familiar with it. In our experience, such blind spots rank among the biggest risks in a manager's career. Each of us has character strengths and weaknesses, but not to know them or fully understand the potentially damaging implications they might have, is simply disastrous. It leads to critical career situations hitting managers like a bolt out of the blue, while their entourage saw it coming from afar. The only way to expose a blind spot is to get feedback from outside, which fortunately more and more companies are doing regularly and in a structured manner.

In the book *The Set-Up-to-Fail Syndrome*, John Donaldson, former CEO of Thomas Cook, talks about how important it is for top managers like him to be given feedback, even if it sometimes hurts to get negative feedback. "When I look back at the way I behaved when I was directing one of the group's two business units, I am encouraged by the progress I have made. [...] If I was the CEO of the manager I was then, I think I'd have fired myself!"

5.2 Resistance to advice leads to failure

Blind spots occur alarmingly often among high-ranking managers. As previously mentioned, this is primarily because managers hardly ever get feedback and rarely think about or question themselves and their own behaviour. Many companies lack the necessary conditions for a culture of constructive criticism, which could, for instance, be established by introducing regular 360-degree feedback or employee surveys. Or, worse still, surveys are carried out but they do not lead to any consequences for staff members.

EXAMPLE

This is often due to a reluctance on the part of managers to have a mirror held up to them. These situations can be particularly frustrating for coaches, as was the case with one of our high-ranking clients from a listed company, whom I had been counselling for some time. He was responsible for around a dozen factories and the results were always good. In less than 15 years, he had worked himself up from the very bottom. In confidential interviews with various stakeholders he had nominated, I was able to get the picture of his manner of communication and management style. The feedback I received from these people was, in a word, catastrophic. One day, our client got a phone call from the company headquarters. The conversation with his boss was surprisingly short and was witnessed by a representative of the personnel department: he was fired, with immediate effect. The news caught him completely off-guard. He had actually been expecting to get a promotion. The reason given was that his aggressive management style was no longer tolerable. Employees and colleagues found him to be unchecked, offensive and hot-tempered. They had repeatedly complained about his angry outbursts and described his behaviour as downright tyrannical. The tragic thing about this was that my coachee's career need not have taken such a turn at all, since he had long been aware of all his character flaws. Moreover, with regard to the results he produced, this man was one of the company's shooting stars. His career had skyrocketed. Whatever he touched turned to gold. Yet this success had led him to disregard the warning signs: continuously surfacing criticism of his style. In other words, his willingness to learn something new about himself and others was very low. His division was in a good position, but his staff no longer produced their best results because he inspired them, but because they feared him. This turned out not to be very long-lived. When he left his division to take on a new job within the group, he fell back into his old way of doing things. Yet only very few at the headquarters really understood why this happened. The company had, for many years, even given him support to work on his management style. But my coachee was not able to change because he failed to understand the implications of his behaviour. And he is definitely not alone in this.

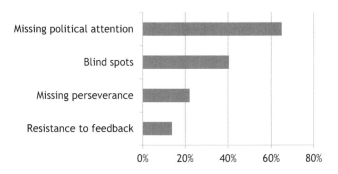

Figure 5.2.1 Four career-jeopardising factors.
Source: Survey by Karsten Drath Dec 2015–Jan 2016.

In the research I conducted for this book, I asked the participating managers about their own critical career situations. 10% admitted that their reluctance to accept advice had contributed to their career upheaval. 22% stated that they had not been assertive enough in their jobs. In 38% of the cases, blind spots were involved and in 65% of the cases the participating managers had not taken the existing political signs in their own surroundings seriously (see Figure 5.2.1).

This shows that focusing on your work is important, but tunnel vision is dangerous. It is vitally important for managers to keep their eyes and ears open, and to listen attentively when being given feedback on their work. Without the motivation to change, any coaching or other support received is questionable to meaningless. At some point in time, the corporate management will be forced to replace that manager because their misconduct is no longer acceptable, despite an otherwise outstanding performance.

EXAMPLE

The same was true for Steve Jobs who, in 1985 at the age of 30, was dismissed from the board of managers from the same company he himself had founded. His autocratic behaviour had lost him any goodwill and credibility he had had with his colleagues. The Apple staff both admired and feared him because of his visionary style coupled with narrow-mindedness, stubbornness and manipulative behaviour. Things went so far that these character traits earned him a name among his staff: Reality Distortion Field. In a speech he gave in 2005, Jobs described this time as follows: "It was awful-tasting medicine, but I guess the patient needed it."

So, what are your strengths and weaknesses? What behaviour patterns characterise you? What is your reputation? The self-image that many executives have about themselves does not always fully agree with how others in their environment see them. Often quite the opposite is the case. A first step to increasing the accuracy of your self-knowledge is therefore to reconcile your self-image with the impressions others have of you. What might at first sound simple is not, in fact. First of all, it is important to get to know the image that other people have of us. In many companies, 360°-feedback is offered these days from a certain leadership position onwards. These are available both as internet questionnaires and in the "handmade" version, which is feedback collected through personal discussions with a coach. Our recommendation is to always use such possibilities. This is especially true if the results are treated confidentially, in other words they are only intended for the recipient. Otherwise, it might be assumed that the statements have been "politically" falsified. But even if no such feedback is offered, you can consult your environment directly. This requires not only some courage but also the ability to listen well. Here are some typical questions from our interviews that you can use for a feedback conversation:

- What do you see currently as my biggest challenges?
- What do you see as my biggest strengths?
- What do you see as my biggest weaknesses?
- How good am I at developing staff?
- How well do I manage to form an effective team?
- How do I behave under stress?
- How cleverly do I deal with politics?
- How well do I market myself and my team?
- How good am I at overcoming silos in the company?
- How would you describe my leadership style?
- What recommendations do you have with regard to my future development?

So far so good. But there is one more difficulty. What happens when you receive such feedback? The greater the deviations between one's internal and external images, the more the feedback hurts. Of course, this applies in particular when the external image turns out to be significantly more negative than one sees oneself. As already described in Section 5.1, *The blind spot*, strong criticism activates defence mechanisms in our personality that weaken the feedback, relativise or refuse it altogether. This is a normal mechanism in order to protect your own self-image. However, it is not always helpful.

Sometimes it takes a downturn in a person's career before they are willing to accept feedback and to work on themselves. Based on what the managers stated in their programmes, the Global Leadership Center of the renowned

Ten Reasons to Reject Feedback:

1. My feedback-providers don't know me well enough.
2. My job forces me to act that way. I am really not like this.
3. This must be an error in the software.
4. Nobody really understands me.
5. They can't mean me.
6. This isn't a good time.
7. My feedback-providers did not understand the questions.
8. My boss wants me to behave that way, actually I am much better.
9. The others just envy my success.
10. It's true but I don't care.

Figure 5.2.2 Ten reasons for refusing feedback.
Source: IGLC INSEAD.

French business school INSEAD has compiled the most common reasons for disregarding and refusing feedback. They are listed in Figure 5.2.2.

What might at first appear amusing to read, is in fact not funny at all. A lack of openness to accepting feedback is one of the biggest risks for managers' careers. You should listen carefully if you see yourself in one or more of these listed statements.

5.3 Executive derailers – what makes managers go off the rails

The reason for managers failing rarely has anything to do with a lack of intelligence, experience or ability. Instead, it is much more the result of illogical, unpredictable and irrational behaviour on the part of these highly qualified and experienced managers, who have the best of intentions. Dotlich and Cairo call these subconscious forces executive derailers, i.e. factors that can derail managers. In their work with managers, they have identified and named 11 of these derailers. Most managers are affected by one to three of these derailers.

It is rarely the case that all these derailers are highly developed in a manager. By contrast, there are only few profiles that show no concentration in any one area. It is, therefore, most probable that you have one or more of these personality traits. Perhaps you are brilliant at structuring and analysing problems and this ability has already spared the company a huge number of bad investments, or set your company apart from the competition. But when you are stressed, your tendency to analyse the causes of matters

Table 5.3.1 Executive derailers

Executive derailers	Typical behaviour patterns
Arrogance	Overly self-confident, arrogant, excessive self-esteem
Excessive caution	Hesitant, resistant to change, risk-averse, slow in making decisions
Habitual distrust	Distrustful, cynical, reacts over-sensitively to criticism, focuses on the negative
Mischievousness	Charming, venturesome, tests limits, seeks thrills
Passive resistance	Appears cooperative from the outside, but is irritable, stubborn and uncooperative on the inside
Melodrama	Moody, easily annoyed, difficult to please and emotionally unstable
Eagerness to please	Wants to please, unwilling to act independently or against the general opinion
Eccentricity	Creative, eccentric in thought and action
Perfectionism	Meticulously accurate and precise, difficult to please, tendency to micromanage
Aloofness	Unapproachable, indifferent towards other people's feelings, not very communicative
Volatility	Dramatic, seeks attention, interrupts others, a bad listener

in detail means that you are unable to make decisions. This phenomenon is not uncommon and is known as analysis paralysis in the literature. As I mentioned before, the large majority of executives do not receive regular, structured and adequate feedback on their behaviour, and here I am not speaking about the annual performance talk, which in any case is seen by many as a farce or, at best, a necessary evil. This means that the blind spots remain and their damaging effect is allowed to unfold.

If managers receive useful feedback and can overcome their resistance to feedback, then many of them are able to use their sharpened awareness to manage their behaviour better and to get their executive derailers under control. This does, of course, presuppose a willingness to change.

So, what are the executive derailers? Dotlich and Cairo have identified the following factors which could jeopardise managers' careers (see Table 5.3.1).

On the following pages I will elaborate further on the individual derailers and the typical behaviour patterns associated with these. You may be familiar with one or more of these derailers. At the end of the overview you can assess yourself.

Arrogance

This derailer is found in people who have a very high opinion of themselves with regard to their own competencies and importance. Executives with this trait are often unable to admit mistakes and learn from experience. They typically think along the lines of: I am right and everyone else is wrong (see Table 5.3.2).

Table 5.3.2 Arrogance

Reflected or ideal behaviour	Unreflected or derailed behaviour
You are willing to fight for what is important to you.	You are not willing to give way in a conflict, no matter what the price.
After comparing other viewpoints with your own, you conclude that yours makes the most sense.	You are convinced that your viewpoint is the most reasonable, even before you have compared it with others.
If your preferred strategy does not work, you take responsibility for this.	If your preferred strategy or idea does not work, you refuse to take responsibility for this.
You critically examine and validate your position on receiving new information.	You interpret new information in the light of your own viewpoint and use this to confirm it.
You can make use of your charisma to consciously influence others.	You dominate others with your charisma.

Caution

Managers with this personality trait have an exaggerated fear of making mistakes and being criticised for them. They find it difficult to make weighty decisions. Frequently, this results in a subconscious resistance to change, which in turn leads to good opportunities being missed (see Table 5.3.3).

Table 5.3.3 Caution

Reflected or ideal behaviour	Unreflected or derailed behaviour
Before you make a decision, you go through the worst-case scenario in your mind to minimise risks.	You focus on the worst-case scenario and are often unable to make timely decisions.
You take your time with weighty decisions, as any wrong decision can have serious negative consequences.	You take your time with every decision, as every decision can have serious negative repercussions.
You reject projects if there are clear indications that the planning is erroneous.	You postpone decisions about projects because you have an unfounded suspicion that the planning might be erroneous.

Habitual distrust

These managers lack social intuition, aplomb and trust. You focus on what is wrong, what runs or could run counter to your interests. You respond to potential conflicts with cynicism and extensive fear of the political damage this might do to you personally (see Table 5.3.4).

Table 5.3.4 Habitual distrust

Reflected or ideal behaviour	Unreflected or derailed behaviour
Before making a decision, you carefully weigh up the pros and cons.	You try to avoid having the sole responsibility for decisions, as you primarily see the potential risk involved in every decision.
You are cautious in dealing with others, as you know that your actions are motivated by your own political or personal interests.	You assume that everyone's actions are motivated by their political or personal interests.
You can take negative feedback and learn from it. You assume that your counterpart is trying to help you.	You find it difficult to accept negative feedback as you assume that your counterpart seeks to harm you with it.
When you give feedback, you try to provide a balance of positive and negative aspects of your counterpart's behaviour.	You only give negative feedback.

Mischievousness

These managers can be recognised by their charming demeanour, coupled with a great willingness to take unnecessary risks. Rules generally only apply to others. They always make exceptions for themselves. The kick managers get out of this means that they are sometimes not able to meet expectations and find it difficult to learn from experience (see Table 5.3.5).

Table 5.3.5 Mischievousness

Reflected or ideal behaviour	Unreflected or derailed behaviour
You question rules and regularly test the boundaries to promote growth and innovation.	You ignore rules and boundaries, as they bore you and you don't think they apply to you.
You make use of your impulsive nature to drive forward new developments.	Your impulsiveness tends to be rather destructive.
You like to take calculated risks and don't take mistakes all too seriously.	You make decisions and take unnecessary risks without giving sufficient thought to the potential consequences.
You use your charm and creativity to move things in your company.	You use your charm and creativity to your own advantage because you like to manipulate others.
If the situation requires it, you use provocation as a tool to stimulate a debate.	You say everything that comes to mind, irrespective of whether it is conducive to your actual goal.

Passive resistance

Managers with this trait tend to be indifferent towards other people's expectations. This means that they are often seen as egotistical, stubborn and uncooperative. The fact that they don't contradict what is being said, does not mean that they agree (see Table 5.3.6).

Table 5.3.6 Passive resistance

Reflected or ideal behaviour	Unreflected or derailed behaviour
What you say and what you do differ when you feel you have no other option.	Generally, what you say and what you do are not the same.
Your environment is generally aware of the motives behind your actions.	Your environment is not aware of the motives behind your actions.
You generally try to avoid conflict, but share your point of view if the situation requires this.	You avoid conflict and very seldom express your opinion.
You are aware of the expectations of others and your obligations towards them.	You are not aware of and not interested in others' expectations or your obligations towards them.

Melodrama

People with this derailer display excessive enthusiasm towards other people or projects, followed by disappointment with those same people and projects as a result of a lack of emotional continuity. Your mood swings influence your decisions (see Table 5.3.7).

Table 5.3.7 Melodrama

Reflected or ideal behaviour	Unreflected or derailed behaviour
You get angry in reaction to a serious mistake or problem arising.	Depending on your mood of the day, you get out of control with minor problems, without being able to articulate why.
Your employees see you as predictable and know what to expect of you.	Your employees find you unpredictable, and do not know where they stand with you.
You generally behave similarly in similar situations.	In similar situations, you sometimes react optimistically and sometimes pessimistically.
You consistently convey positive energy and enthusiasm through your words and deeds.	On one day you spread optimism and enthusiasm with your words and deeds, and on the next day negativity vibes and doubts.
You control your emotions in order to achieve a certain result.	You are controlled by your emotions, without having the feeling that you can influence them.

Eagerness to please

Managers with this derailer tend to strive to be popular with everyone. You find it difficult to act independently and to take what may sometimes be unpopular decisions. Being liked is more important to you than anything else. This frequently results in you perhaps being superficially popular but there being no clearly recognisable direction in your actions (see Table 5.3.8).

Table 5.3.8 Eagerness to please

Reflected or ideal behaviour	Unreflected or derailed behaviour
You are convinced that satisfied employees produce better work.	You are convinced that already one dissatisfied employee could jeopardise the performance of the entire company.
The teams you manage primarily reach decisions based on consensus following ample discussion.	The teams you control either hardly ever reach decisions or only make bad compromises.
You are able to quickly adapt to new situations and circumstances.	You are so flexible that nobody – including yourself – ever actually knows what your position is on any given topic.
You address conflicts and show a real interest in your counterpart.	You do not address conflicts, certainly not directly, and if at all, it is through third parties.

Eccentricity

This derailer relates to the tendency to act in a very colourful, unusual and eccentric manner. Your need to be different from everyone else becomes an end in itself. This frequently leads to these managers being seen as creative, but lacking in practical judgement and tenacity when it comes to implementing their ideas (see Table 5.3.9).

Table 5.3.9 Eccentricity

Reflected or ideal behaviour	Unreflected or derailed behaviour
You have a million brilliant ideas, many of which you put into practice.	You have a million brilliant ideas, which are never put into practice.
With your original and unconventional style you prevent routine and mediocrity.	With your unpredictable and irrational style, you intimidate and frighten your employees.
You have gotten many new initiatives off the ground, whose development you follow and control.	You have gotten many new initiatives off the ground, whose development you do not sufficiently follow and control.
You are able to adapt your unconventional leadership style if the situation requires it.	You refuse to adapt your unconventional leadership style or to stick to behavioural norms.

Perfectionism

This behaviour is about being overly perfectionist, which costs a lot of time and energy and rarely leads to a sense of satisfaction. People with these traits tend to focus on the details and easily lose sight of the overall picture. This means that employees are frequently not able to develop their full potential and feel bossed around. This also leads to an overly long decision-making process (see Table 5.3.10).

Table 5.3.10 Perfectionism

Reflected or ideal behaviour	*Unreflected or derailed behaviour*
You are able to focus on the details if the situation requires this.	You constantly and exclusively focus on the details, which prevents you from seeing the full picture.
You find it sensible to be thorough in preparing a presentation.	You focus more on the aesthetic appeal of a presentation than on its content.
You don't like uncertain or unclear situations, but are aware that you won't always be able to avoid them.	You try at all costs to avoid any situation that is uncertain or unclear, e.g. by imposing a structure.
You manage processes and people with skill and dedication.	You focus so much on processes and interfaces that you frequently forget the needs of the people carrying out the processes.
You know what you can delegate and what you need to do yourself.	You have to do everything yourself, as it would otherwise not meet your expectations.

Aloofness

Managers with this derailer are not interested in or even aware of other people's feelings. They are emotionally detached and come across as intellectually superior. This frequently leads to them having great difficulty reaching their counterparts emotionally, never mind inspiring them (see Table 5.3.11).

Table 5.3.11 Aloofness

Reflected or ideal behaviour	*Unreflected or derailed behaviour*
You create an impartial atmosphere, in which decisions are based on transparent and plausible reasons.	You create a cold atmosphere, in which all human and emotional qualities are avoided.
In the midst of crisis and conflict, you stay present and serene, which gives your employees stability.	In the midst of a crisis or conflict, you are no longer approachable, which unsettles your employees.
You are generally rather reserved, but if the situation requires it, you can build a relationship with somebody.	You come across as reserved and wooden, and you find it difficult to build a relationship with people in relevant situations.
You generally find nurturing relations and building alliances unpleasant, but if the situation requires this, you will personally take care of an important and influential stakeholder.	Irrespective of the situation, you are not able or willing to maintain relationships or to build alliances.

Volatility

Managers with this derailer are always in the limelight. They love grand gestures and a dramatic appearance. They have an engaging personality and a strong need for recognition. They are constantly occupied with being noticed. This means that, under pressure, they are not able to focus on what is essential (see Table 5.3.12).

Table 5.3.12 Volatility

Reflected or ideal behaviour	Unreflected or derailed behaviour
You use your charisma and charm to emotionally touch and inspire others.	You turn every situation into a stage and your counterpart into the audience that is there to admire you.
You use your ability to captivate and inspire people in order to draw the attention of the media, analysts or potential employees to your company.	You use your ability to captivate and inspire people to relish the attention and feel good about yourself.
You are able to make targeted and strategic use of your eloquence to achieve an important goal.	You are constantly colourful and extroverted, irrespective of whether the situation requires this or not.
You are able to scale down your presence, for instance in order to listen to others and to learn something new.	You are not able to scale down your presence and do not or only rarely reflect on what you actually wish to achieve with this.

Self-assessment

Let's be honest, were some of the behaviour patterns uncomfortably familiar to you? In Table 5.3.13 you can gauge the risk of whether and to what extent one or more of these traits applies to you. But beware with these self-assessments that you may also have a blind spot. In personality psychology,

Table 5.3.13 Which traits apply to you?

		Risk		
	None	Low	Moderate	High
Arrogance				
Excessive caution				
Habitual distrust				
Mischievousness				
Passive resistance				
Melodrama				
Eagerness to please				
Eccentricity				
Perfectionism				
Aloofness				
Volatility				

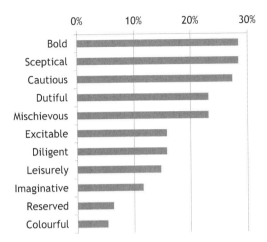

Figure 5.3.1   Distribution of executive derailers amongst the study participants.
Source: Survey by Karsten Drath Dec 2015–Jan 2016.

this is known as the social desirability bias. This is said to be the case if the answers someone gives make them appear more popular or socially acceptable than objective and truthful answers would have.

How honest were you in your self-assessment? And how well do you actually know yourself? The managers who participated in the research for this book were also asked about their executive derailers in the context of the critical career situations they had experienced. The results are presented in Figure 5.3.1.

According to this, it would appear that excessive arrogance and too much self-confidence as well as the rough opposite, namely too much distrust coupled with too much procrastination and weighing things up, are the worst traits in the study participants' self-assessment. This is followed by the tendency to be too perfectionist and having too great an appetite for taking risks. What were least commonly found in the self-assessments were the tendency to need a big stage and an audience and to be in the limelight, as well as its opposite, emotional withdrawal and aloofness.

The type of study presented here is, of course, subject to the phenomenon of social desirability and, therefore, has methodological weaknesses. Correctly done, the derailers of all study participants should have been recorded in a complex personality questionnaire, such as the Hogan Development Survey. However, this would have been too complicated and time-consuming. As we mentioned at the beginning, the majority of those participating in the survey for this book came from Germany, the UK and the USA. According to the Hogan database, which comprises several million records, the following derailers are the most commonly found in these countries (see Table 5.3.14).

Table 5.3.14   Most commonly found career derailers in Germany, the UK and the USA

Germany	Habitual distrust
	Aloofness
	Mischievousness
UK	Aloofness
	Passive resistance
	Eagerness to please
USA	Aloofness
	Perfectionism
	Eagerness to please

What stands out, by comparison, is that the derailer aloofness is to be found amongst the top three in all three countries, while in the results of the study on critical career situations it ended up second to last.

How can that be? This is a good example of the social desirability phenomenon. At the beginning of this chapter I showed that, from a statistical point of view, managers are most likely to fail in their careers in building a functioning team. Empathy and interpersonal skills are needed to build such a team. Indeed, these traits were described by the study participants as the most important prerequisites for long-term professional success. However, in actual fact, many managers do not have this ability, or still have to work on developing it. But that is something nobody likes to hear, of course. This is why there are deviations in the statistics. Self-reflection and assessment are good and important, but they do not spare you from having blind spots. The only thing that can remedy this is to receive external feedback that is as objective as possible, coupled with the will to listen and to work on oneself.

5.4 Are managers prisoners of their own personalities?

Many managers are not able to change their own behavioural weaknesses by themselves. In any case, many do not believe that this is still possible when you are in your late forties or early fifties. After all, "everything somehow still works quite well", as the CIO of a DAX-listed company once told me. "I am much too experienced to change much now." It might not be a surprise that he is no longer with that company. Experience is, of course, not delimiting of behaviour change, as modern brain research has meanwhile sufficiently proven. The key word is neuroplasticity. This term describes the brain's ability to integrate new knowledge and new skills acquired over the course of a lifetime into a complex network of experience. Moritz Helmstaedter from the Max Planck Institute of Neurobiology in Martinsried, Germany, is researching this area. In tests he has proved that the brain is still as powerful in learning at the age of 60, as the brain at the age of 10 years (see Figure 5.4.1). This means no less than that individual patterns for our thinking, feeling and acting at any time and into old age are changeable through repeated processing of other patterns.

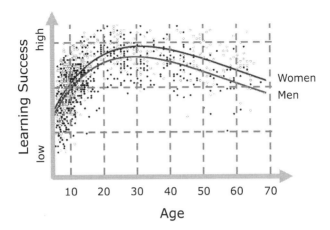

Figure 5.4.1 The principle of neuroplasticity.
Source: Christian Elger, Keynote ICF-Conference "Neuro-Leadership", 2013.

As an absolutely mandatory prerequisite, this does, of course, demand that the manager concerned really wants this. This is easier if you consult an experienced coach or are fortunate enough to have a good mentor. You should at least have a confidant in your personal environment whom you can ask. This might be a team colleague, a superior or a trusted employee. You could ask them how they perceive you – in terms of your leadership style, communication, team management and personal development.

If you receive credible criticism, it is important to systematically work on it. This takes time and patience. You can only improve your behaviour step by step. Important questions to be asked in this context are:

- How am I mentally wired?
- What are my preferences?
- What do I want exactly?
- How am I an obstacle to myself in this respect?
- What are my inner motivations and convictions that trigger certain be-
  haviour patterns?
- How can I get a better grip on this unwanted behaviour?

This kind of work has nothing to do with giving up your personality, as many of our clients fear. It is much more about raising your own potential and integrating more of this into your daily actions. It is more about being yourself, just with more elegance and aplomb. When you spend as much time as I do studying the biographies of successful managers, then it becomes apparent that nearly all of them have had to work hard on themselves in order to get a grip on their limiting and potentially career-damaging traits. The bad news is that this requires a lot of hard work and self-reflection.

But there is also good news: we are not the prisoners of our own personalities and the behaviour preferences associated with them. We have a choice. This characteristic is what distinguishes us from animals. We can choose a form of behaviour that runs counter to the preferences that make up our personality, because the situation requires it or because it will make us more successful. This is what I mean by elegance and aplomb. Everyone can work on themselves. Successful leadership personalities perhaps just do this with more commitment and discipline.

EXAMPLE

Let us take Richard Branson as an example. In order to promote his airline Virgin, he even dressed up as a bearded stewardess with a bright red uniform and matching lipstick. To the *Independent* newspaper he commented: "Every time I am asked to make a fool of myself like this, I feel queasy." In actual fact only a small part of this paradise bird act is part of his personality, but he has learned to play this role because it works excellently. Before Branson became the boss of the airline, he was shy and tended to remain in the background. He had to work hard on himself to adopt this flamboyant role and to feel comfortable with it. This was the only way he could expand his behavioural repertoire and use his popularity to benefit his company.

This example demonstrates how it is possible to enhance your toolkit with additional tools. Working on your own behaviour patterns can also open up other possibilities, as the following example shows.

EXAMPLE

When Cisco's top management decided to improve collaboration through more open communication and empowerment, it was CEO Jahn Chambers who found it extremely difficult. He has always been used to dominating management meetings, and has found it hard to hold back and not express his views on all counts. In 2014, he commented to the *Harvard Business Review*: "In the beginning it was difficult for me to be open to more collaboration. But as I learned to let go of control and give the team more time to come up with the right conclusions, I found the decisions to be just as good or even better than before. But first of all, I had to be patient enough to let the team think for itself."

The American personality experts Zenger and Folkman confirmed these findings. In a study published in the *Harvard Business Review* in 2013, they analysed the results of 360-degree feedback of nearly 550 top managers from 3 different types of organisation: a bank, a telecommunications company and a university. The competencies examined were based on the key skills that have already been described at the beginning of this chapter. Nearly 100 of these managers scored really badly in 1 of the 16 areas of competence. In other words, they performed worse than 90% of the other study participants. Subsequently, the managers were given the opportunity to be supported by a professional coach. After some time had passed, 360-degree feedback was once again used to examine whether and to what extent the evaluations of the protagonists had changed. The result was surprisingly clear. Over 70 of the 100 managers had significantly improved. The evaluations revealed an improvement not just of a few per cent, but of on average 30% compared to the initial assessment. With external support and targeted work, around 70% of the study participants were thus able to turn clear shortcomings into slightly above-average results.

Even well-entrenched behaviour patterns can be changed, simply by consciously acting differently. However, this can only happen if there is the will to change. It is also true that behaviour patterns that run counter to our own personality require us to invest more energy than reaction patterns we have practised since childhood. Self-reflection, impulse control and self-management do not just happen by themselves, but require the continuous investment of cognitive and emotional energy. Every very introverted person who has just given a speech in public will feel exhausted afterwards, when the excitement has subsided. Anyone who is scared of flying and has just overcome their panic to face a flight will be tired after their adrenaline levels have returned to normal.

This energy must be regularly recharged, otherwise it will be like a Formula 1 racing car that is permanently losing fuel. This, of course, requires the basic ability to be in tune with oneself and perceive one's own energy level.

Bibliography

Barsoux, Jean-Louis; How to Become a Better Leader; MIT Sloan Management Review, Cambridge, USA, March 2012.

Dotlich, David L.; Cairo, Peter C.; Why CEOs Fail; Wiley & Sons, Hoboken, USA, 2003.

Drath, Karsten; Resilient Leadership: Beyond Myths and Misunderstandings; Taylor & Francis, Abingdon-on-Thames, UK, 2016.

Hogan, Robert B.; Management Derailment; APA, Washington DC, USA, 2009.

Zenger, Jach; Folkman, Joseph; Ten Fatal Flaws That Derail Leaders; Harvard Business School Publishing, Boston, USA, 2009.

6 Resilience

The art of getting back up

6.1 Why does resilience matter?

As we have seen already, long-term professional success depends on a number of different factors. One of the most dominant factors is the ability to constructively process setbacks and failures. The area of research concerned with this kind of inner resistance is called resilience.

The term "resilience" comes from Latin. The verb *resilere* means to bounce back. The term originated from the material sciences, where it describes the capacity of a body to respond flexibly to an external impact and then to revert back to its initial shape. So, resilience could be translated as "elasticity" or the "ability to recover". Applied to human beings, resilience describes the ability to overcome crises unharmed, to grow through them and, indeed, even to emerge from them stronger than before. A lack of resilience is also known as "vulnerability", which derives from the Latin word *vulnus*, meaning wound.

The concept of resilience was originally applied solely to children who had managed to emerge from difficult conditions – such as war, displacement, domestic violence, poverty, crime or their parents' drug abuse – psychologically healthy and, in terms of their social behaviour, to develop positively. The concept of resilience focused on the protective factors which enabled children to remain mentally healthy, even under such difficult circumstances.

Over the past few decades, the term has increasingly been used to mean a general ability that helps people of all ages to successfully overcome crises. These days, the term no longer only refers to extreme situations, but has generally come to mean the ability to master everyday life and, more particularly, to deal with the pressure to perform in companies. The basic way in which resilience works can be seen in the different phases triggered in response to a crisis. This is illustrated in Figure 6.1.1.

Typically, following a crisis, such as losing your job or your partner becoming severely ill, people enter a phase of reduced performance. This can take the form of emotional instability or dejectedness or a lack of concentration and energy. Depending on the severity of the crisis and on the individual's

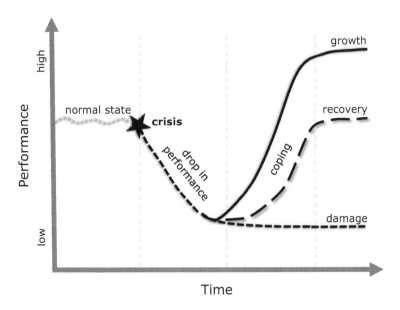

Figure 6.1.1 Schematic diagram of how resilience works.

personality structure as well as the resources available to them, the result may either be permanent harm, for instance in the form of depression, or recovery and thus a return to their original performance levels. Depending on the nature of the crisis, this can take hours, days or even weeks. However, there are also cases in which people grow in a crisis, rising like a phoenix from the ashes and emerging from it even stronger than before. Over the past 60 years, research into resilience has tried to identify the factors that have enabled some people to recover quicker and better from crises than others. You will be introduced to them in the following section.

6.2 Rigid or flexible?

Crises do not simply "bounce off" healthy people, even though we might wish they would. One key point in relation to emotional elasticity and te- nacity is the fact that all individuals – even the most resilient – have to pass through a valley of tears. So, this is not about getting rid of the "valley" altogether, but about reducing it in size. A good example of this can be found in the various structural designs of skyscrapers. Japan is the indus- trial nation with the most earthquakes worldwide. On average, the island state has about 73 earthquakes per month at a strength larger than 4 on the Richter scale. Since land is scarce, the Japanese cities need skyscrapers that can withstand the earthquakes. The first-generation skyscrapers were reinforced and had a high rigidity, without being able to withstand strong

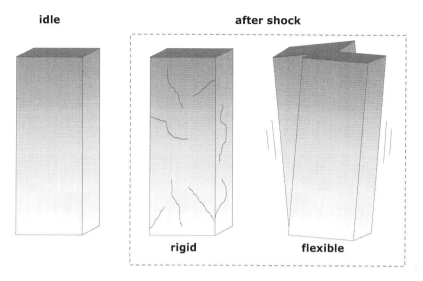

Figure 6.2.1 Resilient (construction) designs for skyscrapers.

earthquakes. Devastating damage with many casualties was the result. Over the past few decades, engineers have developed new methods which allow gigantic buildings to respond more flexibly to external tremors by absorbing vibrations and converting them into movement, while at the same time cushioning them, and thereby preventing the building from swinging dangerously out of control and thus causing destructive resonance vibrations (see Figure 6.2.1). These buildings, which these days are erected in all earthquake-prone regions of the world, frequently have a swinging core or pendulum in the interior. Hence, engineers installed a 600-ton pendulum between the 88th and the 92nd floors of the 500-metre-high skyscraper Taipei 101, the seat of Taiwan's financial centre. When there is an earthquake, the pendulum absorbs oscillations, thus stabilising the rest of the building and ensuring its coherence. The result shows that flexible high-rises can withstand much more powerful earthquakes than rigid constructions.

Mental resilience is very similar. People who have learned to absorb outer turmoil and allow inner vibrations to occur, while at the same time cushioning them instead of reinforcing them, are much better able to deal with crises than those who try to rigidly defy all obstacles they encounter.

6.3 Resilient or tough?

Does the same apply for the human psyche? In a lecture on resilience, I once saw a photo of a lighthouse in a storm-swept sea (illustrated by Figure 6.3.1). The foundations were completely underwater, and only a few metres above the lighthouse keeper was standing on a platform looking towards the

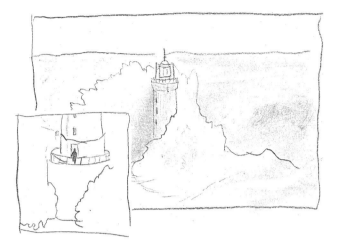

Figure 6.3.1 A beacon in the stormy sea.
Source: © Kara Drath, 2014.

cameraman. The cameraman appeared to be in a helicopter high above the waves. The photo was meant to underline the statement: "Resilient people are as steadfast as a lighthouse in the midst of a stormy sea."

Something bothered me about this metaphor, but for a long time I did not know what it was exactly. Then I read up about the context of the photo and found out that it had been part of a series. Two further shots following that photo showed a giant wave approaching the lighthouse, which eventually completely engulfed the site where the lighthouse keeper was standing. When I saw this, I realised what had been bothering me. If managers equate the concepts of resilience and resilience-based leadership with "encouraging toughness", as some old management books advise, then it is just a matter of time before professional or private circumstances arise that are tougher than them. Of course, a certain amount of discipline also plays an important role. However, the capacity for self-reflection and the conscious perception of oneself as a human being, consisting of body, mind and soul, with one's current needs and sensitivities are at least as important. Figure 6.3.2 shows in a simplified manner how resilient managers will tend to combine reflection with discipline, while "tough" managers will tend to rely exclusively on discipline without much reflection. If both self-reflection and self-control are lacking, I speak of "derailed" managers, comparable to a train that has come off its tracks and is hurtling all over the place, creating havoc. If a certain amount of self-reflection is coupled with a weak level of self-control this is known in research as the "knowing–doing gap" – a phenomenon which I think most managers fall prey to from time to time and which I would also refer to as "ambivalence". This concept describes the fact that in general we

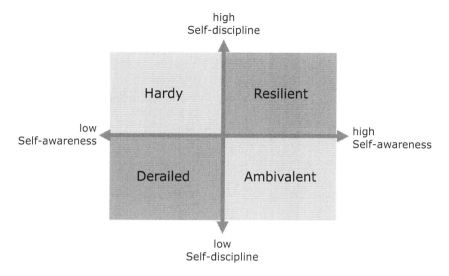

Figure 6.3.2 Resilience combines self-discipline with self-awareness.

all know perfectly well what is good for us, our employees and our company, but that we often do not act upon this knowledge; we ignore it. For example, this might be a manager who knows that he needs to be less tactical and more strategic in his work, but due to the constant time pressure he is under and other motives he is perhaps unaware of, he doesn't do it.

In summary, we can therefore say that resilience is not about uncritical severity towards oneself and others, and certainly not about a lack of self-reflection or self-control. Instead, resilient managers are in a position to combine a high level of self-control and discipline with self-reflection and awareness of themselves as individuals.

6.4 Sense of coherence

Aaron Antonovsky was an American sociologist who emigrated to Israel in 1960, where he worked *inter alia* at the Applied Social Research Institute. At first, he researched the effects of ethnic origin and social status on health and life expectancy. Part of these studies involved analysing various groups of women in 1970, including some who had been born in central Europe between 1914 and 1923. About half (51%) of the then 47- to 56-year-old women were in good mental health. Some of the participants in the study had, as youths, been imprisoned in German concentration camps and witnessed violence, hunger and death. After the war, many of them had been displaced for years until the State of Israel was founded and recognised by the UN in 1949. But even after that the horrors continued, as – within just a few years – Israel was involved in three different wars which threatened to destroy it. To Antonovsky's amazement, around one-third (29%) of these women had good mental health, only 22% less than those who had not experienced the Holocaust directly. This raised the question as to how people managed to remain healthy under such adverse conditions. This issue was to occupy Antonovsky for the rest of his life. In his acclaimed book *Health, Stress and Coping*, he called our health care system's conventional focus on disease-triggering factors into question and coined the term *salutogenesis* (from the Latin *salus*, meaning healthy, and the Greek *genese*, for origin) to describe a new and initially disputed area of research, dealing with factors which keep people mentally and physically healthy. One of his key concepts was a "sense of coherence" – a quality or strong conviction that Antonovsky found to be present in all of the concentration camp survivors he studied. He describes this feeling with the help of four central components:

- Comprehensibility: A belief that things don't just happen, but that they are subject to a higher order and thus can be predicted reasonably well.
- Manageability: A belief that our own skills and experience, and our existing social support and resources, are sufficient to overcome future challenges.
- Meaningfulness: A belief that life is fundamentally meaningful and worth living, irrespective of the current difficulties a person is facing.
- Cohesiveness: The endeavour to reconcile outer events with inner beliefs.

Furthermore, Antonovsky recognised other factors which help people to overcome crisis situations and still remain healthy. He called these generalised resistance resources (GRRs):

- Adaptability: The human ability to adapt flexibly to different crisis situations and to remain largely immune to them as time passes.
- Trustworthy relationships: The inclusion of a person in deep, trusting relationships, e.g. in a family, circle of friends or team of colleagues, so that that person can open up without having to anticipate rejection.
- Belonging to communities: Striving to take up responsibility in institutions, such as the church, school or clubs.

The findings postulated by Antonovsky have not only influenced medicine, but also many other scientific fields over the past few decades. However, Antonovsky was criticised throughout his life for the fact that even though his approach made sense, it was hard to prove. A study from another part of the world came to his aid, although this was only published a good ten years later.

6.5 The children of Kauai

Emmy Werner is an American developmental psychologist and regarded as the grande dame of resilience research. When she first started her research work at the University of California, near Sacramento, the predominant school of thought of previous behaviourists was that insufficient maternal care and emotional attention in early childhood (the father did not play much of a role in this development theory) automatically led to the child's negative development, in the form of psychological and social problems later on. This was continuously substantiated scientifically through a number of studies, which proved that the majority of emotionally ill, criminal or otherwise conspicuous adolescents came from problematic homes.

However, this research approach concealed a logical error. The incorrect conclusion was drawn that because all mail vans are yellow, all yellow cars must therefore be mail vans. Regardless, until that point in time there were indeed no findings about whether children from such problematic homes would have developed negatively anyway. Werner wanted to circumvent this methodological shortcoming by taking a complete and representative cross-section of children from the population as a whole, and observing them over a long period of time to examine in a longitudinal study whether there was, in actual fact, a correlation between parental home and a child's development. She found her survey population 4000 km further west on the Hawaiian island of Kauai. When she began the survey in 1955, Hawaii had not yet been recognised as the 50th state of the USA and mass tourism had not yet taken hold. The people either made their living from agriculture and fishing, or were employed by the US forces, which had their Pacific Fleet stationed there. The living conditions on the picturesque island of Kauai were partly characterised by unemployment, poverty, crime and drug abuse. Werner and her interdisciplinary team of psychologists, paediatricians, nurses and social workers studied a total of 698 children, born in 1955, and collected data at the ages of 1, 2, 10, 18, 32 and 40. Around 210 – which corresponds to around 30% – of the youngsters grew up in difficult conditions: their childhoods were shaped by unemployment, poverty, neglect, divorce and abuse. As was to be expected, between the ages of 10 and 18 a large proportion of these children from problematic parental homes (around two-thirds) displayed learning and behavioural difficulties, got into trouble with the law or suffered psychological problems. However, what was really surprising was that a third of the children developed normally. They successfully completed their school education, did an apprenticeship, found work, had a stable, positive relationship and eventually a family. They were socially integrated, did not become delinquents and did not develop mental disorders. The previous assumption that a child from a problematic parental home inevitably developed negatively was disproved once and for all in 1992 when Werner's work was published in the book *Overcoming the Odds: High Risk Children from Birth to Adulthood*, which caused a minor sensation.

The question as to what all these "resilient children" had in common was, of course, even more intriguing. As Werner observed, these children had so-called "protective factors" which cushioned them from some of the negative consequences of these adverse circumstances. She identified the following factors in her work:

- **Trustworthy relationships:** Since their parents were often not good role models or caregivers for them, these children usually sought other people they could trust and to whom they could become emotionally attached, e.g. siblings, grandparents, neighbours, teachers or priests. What was essential in this relationship was that the child had someone who believed in them and made them feel that they were worth something.
- **Role models:** The mostly same-sex caregivers also unknowingly acted as role models, from whom the child could learn to actively face up to challenges and resolve problems constructively. In this relationship the child was also able to express his or her feelings, which was important in establishing emotional stability and, by following concrete advice, helped to make difficult situations easier for them.
- **Responsibility:** Those children who developed normally, despite adverse circumstances, also had in common that they had to assume responsibility early on, for instance for their younger siblings or by taking on a function at school. Through this responsibility, they learned early on to focus less on themselves and their own problems. They often also experienced their commitment for others as a source of meaning and positive confirmation.
- **Realistic expectations:** What set these children apart from others was that they were able to assess their situation realistically and set ambitious but realistic goals for themselves, which they usually ended up achieving.
- **Self-confidence:** The experience of seeing that they could influence things through their commitment and effort and that they were acknowledged by their peers for a certain kind of behaviour mostly helped these children to develop a healthy and realistic level of self-confidence and a sense of their own self-efficacy.
- **Personality:** Individual personality traits also played a role. So, the resilient children mostly tended to have a more balanced and calm temperament. They also tended to be able to approach others openly and could thus often find sources of support by themselves.

Another important finding that emerged from the data collected by Emmy Werner and her team was that individual resilience did not only have an effect in childhood. A large proportion of the adolescents who initially displayed a problematic development, and drew attention to themselves through delinquency or drug abuse, led normal, successful lives between the ages of 32 and 40. An above-average proportion of women, it seemed, succeeded in disassociating themselves from their negative environment by way of further education, stable relationships and religious commitment.

Emmy Werner and her team's work helped to shift the focus of developmental psychology away from the question of "What makes a person fail in life?" to the perspective "What makes a person succeed in life?" To this day, Werner's findings have been confirmed by numerous studies worldwide. One of these investigations was the Bielefeld invulnerability study of 1989, in which Friedrich Loesel, a German psychologist and criminologist, and his team studied 144 children living in foster homes aged between 14 and 17 in a cross-sectional study, analysing them together with their educators. In this group of adolescents from a total of 27 homes, 54% displayed problematic developments while 46% were developing well. The protective factors identified for these children confirmed Werner's findings. Independently of one another, Antonovsky, Werner and also Loesel came to very similar conclusions regarding the different factors behind resilience. But how does this apply to the findings on successful managers?

6.6 The FiRE model of resilience

How do people manage to develop their full potential under the most difficult circumstances in life? If you talk to individuals who have demonstrated an incredible amount of resilience, they themselves usually regard their achievements as perfectly normal and by no means special. They are often not even aware of their own ability, but just try to cope with life as best they can and simply grasp the opportunities that present themselves. It, therefore, usually takes some time and reflection to become aware of your own ability.

EXAMPLE

Today, Hans-Olaf Henkel is a sophisticated man with an almost aristocratic air about him. Surprisingly, he does not come from a sheltered parental home. After his father fell in World War II, he grew up as a half-orphan and even spent several months in a children's home, which at the time was not a particularly pleasant place to be in. After an odyssey through a total of 14 schools, he eventually managed to complete intermediate secondary school education, after which he began an apprenticeship as a shipping agent. He spent many years going to evening schools to study business administration and economics, as well as sociology. Some 40 years later, after a career in management at IBM and a position as chief lobbyist of the BDI (Confederation of German Industry), Henkel was elected president of the Leibniz Gemeinschaft, a network of German research institutes from various disciplines. Even a butterfly species was named after him.

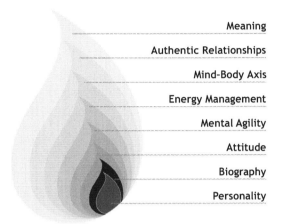

Figure 6.6.1 The FiRE model of resilience.

For our work with managers, we needed a simple yet comprehensive model that minimises the complexity of existing research results without being trivial. We, therefore, combined the various factors of mental and emotional resilience into a spatial construct, which we have called the FiRE model of individual resilience (see Figure 6.6.1). FiRE is an abbreviation for *Factors improving Resilience Effectiveness®*.

It helps managers to develop or practise strategies for maintaining resilience, so that they are better able to withstand difficult situations or crises and, ideally, even come out of them feeling stronger. The spheres model was established with the help of sound concepts developed by a number of renowned psychologists, psychiatrists, sociologists, biologists and brain researchers. These include Lewis Terman's Genetic Studies of Genius, Viktor Frankl's Existential Analysis, Emmy Werner's Resilience Research in Developmental Psychology, Aaron Antonovsky's Sense of Coherence, Jon Kabat-Zinn's research on the Mindfulness-Based Stress Reduction programme, brain research studies undertaken by Klaus Grawe and David Rock et al., Conrad Hal Waddington's research findings on epigenetics, and Robert Ader's psycho-neuro-immunology analyses. These have been described in detail in my book *Resilient Leadership*. The combined findings by Antonovsky, Werner, Loesel and co. provide a comprehensive overview of the contemporary research being conducted on the factors that help to improve inner resilience. The model consists of eight spherical shells resting inside each other and increasing in radius from the inside to the outside. This is supposed to symbolise how the outer layers of resilience, i.e. meaning and authentic relationships, are easier for the individual to influence than the inner core, i.e. one's own biography and personality. In the centre there are the mind–body axis, energy management, mental agility and attitude: four levels that are just as critical for mental resilience and can, with a certain amount of effort, be influenced by the individual.

The sphere Personality

An individual's level of stress resistance is a personality trait which is partly genetically predetermined and partly depends on that individual's early childhood experiences.

Of all spheres of resilience, the personality sphere is the one that is the most difficult to influence. It is only possible to alter basic, underlying character traits such as introversion and extroversion or a person's emotional stability within very strict limits. The main focus of the personality sphere is to become better acquainted with your own strengths and weaknesses in order to have better control of yourself. The inner sphere is of central importance when it comes to becoming better acquainted with yourself and your own character traits, strengths and weaknesses in order to be better able to influence them. Already the inscription handed down by the oracle of Delphi, which is at the heart of Greek antiquity, stated: recognise yourself. This is precisely what this level is about, supported by self-reflection, external feedback and tools from the field of personality psychology.

The sphere Biography

An individual's personality is inseparably linked to their past, which in turn has repercussions for their attitude towards current challenges and future expectations. Basic, subconscious decisions about life, also known as "beliefs" in the field of psychology, can get in the way later on in our professional life. Strategies that were effective in getting attention in childhood and adolescence, are generally still an effective driving force later on in our careers, except that this comes at a high price. Many managers with whom we work have internalised beliefs such as: "If I don't give it my best, I won't be accepted." On the one hand, this deep, underlying conviction releases a vast amount of energy. On the other hand, long-term it also has a negative impact on our social life, our recuperation and sense of personal satisfaction. Such beliefs need to be re-examined and possibly revised. Another aspect of the sphere of *Biography* is the crises and difficult times a person has to cope with in the course of their life. These are important resources when it comes to repeatedly dealing constructively with distressing situations and literally not being pulled down by them.

In summary, the sphere *Biography* is concerned with the resources needed to overcome difficult situations from your past.

The sphere Attitude

A person's inner stance influences his approach to challenges in life. It ultimately determines whether an unforeseen event is seen as an excessive strain or a challenge. Someone's inner stance gives a person's feelings and thoughts direction and thus has an effect on the quality of their actions. Does a manager see himself as a "creator" who shapes his own fortune? Or rather as a "victim" who loses control of the circumstances in his life, who pities himself and blames others for his misery? Such a victim mentality is expressed both verbally and non-verbally; it reduces your own emotional serenity and capacity to think, as well as weakening the quality of your decisions. And yet it is not easy to drop such a victim mentality. We all know that. The sphere of *Attitude* is, therefore, concerned with developing strategies for constructively influencing your inner stance.

The sphere Mental Agility

This sphere deals with the ability and the will to continue to learn, to react flexibly to rapidly changing conditions and to embrace uncertainty and complexity with confidence. More than ever executives need to be able in today's complex and ambiguous world to make far-reaching decisions quickly, even though the data may be contradictory and constantly changing. On the one hand this requires a healthy intuition and, on the other, the self-confidence to be able to live with suboptimal decisions. Above all, however, it requires the willingness to leave one's own comfort zone when entering a new territory, as well as the ability and the will to improvise. Mental agility has something to do with being sceptical of traditional experience and taking for granted that change and disruption are about to happen. It means recognising patterns and gaining new insights from seemingly incoherent data points. Being open to new experiences is a trait, i.e. a behaviour preference which is stable over time. This means that, based on their personality, different people are more or less open to change and ready to leave their comfort zone. In this sphere, it's about learning techniques to further develop this ability in oneself.

The sphere Energy Management

This sphere is a collection of simple, fast-working strategies to consciously improve your energy level and sense of well-being. They are like a first-aid kit for managers and everyone who wishes to work on grounding themselves, recharging, creating more of a distance to everyday problems and, by extension, on being better equipped to deal with difficult situations. The range of potential resources from which new energy can be drawn is immense and different for each individual. It ranges from sport to classical music, spa treatments and theatre outings to DIY work and similarly creative activities. Resources first have to be developed and then applied regularly to have a positive impact. By working at this level, you learn to consciously control your emotions and accompanying thoughts, so that even under great pressure you do not get stuck in the hamster wheel, but are able to calmly deal with situations and maintain a healthy inner distance from them.

The sphere Mind–Body Axis

As humans we consist of body and mind. Both are intricately connected and mutually influence each other. They should, therefore, be paid equal attention. This also applies for managers. However, they often have a lifestyle which, as a result of long working hours and frequent travel, does not allow them to take care of their bodies in an appropriate way. Work on the mind–body axis starts with the amount of sleep and quality of nutrition and goes on to cover various forms of physical exercise, such as endurance sports, yoga and autogenic training, mindfulness and meditation exercises. The MBSR method is a particularly suitable combination of physical movement and mindfulness exercises. The abbreviation stands for Mindfulness-Based Stress Reduction. Regularly practised, these exercises can also reduce the susceptibility of a person to internal crises. This also includes the measurement of physical stress indicators, such as heartbeat variability, with the aim of raising self-awareness. The body is a very useful tool to quickly achieve a healthy inner distance from everyday incidents. This distance helps to reduce the experience of negative stress. The work in this area focuses on using the body to gain greater inner balance and clarity of thought.

The sphere Authentic Relationships

Whom do you speak to if something really gets to you? Who is your own personal supervisory board? Trustworthy, honest relationships are particularly important for managers, since they give them a brief respite from always being the authoritative decision-maker who constantly has to have a solution for every problem. Authentic relationships to friends, close colleagues, mentors or a coach give a manager the chance to voice her doubts and fears. This is what makes such relationships so valuable. The life partner or spouse also plays a pivotal role in this respect, of course. They should, however, not be the only person the manager can turn to for advice. The higher the manager climbs up the career ladder, the less her lifestyle allows her to maintain deep friendships. It is also often difficult to know who is really giving honest advice and who is only pretending to be a friend in order to gain an advantage. The ramifications of these authentic relationships are underestimated by many successful managers. Cultivating such contacts is thus given a low priority until one day you no longer have any friends who want to spend time with you, particularly when the chips are down.

This sphere is, therefore, about creating awareness of these Critical Leader Relationships and about then turning these contacts into more regular and professional ones, into your personal "supervisory board" so to speak.

The sphere Meaning

Professionally committed and successful people often run their lives in the fast-track lane. They put in a great amount of effort, accept a lot of inconvenience for the sake of their jobs and often forgo a fulfilled private life in the process. Only those who see a purpose in what they do – whose actions feel right and meaningful – can withstand professional pressure and susceptibility to life crises. As the American philosopher Henry David Thoreau put it: "It is not enough to be busy. So are the ants. The question is: What are we busy with?"

The sphere of *Meaning* is, therefore, about identifying and developing a manager's personal values, the ones that are really meaningful in his life. The phrase "to make a difference" hits the nail on the head: In what area of your life would you like to make a real difference? What do you want to stand for? For whom would you like to achieve something special?

Bibliography

Anonymous; Veterans Statistics, PTSD, Depression, TBI, Suicide, Veterans and PTSD; 2014.Antonovsky, Aaron; Health, Stress and Coping; Jossey-Bass, New York City, USA, 1979.

Becker, Klaus Juergen; Ho'oponopono, Die Kraft der Selbstverantwortung; RiWei, Regensburg, Germany, 2009.

Berndt, Christina; Resilienz, Das Geheimnis der psychischen Widerstandskraft; Deutscher Taschenbuch Verlag, Munich, Germany, 2013.

Bilinski, Wolfgang; Phoenix aus der Asche, Resilienz – wie erfolgreiche Menschen Krisen fuer sich nutzen; Haufe, Freiburg, Germany, 2010.

Bittelmeyer, Andrea; Karrierefaktor Resilienz, Rueckschlaege besser wegstecken; manager Seminare, Bonn, Germany, 2007.

Brooks, Robert; Goldstein, Sam; The Power of Resilience, Achieving Balance, Confidence, and Personal Strength in Your Life; McGraw Hill, New York, USA, 2003.

Buessers, Peter; Das Konzept der Salutogenese nach Aaron Antonovsky, Eine Perspektive fuer die Gesundheitsbildung; Universitaet zu Koeln, Koeln, Germany, 2009.

Clarke, Jane; Nicholson, John; Resilience: Bounce Back from Whatever Life Throws at You; Crimson Publishing, Richmond, UK, 2010.

Claussen, Andrea; Executive Resilience: Can Body-Self-Awareness Create a Higher Level of Resilience?; INSEAD, Fontainbleau, France, 2013.

Coutu, Diane L.; How Resilience Works: Confronted with Life's Hardships, Some People Snap, and Others Snap Back; Harvard Business School Publishing, Boston, USA, 2002.

Csíkszentmihályi, Mihály; Flow – der Weg zum Glueck, Der Entdecker des Flow-Prinzips erklaert seine Lebensphilosophie; Herder, Freiburg i. Breisgau, Germany, 2006.

Drath, Karsten; Coaching und seine Wurzeln, Erfolgreiche Interventionen und ihre Urspruenge; Haufe, Freiburg, Germany, 2012.

Drath, Karsten; Resilient Leadership: Beyond Myths and Misunderstandings; Taylor & Francis, Abingdon-on-Thames, UK, 2016.

Eidelson, Roy; Soldz, Stephen; Does Comprehensive Soldier Fitness Work? CSF Research Fails the Test; Coalition for an Ethical Psychology, 2012.

Gillham, Jane; Reivich, Karen; Building Resilience in Children, The Penn Resiliency Project; University of Pennsylvania, Philadelphia, USA, 2007.

Grey, Jacqui; Executive Advantage, Resilient Leadership for 21st-Century Organizations; KoganPage, London, UK, 2013.

Jackson, Rachel; Watkin, Chris; The Resilience Inventory: Seven Essential Skills for Overcoming Life's Obstacles and Determining Happiness; British Psychological Society, Leicester, UK, 2004.

Loesl, Friedrich; Aggression und Delinquenz unter Jugendlichen; Untersuchungen von kognitiven und sozialen Bedingungen; Luchterhand, Wolters Kluwer, Munich, Germany, 2003.

Maehrleit, Katharina; Resilienz, Stark wie Bambus; manager Seminare, Bonn, Germany, 2012.

McCann, Joseph; Selsky, John W.; Mastering Turbulence: The Essential Capabilities of Agile and Resilient Individuals, Teams, and Organizations; Wiley, San Francisco, USA, 2012.

McCarthy, John F.; O'Connell, David J.; Hall, Douglas T.; Leading beyond Tragedy: The Balance of Personal Identity and Adaptability; Emerald Group Publishing, Bingley, UK, 2004.

Nicholson, Nigel; Bjoernberg Asa M.; Whom Shall I Turn to?: The Hidden Role of Critical Leader Relationships in Leader Effectiveness; London Business School, London, UK, 2013.

Patterson, Jerry L.; Goens, George A.; Reed, Diane E.; Resilient Leadership in Turbulent Times: A Guide to Thriving in the Face of Adversity; Rowman & Littlefield, Plymouth, UK, 2009.

Reivich, Karen; Shatté, Andrew; The Resilience Factor: 7 Keys to Finding Your Inner Strength and Overcoming Life's Hurdles; Three Rivers Press, New York, USA, 2002.

Schmitz, Christof; Resilienz und Veraenderung, Braucht Change Krisen – und wenn ja: welche?; Manager Seminare, Bonn, Germany, 2009.

Schuler, Markus; Resilience, Wie es um Fuehrung, Flexibilitaet und strategische Weitsicht im Unternehmen bestellt ist; Egon Zehnder International, Zuerich, Switzerland, 2010.

Seligman, Martin; Building Resilience: What Business Can Learn from a Pioneering Army Program for Fostering Post-Traumatic Growth; Harvard Business School Publishing, Boston, USA, 2011.

Siebert, Al; The Resiliency Advantage: Master Change, Thrive under Pressure, and Bounce Back from Setbacks; Berrett-Koehler, San Francisco, USA, 2005.

Siegel, Daniel J.; Das achtsame Gehirn; Arbor, Freiamt i. Schwarzwald, Germany, 2007.

Tardanico, Susan; Entire Management Team Killed, A CEO's Turnaround Story; Forbes.com, New York, USA, 2012.

Toegel, Ginka; Barsoux, Jean-Louis; How to Become a Better Leader; MITSloan Management Review, Cambridge, USA, 2012.

Topf, Cornelia; Krisenstrategien, Rettung aus eigener Kraft; manager Seminare, Bonn, Germany, 2005.

Various; Harvard Business Review; Building Personal and Organizational Resilience; Harvard Business School Publishing, Boston, USA, 2003.

Wellensiek, Sylvia Kéré; Handbuch Resilienz-Training, Widerstandskraft und Flexibilitaet fuer Unternehmen und Mitarbeiter; Beltz, Weinheim, Germany, 2011.

Wellensiek, Sylvia Kéré; Resilienz lernen, Die innere Staerke wecken; manager Seminare, Bonn, Germany, 2012.

Werner, Emmy; Resilienz – Gedeihen trotz widriger Umstaende; Eroeffnungsvor-
trag Internat. Resilienz-Kongress 2005, ETH Zuerich; Auditorium Netzwerk,
Muellheim/Baden, Germany, 2005.

Werner, Emmy; Overcoming the Odds: High Risk Children from Birth to Adulthood;
Cornell University Press, Ithaca, USA, 1992.

Wood, David; Army Chief Ray Odierno Warns Military, Suicides "Not Going to
End" after War Is Over; Huffington Post, New York, USA, 2013.

Zolli, Andrew; Healy, Ann Marie; Resilience: Why Things Bounce Back; Free
Press, New York City, USA, 2012.

7 Mastering what life throws at you

On the basis of the survivors of 9/11, the New York psychologist George Bonanno demonstrated how differently people process strokes of fate. Over a span of two years, Bonanno studied people who had experienced the fall of the Twin Towers first-hand. Some of them had been under such shock that they developed permanent psychoses, became depressed, had anxiety psychoses and other chronic disorders. Others showed either only slight symptoms or none at all. A total of 35% of those who had survived the terror attacks actually showed themselves to be resilient, i.e. they displayed no symptoms or recovered very quickly. This is a remarkable value considering the singularity and gravity of this trauma, but this also coincides with the findings of other resilience researchers, such as Emmy Werner.

In the context of business management, resilience also means the ability not to be defeated by external upheaval, such as failure, conflict or other adversities in your life and even to grow because of them. Yet, in this case, the situations are usually less life-threatening. How can targeted training be used to develop inner resilience? What does an emotional and cognitive workout entail? Managers with pronounced resilience do not allow their negative thoughts and emotions to take control. Instead, they consciously try to work with them constructively. This is a characteristic that is often also known as emotional agility or self-control. In our complex, ever-changing knowledge society, the ability to manage one's own negative and destructive impulses and feelings is becoming increasingly important, also with regard to corporate success. Numerous studies have demonstrated that having emotional agility can help manage stress, reduce erroneous decisions and make you more innovative and efficient.

But how can a manager learn to cope with private and professional crises without falling apart? Is it at all possible to acquire this skill? Current research findings suggest that the concept of resilience in adults may be classified as a personality's raw resilience and acquired resilience, which is the sum of all coping strategies, attitudes and techniques that a person acquires in the course of their life in order to stabilise themselves in times of crisis.

Figure 7.0.1 shows the correlation between these different aspects of resilience.

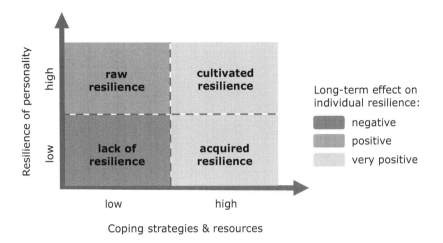

Figure 7.0.1 Different types of resilience.

7.1 Same goal, different reasons

It should be a part of each manager's sense of professionalism to prioritise the cultivation of such skills that increase or at least preserve their own ability to perform. And this challenge will be different for people with a high level of raw resilience than for those who are particularly sensitive.

People with extensive raw resilience typically see no need to take care of themselves and have, therefore, never really cultivated it. They tend not to be particularly empathic. In fact, they are even rather thick-skinned and they seem to have endless amounts of energy and are not easily distracted from their course. They are strict with themselves and with others. These people appear to be completely invulnerable – until they encounter a situation in their life that is bigger and more powerful than they are, and then they find they are not able to deal with it. Through our work, we have encountered numerous cases of managers who were completely devastated by such a situation, because they had not developed strategies to deal constructively with their weaknesses and to get themselves back on their feet. The depths to which these decision-makers then fall can be truly cataclysmic.

By contrast, people with a low level of raw resilience are only too familiar with their dark sides and inner demons. They tend to be sensitive, more easily unnerved by conflicts and uncertainty, and tend to worry a lot. As far as possible, they have accepted this situation and more or less consciously developed strategies to stabilise themselves. They do not feel at all invulnerable and know their own limits. The legendary British Prime Minister Winston Churchill, who led Great Britain through World War II, called the dark phases of his life "the black dog". For this group of decision-makers it is important to become aware of their inner resilience and to continue to cultivate and professionalise their acquired resilience.

From research on resilience, we know today that having a high level of raw resilience is a factor that allows personality factors to remain stable over time; in other words, it limits people's inner growth. By contrast, a low level of raw resilience or a high level of sensitivity might hold many risks but it also enables the potential for greater inner growth.

7.2 Mental weight training

Even if there are different levels of motivation for improving one's resilience, the path to get there is the same for everybody. Work in itself, particularly when it concerns working on your own resilience, is nothing more than mental and emotional power or fitness training. There is no point in signing up to a gym to get physically fit if you are not going to go there. Reading a book about fitness and going once a month for a workout will not have any effect either. It also makes no sense if you go to the gym only to spend time at the bar or in the spa if you are actually trying to increase muscle mass and reduce fat. Conversely, fitness training has always only proven to work if you are disciplined enough to go there twice or three times a week over a longer period of time, if it makes you sweat and you even end up struggling against your own pain threshold.

The same goes for mental fitness. Working on your own resilience should be understood as an inner process, which can last for months or years. Reading a book or going to a seminar is a good start, but no more than that. The real work happens inside you, through critical self-reflection and observing yourself, as well as trying out new thought and behaviour patterns. This may mean looking into the dark corners of your closet and perhaps owning up to a few unpleasant truths. Perhaps you need to do away with some old habits and leave your comfort zone. Working on yourself requires taking yourself seriously, maybe for the very first time, and applying the same diligence and long-term dedication to yourself as you would to any other project. Working on yourself is not always comfortable, but it is worth it. And, as with physical exercise, this work can be done alone, in groups or under the supervision of a personal trainer or coach.

Another important aspect, which needs to be given some thought, is the moment you actually start training your resilience. Someone who wants to learn how to sail is typically not going to start at wind force ten, but rather when the wind is more manageable, at perhaps wind force three. The same applies to resilience. It is more effective to train inner resilience before the occurrence of a serious career situation and not when the damage has already been done.

7.3 Working at different levels

Based on our own individual preferences, work on our own inner strength certainly can and should take place at different levels. The eight spheres of the individual resilience model can give us sound guidance in this respect in order to identify possible approaches. There is no specific order in which to work

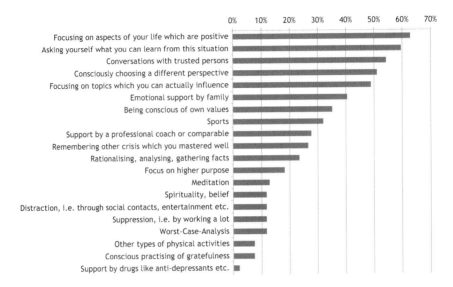

Figure 7.3.1 Practised coping strategies for critical career situations.
Source: Survey by Karsten Drath Dec 2015–Jan 2016.

through the individual spheres. But it certainly makes sense to work on as many levels as possible in order to achieve the best and longest-lasting effect.

In my research for this book, the participating managers were asked, among other things, which strategies they used to successfully process difficult career situations and to ideally emerge from them stronger than before. The results were very informative (see Figure 7.3.1) and showed that nearly all eight spheres of resilience were, in fact, used by managers. However, the statistics also revealed that some highly effective methods are only very occasionally applied. More on this later on.

7.4 Taking stock: how satisfied are you with your life?

It can generally be said that a manager's resilience will be particularly challenged if crises or setbacks are experienced in several areas of his or her life.

EXAMPLE

The example of Swisscom's former CEO, Carsten Schloter, highlights this. When you are leading a fast-track life, losing your own family can quickly throw you off-track, particularly if power struggles and other critical career situations happen at the same time. The more areas are deemed to be unfulfilling or perceived as problematic, the more this will have a negative impact on the amount of resilience at a person's disposition.

Figure 7.4.1 Line.

What about you? What is your life situation like? How satisfied are you in general with the areas of your life? Use the questions in the following sections to reflect on each area of your life. Give yourself enough time for this. Be as honest with yourself as possible. Then rate that area on a scale (see Figure 7.4.1) from 0 (meaning "not at all") to 10 (meaning "completely").

Career

- How happy are you with your choice of career?
- How satisfied are you with your current career level?
- How do you compare with your peer group, e.g. former fellow students?
- To what extent do you love what you do?
- All in all, how much do your job and your career fulfil you on a scale from 0 to 10 (0 = not at all; 10 = completely)?

Money

- To what extent do you have enough money to live life without being worried?
- To what extent do you have enough money to live out your need for freedom and autonomy?
- Do you have enough money to fulfil your need for status and personal fulfilment?
- All in all, how happy are you with your financial situation on a scale from 0 to 10 (0 = not at all; 10 = completely)?

Relationship

- How comfortable do you feel in your partnership?
- How much do you trust your partner and how open are you with one another?
- How much does your partner inspire you?
- How fulfilling is your sex life in your relationship?
- Do you feel loved by your partner?
- All in all, how much does your relationship fulfil you on a scale from 0 to 10 (0 = not at all; 10 = completely)?

Family

- To what extent does your family give you its wholehearted support?
- How harmonious and relaxing is your family life?
- To what extent does your family catch you if you are feeling down?

- How much time do you spend with your family? How happy are you with this?
- All in all, how much does your family life fulfil you on a scale from 0 to 10 (0 = not at all; 10 = completely)?

Friends

- To what extent does your circle of friends give you its wholehearted support?
- Do you have friends whom you can completely confide in?
- Are you open towards your friends? To what extent do you confide in them?
- To what extent do your friends catch you if you are feeling down?
- How much time do you spend with your friends? How happy are you with this?
- All in all, how much does your circle of friends fulfil you on a scale from 0 to 10 (0 = not at all; 10 = completely)?

Social engagement

- To what extent are you involved in political, social, church or other forms of volunteer work?
- To what extent do these activities give you a sense of satisfaction?
- To what extent do you receive positive feedback, confirmation and recognition from this kind of work?
- How much time do you spend on these social activities? How happy are you with this?
- All in all, how much do social activities fulfil you on a scale from 0 to 10 (0 = not at all; 10 = completely)?

Personal growth

- How well do you know your strengths and weaknesses?
- Are you generally at peace with yourself as a person?
- To what extent do you love yourself?
- Have you set yourself any goals for your own development?
- How much does your lifestyle enable you to grow as a person and manager?
- All in all, how happy are you with your personal development on a scale from 0 to 10 (0 = not at all; 10 = completely)?

Health

- How happy are you with your physical state of health?
- Do you take good care of your body? How far do you take care of it?
- Do you sleep enough? To what extent do you feel strong and well-rested?
- To what extent do you have a healthy diet?
- All in all, how happy are you with your health on a scale from 0 to 10 (0 = not at all; 10 = completely)?

Body

- To what extent do you feel comfortable in your own skin?
- How happy are you with your level of fitness?
- How attractive do you feel?
- To what extent do you like your body as it is?
- All in all, how happy are you with your body on a scale from 0 to 10 (0 = not at all; 10 = completely)?

Mood

- To what extent are you emotionally stable?
- How often do you feel joy and satisfaction? How happy are you with this?
- How often are you preoccupied with gloomy thoughts and worries? To what extent are you happy with this?
- All in all, how happy are you with your emotional stability on a scale from 0 to 10 (0 = not at all; 10 = completely)?

Higher power

- To what extent do you believe in a higher power?
- To what extent does your faith help you to cope better in difficult times?
- What role does spirituality or religion play in your life? How happy are you with this?
- All in all, how happy are you with your spiritual life on a scale from 0 to 10 (0 = not at all; 10 = completely)?

Meaning

- Do you know what values you believe in?
- To what extent does your lifestyle reflect the values that are important to you?
- How meaningful is your life to you?
- To what extent are you striving for a higher goal that you wish to achieve in this lifetime?
- To what extent is the life you lead inspired by other people?
- All in all, how happy are you with your emotional stability on a scale from 0 to 10 (0 = not at all; 10 = completely)?

The result

So far, so good. Now enter your scale values in Figure 7.4.2. Each circular segment stands for one area of your life and each dotted segment corresponds to 20%. Starting at the centre enter your scale values and hatch that area for the sake of better visibility. You might also want to ask a person you trust to give you feedback in this way.

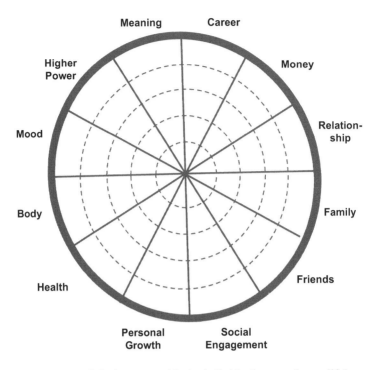

Figure 7.4.2 How satisfied are you with the individual areas of your life?

What thoughts cross your mind when you look at these areas of your life? If the area you completed was a wheel, how well would it roll, how bumpy would the ride be? Which areas of your life do you focus on too much? Which areas of your life need more energy and focus invested in them?

7.5 Personality: how are you wired?

As I described before, an individual's basic make-up will have a strong impact on their resilience. The initial aim should, therefore, be to reflect on the aspects and facets of your own personality: How would you currently handle setbacks? Which of your personality traits are helpful, and which are more of a hindrance? How well are you generally able to handle yourself? Into what thinking trap do you tend to fall under great emotional pressure? Have a look at Figure 7.5.1 to recap your favourite thinking traps.

The SWOT analysis is a strategic management tool, which was developed as early as the 1960s by the Harvard Business School. SWOT stands for Strength, Weakness, Opportunity and Threat (see Figure 7.5.2). Even if this method was actually intended for corporate strategy development, it is also ideal for assessing one's own inner resilience. The method itself is not what

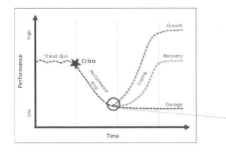

Catastrophising

Making a crisis out of a problem

Generalising

It always rains on me

Maximising Negative, Minimising Positive

Just another failure

Mind Reading

Taking events too personally

Emotional Reasoning

Because I feel it, it must be true

External Locus of Control

It's somebody else's fault

Mental Rumination

Thinking in circles

Figure 7.5.1 Common thinking traps.

Strength	Weakness
Opportunity	Threat

Figure 7.5.2 Template for your SWOT analysis.

is important but the deep self-reflection associated with it, which in our experience is a challenge for many managers. By nature, managers are pragmatic achievers, not abstract thinkers. That is undoubtedly a good quality, but also entails risks, especially when it involves observing themselves and critically questioning their own actions.

Take your time for self-reflection with the SWOT analysis. How would you currently handle setbacks? What works well and what does not? What

Strength	Weakness

– *Usually at ease*
– *Can handle stress well if I exercise and sleep well*
– *Disciplined and can work hard if I am inspired by the topic*
	– *Ambiguity is worrying for me*
	   => Catastrophising
	– *I tend to avoid conflicts*
	– *Tendency for self-doubts*
	   => Maximising negative
	– *Difficulty with saying "No"*

Opportunity	**Threat**
– *See ambiguity more as a possibility* – *Find a more constructive approach to conflicts* – *Take better care of my own interests*	– *If I am not taking good care of myself I can go into a downward spiral*

Figure 7.5.3 A sample SWOT analysis.

do you want to improve in future and what do you want to avoid under all circumstances? You can also use the analysis as a scheme to obtain feedback from people about your level of resilience. Figure 7.5.3 provides an example of a completed SWOT analysis.

Humans develop characteristic behaviours not without reason. Especially under pressure, the oldest parts of the human personality often become dominant: the so-called traits. As a reminder, these are time-stable behavioural preferences that are difficult, if not deliberate, to change. We had a look into the correlation between these traits and professional success in Section 2.6, *The old question: nature or nurture?* In order to understand the external image that the environment has of a manager, it makes sense to complete it by surveying the traits, as an inside view of the personality. The traits of a human can be determined by personal psychological testing. The most established methods for this are known as the group of Big Five methods. This five-factor model is one of the oldest and best-studied psychometric procedures. It has been referenced in more than 3000 scientific studies over the past 20 years. According to this model, the personality of a person can be distinguished by means of five dimensions:

- Need for stability
- Extraversion
- Originality
- Accommodation
- Consolidation.

As described above, the instruments of the group of Big Five methods capture many aspects of human personality. However, three factors play a special role in the degree of self-guidance that a person is able to achieve by virtue of his or her personality. In my book *Resilient Leadership,* I explain that these factors constitute the so-called *raw resilience* of a person. Current research findings suggest that the construct of inner resilience in an adult is subdivided into the "raw" resilience of an individual's personality, and also into the "acquired" resilience, which represents the sum of all self-management or coping strategies that a human develops in the course of his or her life.

Let's first take a look at *raw resilience.* We might imagine that you are startled by a very loud bang. Involuntarily you will close your eyes for a moment – provided you are healthy and conscious. This reaction is called the startle reflex or the moment of shock. The duration of this moment of shock in every human being allows initial conclusions to be drawn about their neurological resistance to surprising developments in the environment. This trait is part of the "raw resilience" because it develops early in life and is partly even inherited. By contrast, *acquired resilience* is composed of a combination of many different aspects.

For the interpretation of the Big Five, it is important to understand that these are qualities of a personality, not competencies or strengths or weaknesses. Therefore, there are basically no good or bad expressions, even if some expressions are certainly more socially desirable than others, such as extraversion. However, the area of raw resilience is an exception. This aspect of the personality is represented by three of the five factors of the Big Five. These are need for stability, extraversion and originality.

Need for stability

This factor reflects individual differences in experiencing and coping with challenging situations. High scores correspond to a high susceptibility to negative stress, but also stand for empathy. People with a high level are more likely to be easily disturbed by environmental events. They tend to be more insecure, more worried and generally need more time to recover from stress. They can anticipate problems well and often have a pronounced ability to empathise with other people. Low levels represent a high level of resistance to stress, but also tend to represent a less pronounced ability to empathise with others. People with a low expression are more calm and balanced and rarely experience strong emotional arousal. Also, they tend to generally perceive feelings as less intense.

Extraversion

This characteristic describes differences in dealing with other people, especially in situations that are perceived as energy-consuming or energy-giving. High values mean that someone gains energy from being active and in contact with many people. These people are often sociable, person-oriented, warm, optimistic and easy to enthuse. Low values mean that someone is more likely to draw energy from being in touch with just a few people and having some peace and quiet. These individuals are often more restrained in their social interactions. They prefer one-to-one conversations and often like to be independent.

Originality

This factor describes how a person deals with external changes that are not actively driven by him or her. Depending on the value, a person may have a tendency to feel deprived of energy in reaction to external change or she might even feel inspired. High values stand for attributes such as ingenuity, curiosity and a preference for the unknown. Low values indicate a preference for predictability and plannability as well as a preference for the known.

Protective/risk factors and resilience

Today, we know from resilience research that in the Big Five logic, a low level of "need for stability" can be considered a protective factor. The background is that, given a low level of this value, there is simply no longer anything that disturbs us. A high degree of extraversion is also considered a protective factor. It is easy for people of this stature to talk to others about their inner world, an aspect that is central to inner stability. The same is true for originality. High values correlate with a tendency to embrace change more easily which helps to better cope with an ever-changing environment. Conversely, high scores on the "need for stability" scale are seen as a risk factor for raw resilience, as people with this property are generally more easily stressed. Figure 7.5.4 should clarify this connection.

And what about your level of raw resilience? What, in your opinion, are your scores for the factors "need for stability", "extraversion" and "originality"? By estimating the expression of these so-called sub-traits, you can roughly estimate your level of raw resilience. Figure 7.5.5 is intended to

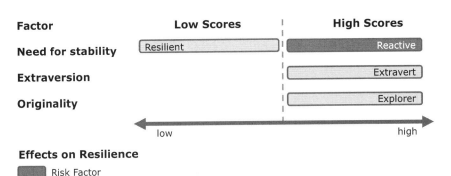

Figure 7.5.4 Constituents of raw resilience.

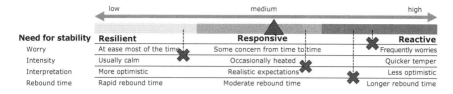

Need for stability	Resilient	Responsive	Reactive
Worry	At ease most of the time	Some concern from time to time	Frequently worries
Intensity	Usually calm	Occasionally heated	Quicker temper
Interpretation	More optimistic	Realistic expectations	Less optimistic
Rebound time	Rapid rebound time	Moderate rebound time	Longer rebound time

Figure 7.5.5 Estimating your own traits.

Need for stability	Resilient	Responsive	Reactive
Worry	At ease most of the time	Some concern from time to time	Frequently worries
Intensity	Usually calm	Occasionally heated	Quicker temper
Interpretation	More optimistic	Realistic expectations	Less optimistic
Rebound time	Rapid rebound time	Moderate rebound time	Longer rebound time
Extraversion	**Introverted**	**Ambiverted**	**Extraverted**
Warmth	Holds down positive feelings	Shows some positive feelings	Shows a lot of positive feelings
Sociability	Prefers working alone	Occasionally seeks out others	Prefers working with others
Activity mode	Prefers being still	Moderate activity level	Physically active
Taking charge	Prefers independence of others	Accepts some responsibility for others	Enjoys responsibility of leading
Trust of others	Is sceptical of others	Is somewhat trusting of others	Readily trusts others
Originality	**Preserver**	**Moderate**	**Explorer**
Imagination	Implements plans	Creates and implements equally	Creates new plans and ideas
Complexity	Prefers simplicity	Balance of simplicity and complexity	Seeks complexity
Change	Maintains existing approaches	Is somewhat accepting of changes	Readily accepts changes
Scope	Attentive to detail	Attends to details if needed	Resists details

Figure 7.5.6 Estimation scales for the traits of need for stability, extraversion and originality.

illustrate this process for the trait "need for stability". Start with aspects of "worry" and mark on the appropriate scale which description best suits you. Hand on heart: Does "at ease most of the time" describe you well? Or is "frequently worries" a better depiction? Mark the scale value that best describes you. Use the full width of the scale for this. Repeat this step for all other sub-traits such as "intensity", "interpretation" and "rebound time". If you've estimated all your values for all sub-traits in this way, you may average them from top to bottom. This then describes the expression of the trait in your case.

The crosses represent the values for the individual sub-traits. The triangle represents the graphically estimated mean value. This is of course only a rough appraisal and not to be confused with a scientific test. However, in my experience, this graphical estimate yields quite useful tendencies. Using Figure 7.5.6, you can do the test for yourself.

7.6 Biography: how you can draw strength from your past

The way a person sees their life history, particularly their view of the difficult phases and experiences, is crucial for their attitude towards the present
and future, and thus for their own resilience. Since the human memory is
organised in stories and pictures and does not distinguish between sensory
impressions, factual content and emotional evaluation, our life history is
not static. Instead, it is changeable, particularly with regard to the emotional evaluation of past occurrences. In order to strengthen your inner resilience, it therefore makes sense to engage more intensely with your own
history, and to ask yourself the following questions for instance: From what
phases in my biography can I still draw strength today? Which ones drain
my energy if I think about them?

How has your life been up to now? What is the first thing that comes to
your mind? Most people will spontaneously remember a handful of events
that have shaped their life so far. These events stand out in their memory
like a lighthouse that can be seen many kilometres along the coast. Others
fade by comparison.

Our memory is not objective, but shaped by emotions. The story that a
person tells about his life defines his attitude in the present. It is, therefore,
useful to concern yourself in detail with your past. While it may seem like
our life story just happened to us, a person's biography can in fact also be
understood as a collection of resources. In our experience most life stories
include three major parts:

- Positive events: remembering such moments gives strength.
- Negative events: the fact that these crises have been overcome and overcome is proof of the ability to handle crises well.
- Insights and decisions: these insights and control impulses are an expression of self-guidance.

Some find it uncomfortable to deal with their past. Particularly stressful
situations in childhood have often been neatly stored away and lie dormant
in some seemingly forgotten area of the brain. The confrontation with these
memories is sometimes very uncomfortable and stands in sharp contrast to
today's aplomb and strength. Nevertheless, we encourage managers to take
a look at these hidden areas in their closets, since that is the only way they
will become less terrifying.

A person's own life history can be described either in great detail or in a
very rudimentary form. We encourage our clients to describe it in as much
detail as possible and with as many facets as possible. The only thing that
counts is what is important to the narrator.

What life events have most distinctly shaped your life? What decisions
have you made? What are you proud of? What still gives you strength today?

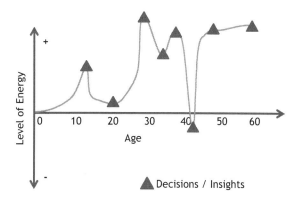

Figure 7.6.1 Documentation of main events in your own life story.

Figure 7.6.1 shows one way of documenting your life story and of visualising the development of your life energy over the course of time. It is best to proceed as follows:

- First create an overview of the main life events, starting with your childhood.
- Then state the degree of life energy or well-being that you felt at the time for each event (+10 for very high to –10 for very low).
- Visualise these events in a diagram like Figure 7.6.1.
- Now add to this the key insights you have gained in your life. What fundamental decisions have you made? Present your decisions and insights in the diagram.

What do you notice? What patterns do you recognise in your life? I am sure that you had already come to terms with many difficult situations in your life. How can you make use of these experiences today?

One insight that people usually have during our workshops is that the most distressing periods in their life often also contained the most profound insights and lessons for them. For many, it is also very inspiring to see how their own fundamental decisions about life have been influenced by these lessons.

7.7 Attitude: from victim to shaper mode

A manager's attitude or inner stance is decisive for the way in which he deals with stressful situations. It, therefore, has a substantial influence on her inner resilience. It will essentially determine whether a difficult development is seen as a challenge, as an incentive to do your best or as an excessive burden that will eventually lead to inner resignation.

The importance of the inner attitude is underestimated by most people. An excursus into the pharmaceutical industry should illustrate that. The licensing of drugs is an expensive thing for a good reason. At the heart of the approval procedure are clinical studies in which the effectiveness of a drug is tested in comparison to a so-called *placebo*. The word *placebo* in Latin means "I will please". It is a medication that contains no active pharmaceutical ingredients. The effectiveness of a drug is referred to in clinical trials as "effect strength". In such a clinical trial, the effectiveness of a new drug is tested on a group of patients, while a control group is given a placebo that looks and tastes exactly like the drug. It is important to note that the placebo is administered to patients under the claim that it is, in fact, the real drug. The fascinating thing about this is: the effect strength of such placebos in clinical trials typically reaches a magnitude of 30–50%! This means that even in the most conservative clinical studies at least 30% of the effect of a drug comes from the fact that the person believes in its effect. The effect size of placebos is thus about as high as the effectiveness of most antidepressants.

A person's inner stance is somewhat instinctive, in other words it is typically unconscious, but it can be perceived and can, therefore, be consciously influenced with some practice. Central to this is where a person sees the authority that has control over her destiny. If this authority is located within the person herself, then one speaks of an "internal locus of control". Such people can be recognised by the fact that they see themselves, and only themselves, as being responsible for their fate. We also refer to this attitude as a "shaper mode". On the other hand, if a person perceives destiny as a power that he or she is helplessly exposed to and which cannot be influenced, this is also referred to as an "external locus of control". People with this belief often blame others for events or mishaps, which is why we refer to this as a "martyr mode". Every person has a tendency towards one of these two attitudes because of her personality and biography. However, this is not necessarily predetermined, and can be changed by working on yourself.

Below, I will give you a few tools that you can use to consciously perceive and improve your inner attitude.

Resilience researchers unanimously agree that a high level of self-responsibility is an essential aspect of inner energy that helps people to survive crises unharmed. This specifically means that people who assume full responsibility for their past, present and future tend to be able to mobilise more inner strength and resilience than those who do not.

For the purposes of simplification, we can divide our life into three different areas (see Figure 7.7.1):

1 The first area of control can be determined by ourselves directly. This includes, for instance, our own body, family, team of colleagues and our relationship with employees, colleagues and superiors. In this area, everyone can influence things directly and make a difference.

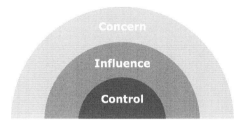

Figure 7.7.1   The circle of control model.

2   The second area of influence includes all aspects of life which a person influences indirectly. This includes, for example, the atmosphere at work, the strategy of a business unit, and innovations or the promotion of certain initiatives.
3   The third area of concern, in contrast to the others, can hardly be influenced at all, even with the greatest possible effort on behalf of the individual. This is an area you can only worry about, e.g. global warming, the Middle East conflict or corporate strategy.

In which of these areas do you invest the greatest part of your energy? Where do you directly or indirectly exert influence and take responsibility for what happens? And in what area do you invest a lot of time getting worked up about things you cannot influence?

Particularly in companies affected by many changes, we frequently encounter a number of high-ranking executives who invest a lot of time and energy in complaining about things that have gone wrong, but that can't be altered. They do not make use of the opportunities for action available to them during this time, but are concerned with issues they cannot change.

This kind of rumination may be human, but it is not particularly constructive. By contrast, people with a high level of resilience are much more concerned with areas which they can directly control or indirectly influence, and spend comparatively little time worrying about areas outside their sphere of influence or that lie in the past. This is accentuated even further if personal setbacks are added to the equation and the manager adopts a victim role in which he can no longer fend for himself. Thus, through their own doing, the area they can control or influence is then artificially reduced in size (see Figure 7.7.2).

The problem is that these managers are often not aware of what they are doing, not even when it is pointed out to them. This knee-jerk habit of making others responsible for their misfortunes has often been well-trained over a long period of time. If this problem is addressed it frequently leads to denial or aggressive reactions. Does this apply to you, too? Where do you take on the martyr mode? What is the benefit of being a martyr and not taking

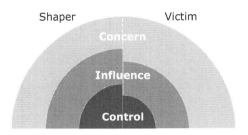

Figure 7.7.2 The victim mentality reduces one's own room for manoeuvre.

responsibility for yourself? How does it improve things? How does it make things worse? What do you need to do for yourself to be able to drop this role?

To feel like a victim entails emotions like fear, anger, shame, helplessness and sometimes even hopelessness. All of these are not particularly pleasant or even desirable feelings. It is all the more surprising that some people spend a long time in the martyr mode and constantly refuse to leave. Some spend many months there and some even longer. But if an energetic state lasts for a longer period, it does not happen without a reason. This is true for nature, in general, and for the human psyche, in particular. The victim attitude must therefore also have certain advantages. And that is exactly the case. The background is a phenomenon known in medicine as a secondary morbid gain. Recall the example of the ill child in Section 4.4, *Managers as victims*, whose illness was subconsciously prolonged on account of what benefits accompanied it. But what is the secondary gain a manager can draw from his victim attitude? There are different aspects here:

- **Guilt:** A manager in the martyr mode is not guilty, because she was indeed played badly by others. Good and evil are clearly distributed.
- **Moral superiority:** He is emotionally in the right and morally superior to the adversary. He deserves solidarity and support from others.
- **Responsibility:** She is not responsible for the events, because she cannot do anything in this situation. Her hands are tied.
- **Encouragement:** When something bad happens, one can expect approval and sympathy from others.
- **Tolerance:** If someone has lost a lot, people usually are more tolerant of misconduct and derailments, because this person deserves to be taken care of.

So, there are some valid reasons to critically question yourself when in the martyr mode. But this is easier said than done, because in such stressful situations our brain is flooded with adrenaline and noradrenaline which are created in its pain centre. This usually leads to thought patterns that are not very helpful, as I described in Section 4.5, *Watch out, thinking trap!* The first step in abandoning the martyr mode is therefore to admit to yourself that you are even in it at all.

Changing the perspective

One of the easiest strategies to cope with setbacks and challenging situations is to consciously change the perspective through which you are viewing this life event. Please join me on a small journey. Imagine, you see yourself from above, i.e. from up in the air. Perhaps you see yourself brooding alone over a problem and scratching your head or you see yourself pacing up and down like a tiger in a cage. Perhaps you're talking to others or taking a walk to let off steam. Now please gradually zoom out of the picture. The image of your own person is getting smaller. The contours of rooms, houses and streets come into the picture. You continue to zoom out of the picture. Now street blocks and neighbourhoods are visible. You increase the distance even further. Now you can see whole cities. A moment later you see the outlines of countries, and then continents. Notice how the distance to your problem keeps on increasing. The curvature of the Earth is already clearly visible. Then zoom out even further until you finally see the Earth in all its beauty. The trip goes on. The Earth gets smaller. The moon, in its orbit, comes into view. Even near-Earth asteroids are now visible. After a short while, the sun and the planets Mars, Venus and Mercury come into view and then become smaller and smaller. Thereafter, the outer planets of our solar system push into the picture. Our solar system is getting smaller and smaller. A little later, it disappears in the Oort Cloud, a collection of innumerable comets and asteroids. Neighbouring solar systems become recognisable. Finally, you can even recognise individual constellations. They appear much bigger here than from Earth. Finally, our galaxy, the Milky Way, becomes visible with its majestic appearance (see Figure 7.7.3). Here we stop the mental journey.

Now ask yourself the following question:

Seen from this perspective, how important is my problem, really?

Figure 7.7.3 Changing perspectives.
Source: Fotolia, Fotolia Premium.

Linger a moment on this issue. What answers come to your mind? This exercise belongs to the so-called disassociation techniques. Disassociation comes from Latin and means "separate, divorce". By changing the inner view, there is a gradually increasing separation of observer and problem, which gives the person experiencing the problem more distance from the stressful situation. After completing this mental journey, the onerous situation is still there, but it is embedded in a different context and thus relativised in its impact. Regularly practised, techniques such as these can significantly increase one's self-control in stressful situations.

Transforming inner beliefs

In no other species is the offspring so dependent on the care and protection of the family in order to learn what is essential for survival. From an evolutionary point of view, therefore, it has always been of fundamental importance for humans to be part of a social group, be it a family or a tribe. Some 100,000 years ago, being expelled from it meant certain death for our ancestors. However, for social groups to function, all parties involved must be in agreement on the status of the individual in the group. Hierarchies help to organise a social fabric of people. This is the only way we can explain how when two group members meet for the first time, the neural brain structures, which are also responsible for the processing of numbers, are activated. The brain evidently "calculates" the status of one's own person compared to another. Because of our ancestors, we are therefore anxious to get along well in a social system. The first system people get to know is the family into which they are born. A souvenir from our childhood and adolescence is so-called beliefs, which are basic decisions about life that we made in our childhood. As a child, each person makes formative experiences, from which he draws conclusions as to how best to cope in his family. Please note that the existence of a belief is not to be confused with the assumption that one's parents have done something wrong. This manifested childlike logic works even if your own parents were loving and supportive. Beliefs can generally be understood as childlike strategies to gain parental attention and care. Ideally, children are looking for love and attention. If, for some reason, they do not get this, they develop strategies to receive any kind of attention, because children cannot develop without it. Once learned, these strategies remain active until adulthood, although the frame of reference has changed completely in the meantime. A person's own family and employer have taken the place of their original family, and the small boy or girl has meanwhile become a successful manager. And yet those beliefs are still active, as can best be seen when a manager is put under great pressure. This is when such a belief becomes truly dysfunctional.

Since beliefs have been typically formed during infancy and still determine our behaviour today, the corresponding neuronal patterns are very strongly manifested. From a neurobiological point of view, such structures cannot be deleted or resolved. Rather, it is important to identify them and transform them into new behavioural strategies that are more appropriate to the current life situation. These new beliefs should then repeatedly be tried and practised. At the beginning this feels very unusual, like a new step sequence in dancing. But, over time, one acquires the new belief through constant application.

Typically, in our childhood, we made a lot of decisions about how to best manage life. So, there can in fact be more than one belief. But usually one of these mental patterns is dominant in our everyday life. Since we were once small and grew up in more or less intact families in the absolute majority of cases, these beliefs are very similar. Frank Farrelly, an American psychotherapist and founder of Provocative Therapy, coined the phrase "The Most Personal Is the Most Universal".

In order to be able to identify that belief, it is useful to start with the following logic: "If [behaviour], then [negative consequence]", so that both the decision linked to the behaviour pattern and the consequence are described.

To get to grips with your dominant belief, ask yourself the following question:

> Suppose that I have a typical behaviour pattern that frequently gets in my way and makes my life unnecessarily difficult, what behaviour pattern would that be?

In our work with clients, we typically receive answers like the ones below to this question:

a   I tend to work too much.
b   I try to smooth things over and please everyone around me.
c   It makes me angry if my performance is not rewarded.

In the next step we ask the question:

What is the basic assumption underlying this typical behaviour?

Typically, we receive answers like the following to this question:

a   Through a lot of work, I make sure that everyone can see how good I am.
b   If I solve conflicts and create harmony, then I will be recognised.
c   Only performance counts.

In the subsequent step, we translate the belief into an if-then logic. It is important to formulate the sentence in the language of the child, as it is then more direct and powerful. For example, in the case of the aforementioned life assumptions, this could lead to the following beliefs:

a   Only when I am strong will I be loved.
b   If I do not please others, I get in trouble.
c   If I do not give everything, I will be doomed.

Figure 7.7.4 Cost–benefit analysis of a belief.

From our experience, people's beliefs tend to be rather similar, which makes it easier to find the right set of beliefs for a particular person. Whether the elicited belief "fits" can only be perceived by the person themselves, although it is usually relatively clear whether a belief feels right for someone or not because it feels right and quite uncomfortable at the same time.

The next step is about performing an emotional cost–benefit analysis of the belief. Even if a belief is frequently perceived to be disturbing, it was nevertheless a useful coping strategy in the past and needs to be appreciated as such. No belief is completely good or bad. Instead, each belief has useful aspects and also a price to be paid for it. The cost–benefit perspective is the result of extensive self-reflection. Within a coaching process, this work can certainly take an hour or more. Figure 7.7.4 shows the results of such a reflection.

The last step towards the transformation of beliefs is the actual creative process. Here the aim is to combine key aspects of the original belief in new ways, so that it provides the same benefit but at considerably reduced cost.

To make this possible, another element is needed. For this, the following question is important:

> From today's point of view, what is even more important to you than living your beliefs?

Behind this question lies the search for a value of utmost importance to the adult. Maybe it's about creating something. Maybe integrity is central. Or maybe it's about trusting yourself. The highest value has the function of a stirrup, with the help of which it is much easier to sit up again, if you have fallen heavily from a horse.

Figure 7.7.5 A transformed belief.

The new belief created in the process should represent a challenge that, realistically seen, generally appears to be achievable, and does not make the person feel overburdened. The new belief must be powerful, so it is really important that the words ring true for the person (see Figure 7.7.5).

What is your transformed belief? Once you have found a new belief, it needs to be practised. This only works if initially that person regularly re-members the new thought pattern. This will only happen with the help of various visual memory aids. Images, such as a nature picture or a painting, which the person concerned associates with a certain belief, but which do not mean anything to anyone else, are practical and therefore also very pop-ular. You may also find certain objects, music or rituals that link to your new beliefs. The more sensory channels you address, the better you will be

---

EXAMPLE

Thomas Weber's (altered name) striving for harmony was nearly his downfall. His career was going from strength to strength after he re-turned from an assignment in China, but then stagnated because he was not able to assert himself against some dominant colleagues. His

(*Continued*)

belief was: "If I say what I think, they will trample all over me." With his coach's help, he found out what lay behind his strong need for harmony and his tendency to want to please. And he found out that two things were more important to him than his need for harmony, namely to create and to improve things. So, his new belief, which he practised every day, was: "Only if I show myself, can I change things for the better!" He was subsequently able to anticipate challenging situations and to overcome his need for harmony. In the process, he also learned to assert himself. Further career steps followed.

able to connect to your transformed beliefs when it matters. What memory aid would be suitable for you (see Figure 7.7.6)? What could help you remember your new beliefs at least once a day?

Consciously practising gratitude

With around 1.1 million civil and military staff members and a budget of more than 200 billion US dollars, the US Army is one of the biggest, most complex and arguably most expensive organisations in the world. It can hardly be suspected of being excessively open to trying out new ideas or being prone to philanthropic gestures. But the army has a big problem. In 2013 more soldiers died by committing suicide than under hostile fire. In reaction to this development, George W. Casey Jr., a retired American four-star general and former chief of staff of the US Army, launched the world's biggest resilience-boosting programme under the name of "Comprehensive Soldier and Family Fitness" in October 2009. This programme has now been running for several years and has been assigned a budget of 140 million US dollars. Using various measures, it is intended to prepare around one million

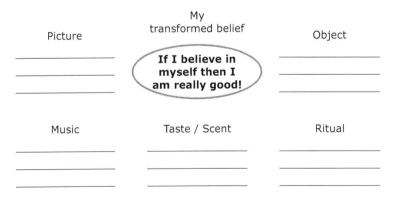

Figure 7.7.6 Memory aids for your transformed belief.

members of the US Army and their families for the traumatic experiences of a long-lasting military deployment. The measures include voluntary on-line courses, an online portal for soldiers and families to make a confidential self-assessment of their personal resilience situation as well as a ten-day train-ing course for members of the US Army who have been especially released from other duties to become so-called Master Resilience Trainers (MRT).

The conceptual roots of the programme are largely to be found in the so-called Penn Resiliency Program developed by Jane Gillham, Karen Reivich and Martin Seligman in 1994 at the University of Pennsylvania. In this pro-gramme, elements of cognitive behavioural therapy are combined with pos-itive psychology to form a curriculum designed to help students cope better with stressful and frustrating situations. In more than 20 independent stud-ies it was meanwhile possible to prove that the incidence of medium to se-vere symptoms over a period of up to 24 months could be reduced compared to a control group. It was also possible to verifiably reduce the incidence of fear and feelings of helplessness. On the other hand, optimism and general well-being increased.

Interestingly, one of the programme's central interventions is the practice of gratitude. In army jargon, it was given the bold name: Hunting the Good Stuff. Essentially, the exercise consists of reflecting daily on the good things that one has experienced on that day. Every day, programme participants are to note down at least three incidents for which they feel truly grateful. This appears much simpler than it actually is. Try it yourself.

EXERCISE: PRACTISING GRATITUDE

For which three incidents, encounters, talks, gestures etc. do you feel grateful? Write them down.

This does not refer to general events, such as the fact that you are alive or that there are people that you love. Rather, this is more about the small things that have happened today.

And now imagine that you are in a war zone, in a hot, sandy environment surrounded by strangers, who want to kill you, far away from your family, for many months. How difficult must it be for those soldiers to find three events daily that they feel grateful for? That is really hard work. The trick is that you can't be a victim and be grateful at the same time. Try it. Self-pity, despair, righteousness and passiveness are difficult to feel when you are concentrating at the same time on incidents that you feel deeply grate-ful for. Hebb's rule is the neurobiological basis for this exercise. Already in 1949 Canadian psychologist Donald Hebb advanced the hypothesis that has since been sufficiently proven: "What fires together, wires together". This means that neurons from different areas of the brain, which are regularly and simultaneously stimulated, develop ever-stronger networks over time until they eventually become an independent stimulation pattern. The more often you consciously feel gratitude, the more the neuronal paths that are responsible for this emotion are strengthened and fortified. At the same time, this daily practice trains your awareness and you start to focus more on those things during the day which you see positively.

But this exercise also works the other way around, almost as a litmus test. Imagine that you try in the afternoon or in the evening to find three events from today which you can be truly grateful for and nothing comes to mind after a quarter of an hour. In this case there are three possible scenarios:

1   You just woke up.
2   You have a truly terrible fate.
3   You are in the victim position.

Gratitude or humility are important qualities when it comes to abandoning the martyr mode. While you can be proud of many achievements in your life, there are many more fundamental things in your life which enabled your success, but are totally outside of your control. This includes the country and family you were born into. Your access to health care and education. The fact that you grew up in peace and without the threat of losing your life, and much more. Keeping this in mind now and again helps to reduce the stress of inconvenience. In our resilience workshops and in our one-on-one sessions with our clients we regularly use this method. The results are really astonishing. Already after just a few weeks, managers report noticing considerable changes in their sense of well-being, their aplomb and in their ability to maintain a healthy distance from difficult situations.

7.8 Mental agility: getting comfortable with leaving the comfort zone

Mental agility describes the will to constantly question existing concepts about needed skills, trends or market dynamics and to relearn them if necessary. Current keywords for this are hype topics, such as Digitalisation, Internet of Things and Industry 4.0. The problem with this is that especially executives with a lot of professional and life experience unilaterally assess the value of experience as being crucial to success in meeting new challenges. However, in the face of disruptive change which can potentially destroy entire business models within a few years, experience can be the least useful asset to survive.

Everyone operates in a certain mental comfort zone. But what happens when we get confronted with a new challenge? Assume you get a tempting job offer – the only thing is that it is in China. You have the choice of accepting the offer or rejecting it. If you don't accept the challenge, nothing happens. Everything stays the same and life still takes place in your previous comfort zone. On the other hand, if you do choose to embark on this adventure, you and your family can expect many new experiences that are far from being only positive. Language, climate, culture, food, political system – nothing is familiar. This initially costs a lot of energy. Of course, such an experiment can also fail if you feel too overwhelmed by the challenges you realisethe situation provides. In this case, the adventure potentially leads directly into martyr mode.

However, with a bit of luck, you and your family get used to the new circumstances after some time. Maybe you even like the new environment and you can find like-minded people, maybe new friends. In this case, your comfort zone begins to increase, taking on board these new and unique experiences.

An executive has countless such learning opportunities throughout his career. This can be, for example, the acquisition of new skills or the assumption of more responsibility. And each time, he has the opportunity to take on this challenge, and either to grow with it or to fail. Alternatively, he can also avoid these situations and remain at his usual level of competence and comfort. Figure 7.8.1 illustrates this.

To question existing comfort zones and proven recipes for success is always an individual decision. Nobody can relieve you of this, but you can ensure that the quality of your decisions becomes more holistic. Again, the old surgeons' saying applies: "do it often, do it well".

From a neurobiological perspective, mental agility is a routine in expressing and consolidating new neuronal structures. This brain transformation

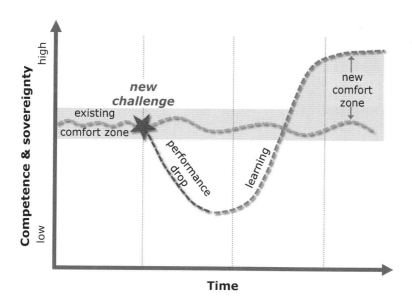

Figure 7.8.1   Mental agility.

capacity is also called neuroplasticity. In order to cultivate this ability, it essentially requires three components:

a A good reason. We know from modern brain research that brain neuroplasticity exists at any age, when the challenge ahead is emotionally stimulating and related to a person's goals and values.
b Sufficient physical and mental resources. This includes enough sleep, exercise, a healthy diet and a reasonable amount of stress. If a person is already experiencing high levels of negative stress, this is not the optimal time to train mental agility.
c Training. Practice with low-risk challenges. Get to know new people, for example, who have different interests than you. Travel to countries you do not yet know. Learn a new hobby or try a new language. Anything that promises new experiences and leaving the comfort zone is allowed.

But a high level of mental agility is not the only thing that is helpful in dealing with being outside the comfort zone. Recent studies suggest that a strong will to learn makes you happier, more successful, and even positively impacts your longevity.

EXAMPLE

A 2016 Yale University study looked at the reading behaviour of 3635 Americans over the age of 50 years. The team, led by Becca R. Levy, came to the conclusion that those study participants who read a book for more than 3.5 hours a week lived an average of two years longer than those who did not read. Additional benefits of reading regularly were increased cognitive performance and a greater sense of satisfaction in life. However, this probably does not mean reading just anything. Decisive for the positive effect was apparently the intense intellectual and emotional engagement with the reading material. In contrast, the positive effect did not occur when only newspapers or magazines were read. Here, a positive effect could only be discerned with seven hours of reading a week or more.

7.9 Energy management: your first-aid kit

Which mechanisms have you developed to reduce stress when you are feeling tense? How do you boost your energy when you are about to go into an important meeting? Which tools do you use to be better organised? What do you consciously or subconsciously shy away from? These are all resources that you have developed for yourself. Resources are skills that enable us to

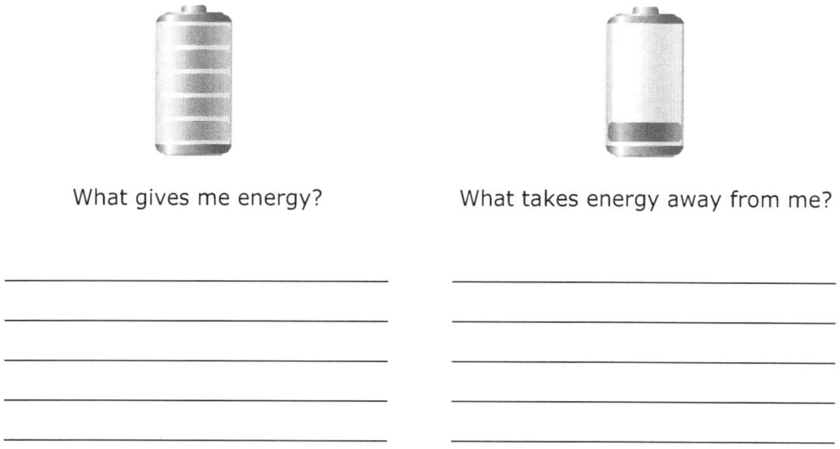

What gives me energy?

What takes energy away from me?

Figure 7.9.1   Your individual energy balance.
Source: Fotolia, Arcady.

handle our emotions. The more resources you have and the more flexibly you can make use of them, the better. They help you to handle challenging situations better and thus improve your individual resilience. At the other end of the spectrum there are situations, behaviour patterns or certain people who, for some inexplicable reason, drain you of energy, like an electrical battery which suddenly loses more energy when it is cold than when it is warm. You often only notice in hindsight that you have been dealing with an energy thief.

Take a few minutes for a first assessment of your energy balance (use Figure 7.9.1). What gives you energy? What makes you lose energy?

Human beings have the unique ability to draw strength from a thought, an activity or even a lifeless object. This is one of the aspects which distinguishes us from other animals. In terms of resilience, the sphere of resources covers all the skills that a person has developed to control himself emotionally. This also includes the abilities to reduce stress and clear one's head, to stimulate oneself and calm oneself down again, to channel the flow of ideas in a certain direction, to consciously change one's emotional status and recharge one's batteries. In summary, the term "resources" can be used to describe all thoughts, activities and objects that allow a person to get closer to a desired emotional state or adopt an inner attitude in order to be better able to deal with challenging situations and hence to improve their individual resilience. In our view there are various kinds of resources that vary considerably from person to person (see Table 7.9.1).

Table 7.9.1 Various kinds of resources

Resource	Description
Roots	Thoughts, activities and objects that ground you, bring you into contact with your own body and help to release blocked energy
Wings	Thoughts, activities and objects that help you to build up a certain energy or attitude and to bundle your energy, strength and optimism
Tools	Organisational aids and administrative support for increasing one's own efficiency
Energy thieves	Behaviour patterns, people and situations that drain you of energy or prevent you from reaching your desired inner state

Roots

What are your root resources? What helps you to calm down and reduce the level of inner activity? Roots ground you, put you in touch with your body and help to release blocked energy. They also help you to develop a greater inner distance from the problems of everyday life (see Table 7.9.2).

Table 7.9.2 Examples of root resources

Thoughts	Activities	Objects
Memories of happy moments, e.g. a holiday	Exercise, e.g. running, walking or yoga	Images that trigger happy memories
Thinking rituals, e.g. focusing on the positive	Wellness, e.g. sauna or massage	Certain music, e.g. classical music
Relaxation exercises for the mind, e.g. dream journeys	Manual or physical work	Fire, e.g. candles or an open fireplace
Meditation	Laughing or smiling	Certain comfortable clothes

Wings

Wing resources (see Table 7.9.3) help people to build up a certain energy or attitude, and thus to raise the level of inner activity. These techniques generate strength and optimism, they bundle energy and help you to rise above your current difficulties. Used in the right situation, they create a certain "build-up tension" inside. This makes it easier to rev up your own energy and consciously identify with your actual goals, so that you are better able to mentally prepare for and adjust to a challenging situation.

What helps you to grow wings?

Table 7.9.3 Examples of wing resources

Thoughts	Activities	Objects
Visualisation, especially of successful moments	Physical activation, e.g. through faster walking or running	Illustrations which symbolise goals, attitudes or beliefs
Conscious remembering of positive beliefs	Rituals, e.g. reading texts or affirmations out loud	Listening to certain energising music
Consciously thinking about a higher goal one wishes to achieve	Recharging, e.g. through enough sleep and good food	Talismans, i.e. objects that have a positive, subjective meaning
Reflecting on what a real or fictional role model would do	Consciously creating a supportive, positive environment	Selected clothing in order to feel perfectly prepared

Tools

Another group of resources are "tools", in the broadest sense of instruments and support structures that make your working life easier. They might not be able to recharge your batteries, but they make sure that they do not discharge as quickly. One example of a tool is the management of priorities, for instance by means of the Eisenhower Matrix (see Figure 7.9.2). This tool is both easy to understand and also provides an effective structure in order to tackle the omnipresent mass of tasks. It is surprising how many managers these days are familiar with these and similar methods, and yet they do not make use of them. This method was originally developed by the American General and President Dwight D. Eisenhower. Since it distinguishes between

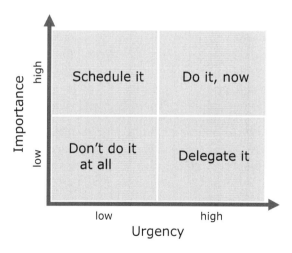

Figure 7.9.2 The Eisenhower Matrix.

urgency and importance, it is a particularly useful tool to use under time pressure to allocate the scant amount of time available more effectively.

The mantra "Who can do it 80% as well as you?" helps to delegate tasks in a structured manner and earlier on. Another example of a tool is actively managing your agenda. Many managers with whom we work have their electronic schedules open for anyone to see. So, there is actually some truth in the expression "I am not the master of my agenda!" This gets worse, the more different time zones are added to this. However, with little fuss and difficulty this plight can quickly be ended. By limiting access and reserving some time for recurring serial appointments for sport, networking and strategy or for an all-round check-up, you make sure that you keep control of your agenda and do not neglect your needs.

The top asset among the support structures is, of course, a well-functioning, canny and intelligent assistant. There is nothing that can keep a manager's back clear or reduce his or her stress level better than an executive assistant. Here you should be picky in your choice and invest plenty of time in giving a good briefing and regular feedback.

What resources and support structures have you created for yourself? What could help you to expand them even further?

Energy thieves

The fourth group of qualities which we would like to analyse in the context of resources is how to deal with energy thieves, i.e. people or things that draw our energy and deplete our energy reserves. The resource, in this case, entails having a strategy that is appropriate for dealing with negative influences. One example of energy thieves are people with a very negative basic attitude, e.g. because they have chosen to stay in martyr mode. One strategy could be to avoid such people, or, if this is not realistic, to minimise contact with them. However, this is not always realistic, for example, if they are colleagues or even supervisors. Here it helps to consciously determine the time, place and length of the contact. It is helpful, for example, not to allow such people to tear you down by talking to you at length at your own desk. Rather, you could signal that you are not available right now and postpone the conversation to a later date. With this you can determine the time, place and duration of the conversation, which will cost you much less energy.

Another group of energy thieves are smartphones. On the one hand, these technical marvels are a real blessing, as they are immensely helpful. At the same time, they are also a curse, especially if you let them dominate your behaviour too much. In our workshops we often ask the participants how long they think smartphones have already existed for. The estimated period is often 15 to 20 years. In fact, Apple released the first iPhone only in 2007, about 10 years ago. In this short time, it has drastically changed our working and communication behaviour. Not only for the better.

Christian Montag, a psychology professor at the University of Ulm, Germany, found out in a study conducted in 2016 that a typical German smartphone user looks at their phone 88 times a day, 35 times alone to check whether a message has arrived. This figure is likely to be even higher for many executives. Other studies have shown that lack of access to a smartphone can lead to increased heart rate, blood pressure and even anxiety. This phenomenon is also described in the literature as "Smartphone Separation Anxiety".

Another problem with smartphones are the visual, auditory and tactile stimuli that emanate unprompted from them and that immediately draw the attention of the owner regardless of the current activity. In particular, the so-called default mode network of our brain, a system consisting of parts of the prefrontal cortex and the parietal and temporal lobes, is affected. When our brain has no concrete tasks, it switches to a state of unspecific alertness that is not to be confused with the state of sleep. It then looks like a radar in all directions to a variety of external and internal stimuli, e.g. in the form of thoughts or sensory perceptions from the outside world. Brain researchers assume that this network has a strong coordinating and balancing function for the entire brain and that it is therefore important that the brain keeps returning to this state of rest. On the other hand, if it is permanently confronted with uncontrolled stimuli, such as smartphone signals, it is always "on the go", which leads to an inhibition of the default mode network. In the long run, this can have a negative impact on one's concentration, short-term memory and one's ability for strategic planning and action. This connection between this type of multitasking and reduced cognitive abilities has been proven by means of brain imaging techniques.

Smartphones have the tendency to make the barrier between work and private life disappear. This has both advantages and disadvantages. This is why it is important to cultivate a good management of mobile communication technology, but this requires a high degree of self-discipline, as we have experienced in our work with managers time and again. In particular, it is extremely difficult for executives not to react to the signals from their smartphone, because a crisis could occur at any moment, which requires their immediate attention.

A strategy that we consider useful for handling these devices is therefore to define times and places in which you do not use them. We also call that *digital detox*. Here are some examples of such digital detox zones:

- immediately after getting up,
- just before bedtime,
- while eating,
- during important discussions,
- during a specified time window on the weekends,
- during set times on vacation.

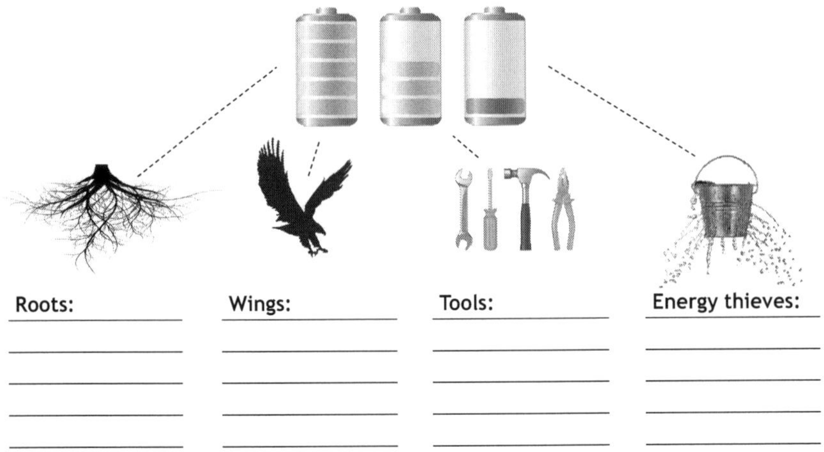

Figure 7.9.3 Overview of energy management.

As described above, it is important to disable all visual and audible signals within these zones to protect yourself from spontaneous smartphone stimuli. This also applies to vibration alerts and smartwatch connections. Smartphones are not necessarily bad per se. However, we have found that most executives have not cultivated conscious use of them yet. It is necessary to change this.

Overview

Figure 7.9.3 illustrates an energy management overview. What are your energy thieves and what strategies have you developed to deal with them? How will you now put these newly acquired behaviour patterns into practice? How will you ensure that your intention is not forgotten? How will you monitor the implementation of your goals? It would be useful to regularly record your results, both positive and negative, and especially to keep track of your insights in a coaching logbook. So that you do not forget anything in the hustle and bustle of everyday life, you might find it helpful to make this a fixed appointment in your schedule.

7.10 Mind–body axis: how to strengthen your body, soul and mind

René Descartes, a 17th-century French philosopher and naturalist, postulated the separation of mind and matter as two completely independent "substances" with his phrase "I think therefore I am."

This claim, which is also referred to in the literature as "Cartesian Separation", has decisively shaped the Western image of man and our relationship to our bodies. For many in the Western world, for example, the body is essentially a transportation vehicle and a visual object that has no connection whatsoever with our mental and emotional inner life.

The assumption that thoughts, emotions and physical condition are independent of each other is clearly refuted today. Not only does the psyche, with its emotions and thoughts, influence numerous processes in the body via the brain, including the immune system and even parts of our genetic make-up. The reverse is equally true: the body influences the cerebral metabolism and, by extension, also a person's psychological balance and mental capacity, e.g. through sport or meditation.

Those who understand and can make targeted use of this interrelationship will have a decisive impact on their resilience. Unfortunately, the practical implications of this insight have been slow to materialise. This is because people in the Western industrialised nations tend to one-sidedly overrate intellectual capabilities. This is particularly noticeable with managers, as primarily cognitive-oriented natural and economic scientists are to be found among them.

Check your attitude towards your body

Be honest: Do you feel comfortable in your own skin? Do you like your body? What do you like about it? What is your body to you apart from a means of getting around and a showpiece? Do you know what condition your body is in? Many people have a very difficult relationship with their bodies. Most of them do not like the way they are. Some simply ignore it or resign inwardly about it, others make a total body cult out of it by permanently trying to optimise it through sport, diets and surgical measures.

Without our body we are nothing and yet many only realise that when their bodies do not function well anymore. With regard to resilience, it is particularly important to develop an appreciative and accepting attitude towards your body. It is therefore crucial to perceive physical signs, develop a good subjective body feeling and become aware of your body's energy level.

Perceiving your body is about noticing and understanding your body's signals. What does you good, what doesn't? Do you notice when you are hungry, thirsty or tired? Or do you perhaps just get fleeting sensations such as a slight tightening of the abdomen, moist palms or a lump in your throat? What do these signals tell you?

Developing a feeling of your body is about having a sense of inner harmony with your body. Does it feel good and right to be in this body? When was the last time you felt really good and comfortable in your body?

Your energy level is part of your body sensation, which in turn depends on such factors as having enough sleep and a balanced diet. Sometimes you

feel like you're bursting with energy and sometimes you feel more like loung-
ing on the couch.

Now it is not necessarily the case that someone with a high level of energy
and a good body sensation, such as a top athlete, automatically has a high
level of resilience. However, someone whose body is completely charged
with energy is more likely to feel balanced and better able to handle stress.

The foundational drivers of the brain

The South African neurologist and brain researcher Etienne van der Walt
has analysed countless scientific studies that make statements about the optimal performance of the brain and how it can be influenced. In his many
years of research work, he has identified four key factors, which have been
labelled as the foundational drivers for optimal brain–body performance.
These are sleep, nutrition, exercise and meditation (see Figure 7.10.1).

Choosing an active lifestyle

Most executives spend too much time sedentary. It should not really be news
that this does not have much of a positive effect and could potentially lead to
physical side effects such as obesity and back problems. Van der Walt therefore advocates a lifestyle characterised by regular movement. 10,000 steps
a day is roughly the amount of exercise that a healthy adult should aim for.
Pedometers and fitness bracelets are effective companions here as they record
movement, visualise it and also make it comparable with like-minded people.

On four days per week, training sessions of at least 40 minutes and medium intensity generating a heart rate of at least 130 BPM should be sched-
uled. Van der Walt also advises to include short intense intervals of 2 to 3
minutes in these workouts to switch between anaerobic and aerobic exercise,
as this alternation has been shown to have a positive effect on brain metabolism. The sport itself is secondary. The core muscles should also be trained
once a week, according to the South African brain researcher.

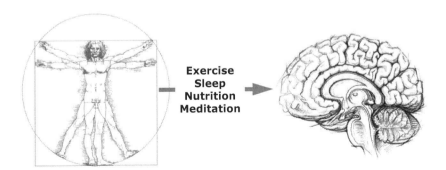

Figure 7.10.1 The foundational drivers of brain–body performance.

The benefits of regular exercise are numerous from the point of view of brain research:

- Regular and adequate exercise stimulates the growth of new blood vessels in the brain, a process also known as angiogenesis. This better provides the brain with oxygen.
- Through regular moderate exercise, new neurons are formed in the hippocampus and also stimulate the expression of neural connections, a process that positively influences the neuroplasticity of the brain. This process, also known as neurogenesis, promotes mental agility, improving our capacity for creative and innovative thinking.
- Varied exercise reduces the level of chronic stress and its harmful effects on brain performance. This improves the ability of the brain to buffer the stress response of the activated pain centre and, thus, deal better with strong emotions such as anger and grief.
- Through regular training, the brain emits so-called endocannabinoids, such as endorphins, the happiness hormone that has been proven to have a positive effect on anxiety, mild depression and physical pain.
- A daily half-hour walk also reduces the risk of a stroke by 20%.

Figure 7.10.2 shows the effect of your lifestyle on your physical performance as you become older. The two different lifestyles are an active one, according to the definition of van der Walt, and a more sedentary one like many managers have. As you can see, the longevity is the same in both cases. However, a person with an active lifestyle stays in the physical performance zone

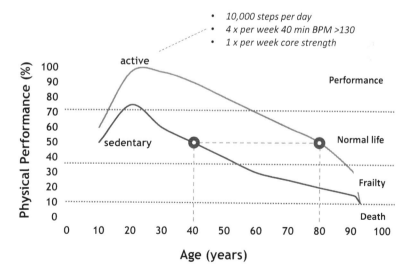

Figure 7.10.2   The link between lifestyle and physical performance.
Source: Fitzgerald et al. (1997).

well into their sixties, while a person with a sedentary lifestyle already enters the frailty zone in their mid-fifties. Or, put differently, an 80-year-old person with an active lifestyle can outperform a 40-year-old with a sedentary lifestyle. That is a pretty compelling piece of data, I find.

Getting the right level of sleep

By means of research van der Walt has identified sleep to be the second foundational driver for optimal brain–body performance. Many executives are known for their discipline and commitment. In our experience working in top management, 80-hour workweeks are normal and are often considered the equivalent of high performance. Of course, this also affects the employees. Anyone who has such a boss and wants to make a career of their own at some point, also does not finish working at 5 pm, but often works late into the night.

EXAMPLE

Bill McDermott, CEO of SAP, describes in his biography *Winners Dream* how he has worked his way up from very humble circumstances to being at the helm of the highest-valuated company in the DAX. He also mentions that his working day starts at 5 o'clock and often goes well past midnight.

From recent findings in brain and sleep research we now know that this form of self-exploitation does not lead to optimal performance and certainly not to an effective level of resilience which depends, among other things, directly on the quantity of sleep, i.e. how many hours we sleep during several consecutive nights. Another factor is the quality of sleep, i.e. to which degree we can sleep through without interruption. According to the US National Sleep Foundation, adults require 7–9 hours of uninterrupted sleep (see Figure 7.10.3).

The exact amount of sleep which a person needs is determined by their genetic code. About a third of executives we work with claim that they only need six hours or less to feel rested. Unfortunately, the facts speak a different language. Researchers at the University of California in San Francisco have in fact identified a DNA sequence which causes adults to require only six hours of sleep a night. The bad news, however, is that this gene is very rare in humans, occurring in less than 3% of the total population.

In 2014, Daniel Gottlieb, an associate professor at Harvard Medical School, published a study that linked the amount of sleep needed to two different regions of human DNA. In the study, researchers analysed data from more than 47,000 people of European descent who took part in several

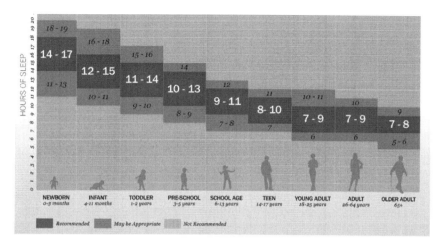

Figure 7.10.3 Amounts of sleep needed.
Source: National Sleep Foundation, USA.

ongoing studies in Europe, the USA and Australia, as well as nearly 5000 African Americans. Researchers compared humans' genetic information to the amount of time they slept on an average night.

The first DNA region was associated with above-average sleep. Previous research has also linked this region to a lower probability of attention-deficit hyperactivity disorder (ADHD). The other region was associated with shorter sleep times, and previous studies had linked the DNA regions to an increased risk of depression and schizophrenia.

Furthermore, research has shown that both sleeping too much and not sleeping enough correlate with an increased probability for health problems such as obesity, diabetes, high blood pressure, heart diseases, psychiatric illness and even premature mortality.

Sleep not only helps with physical recovery, it primarily also enables central brain physiological processes that keep the brain healthy. Like any other organ, the brain produces toxic metabolic substances. These are removed from the brain, which counteracts degenerative diseases of the brain. However, this can only happen during our sleep.

In addition, even more intriguing events occur during each sleep phase in our heads. Our brain basically has two different ways of dealing with information. One processes information consciously, the other unconsciously. The areas that deal with conscious thought processes are, for instance, the prefrontal cortex in the frontal lobe of the cerebral cortex. These structures require much more energy to operate than the areas that are responsible for unconscious processing in the limbic system. Therefore, for reasons of energy efficiency, most of the processes in the brain run unconsciously and thus beyond perception. Modern brain research assumes a ratio of unconscious to conscious processing in the order of

10,000. However, in order for these unconscious processes to proceed, a person first of all needs sufficient sleep. Only when we sleep enough can the brain start to consolidate content from the short-term into the long-term memory where it is integrated into existing memory engrams. For this process, which we also call "learning", the hippocampus is responsible. The so-called REM phases, which usually occur during the second half of the night, are of crucial importance here. REM stands for Rapid Eye Movement. During these phases, which occur four to five times a night, provided there is enough sleep, the brain works on current problems and tries to resolve them through creativity and experience. So, when we are dealing with a problem and decide to first of all "sleep on it", then this certainly has a scientific justification. We are mostly not consciously aware of this phase, but sometimes we can remember more, sometimes fewer of the dreams that occur in these phases and represent our scenic reminiscences of this processing activity.

During these REM phases, the muscle tonus of the entire body is greatly reduced, probably to ensure that the sleeping person cannot put her dreams into action and thus endanger herself. Figuratively speaking, these phases are of particular importance for tidying up the internal hard drive.

As people get older, they tend to wake up more during the second part of the night. People who experience a lot of negative stress often find it difficult to then fall asleep again. This disruption of the sleep cycle not only impairs the brain's physical regeneration, but also cognitive performance and emotional stability. Figure 7.10.4 shows the typical sleep cycle of a healthy adult. The REM phases of sleep are highlighted.

When the sleep cycle is disturbed, be it through inadequate or poor sleep, it will have many physical, cognitive and emotional effects over time. With advancing age, it also takes longer to compensate for an accumulated sleep deficit, making coffee our second most important resource in the world after oil. Travelling across time zones further aggravates the problem, because while the amount of sleep needed decreases slightly with age, the ability to adapt to a different time zone also decreases.

As already mentioned, a prolonged lack of sleep has multiple severe consequences.

Physical

- The level of cortisol increases, which among other things affects the functioning of the immune system. As a result, the likelihood to catch a cold is increased when a person permanently sleeps too little.
- Because of the increased cortisol levels, the functioning of the pancreas is also affected resulting in an increased tendency to gain weight.
- After many years, once a sleep deprivation has become chronic, the symptoms can get much more severe. As mentioned, diabetes, high blood pressure and heart diseases can be the consequence.

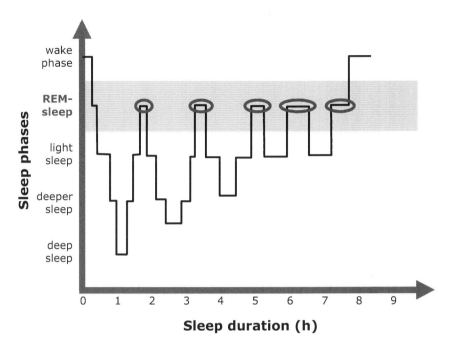

Figure 7.10.4   Characteristics of a healthy sleep cycle.

Cognitive

- Cognitive performance, attention span and IQ decrease. One hour of too little sleep per night costs us about one percentage point of our intelligence. The second hour already costs significantly more. Fortunately, the intelligence returns when you sleep enough again.
- Our decision-making behaviour becomes more conservative, that is, one leans more towards decisions that have already been made in similar ways in similar situations. This reduces the ability to be creative and innovative.
- Lacking sleep is cumulative. For example, 4 hours of sleep per night for 5 days affect your mental capacity as much as 24 hours without sleep. The same amount of sleep over a period of 10 days, however, interferes with one's decision-making authority as much as 48 hours without sleep.

Emotional

- The capacity for emotional self-regulation decreases as the tendency for depressive episodes increases. Recent studies suggest that two hours of sleep deprivation per night over a longer period of time leads to a 24% increased likelihood of a depressive episode.

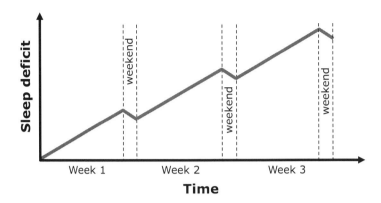

Figure 7.10.5   The cumulative nature of sleep deprivation.

As already mentioned, sleep deprivation is cumulative, which means that the missing hours of quality sleep add up over the weeks and months. Even long sleep phases on weekends are therefore usually not sufficient to compensate for regular sleep deprivation, as Figure 7.10.5 is intended to illustrate.

Not to be underestimated is the effect of a power nap to restore a certain mental freshness. The best time lies between 1 and 2 pm, because at this time our metabolism typically gets more unstable and our efficiency and ability to concentrate are reduced. The perfect nap should last a maximum of 30 minutes. If it takes longer, then the mind and body have difficulty getting back "up".

Nutrition drives performance

Nutrition is considered the third foundational driver by van der Walt. Our brain is a rather greedy organ, being responsible for around 20–25% of the body's energy consumption while constituting only about 2% of its weight. The reason for this is the permanent processing of large amounts of information, sensory impressions and emotions.

To be able to do this, you need a continuous energy supply and therefore a sensible long-term diet. The energy supply of the brain is ensured mainly by various forms of carbohydrates. The so-called glycaemic load of the food supplied plays a central role in the quality of the energy supply. The term glycaemia comes from the Greek language and means something like "sweet blood". Foods with a high glycaemic load (GL) quickly raise the blood sugar level, but only for a short time. A well-known example of this is glucose, which belongs to the family of simple sugars. The subsequent rapid drop in blood sugar level causes an undersupply of the brain. It then signals to the body via the insulin secretion of the pancreas to supply it with even more glucose.

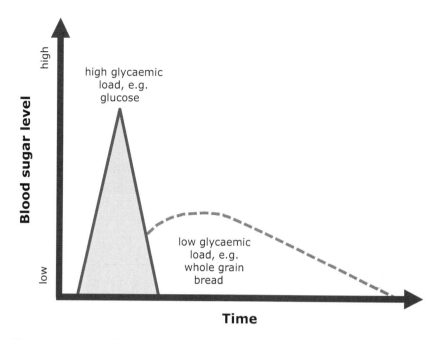

Figure 7.10.6   The effects of nutrition on the glycaemic load.

This phenomenon applies in a similar way to all foods that contain simple sugars like glucose and fructose. Foods with a lower GL are e.g. complex carbohydrates such as whole grains. These multiple sugars must first be split up by the body into simple glucose. As this process takes time, the blood sugar level does not skyrocket as quickly and rises less sharply, and it also decreases more slowly, resulting in a more even supply of nutrients to the brain. Figure 7.10.6 illustrates this relationship.

The brain scientist's recommendation for optimal energy supply to the brain is therefore: reduce your consumption of sweets, biscuits, chocolate and ice cream because they cause unnecessary peaks in the blood sugar, followed by a rapid energy drop. Instead, replace them with unsweetened whole grain foods.

From the glycaemic point of view, foods containing artificial sweeteners are better than products with high sugar content. However, there are many concerns about the long-term effects of these substances, which is why a cautious approach to "diet products" is recommended.

To turn glucose into energy, it must be oxidised by the brain with the help of respiratory oxygen. This metabolic process creates oxygen radicals that can damage neurons in the brain. Since these can hardly regenerate, the nervous tissue in the brain is very susceptible to slowly accumulating damage. If the cell damage accumulates over decades, it leads slowly but

Table 7.10.1 Foods with a high concentration of antioxidants

apples	brown rice	cucumber	potatoes
artichokes	cabbage	green tea	red grape juice
asparagus	cherries	linseed	red wine
beans	citrus fruits	nuts	tea
berries	cocoa	onions	tomatoes
broccoli	coffee	plums	whole grains

inevitably to pathological changes. Neurodegenerative diseases, such as various forms of dementia and Parkinson's, as well as the promotion of inflammatory processes, such as encephalitis, may be the result.

To prevent this, it is important, on the one hand, to strengthen the protective systems of the brain against oxygen radicals. Foods that are rich in antioxidants make a significant contribution to promoting these protections. In general, many of these antioxidants are found in the foods listed in Table 7.10.1.

Those who find this list too long can remember van der Walt's simple rule: five servings of fruit or coloured vegetables per day are enough to meet the need for antioxidants. And by the way, these foods are also recommended in terms of their glycaemic load.

Certain foods are now known to boost inflammatory and degenerative processes in the brain when too much of them are consumed. First and foremost, these are the so-called AGE. This abbreviation stands for "Advanced Glycation End products". They are caused by the reaction of protein with sugar. They are waste products for our bodies. As such, they cannot be metabolised. They only mean excretory work for the kidneys. And their elimination is only partial. The rest is stored in the body and can lead to permanent health problems. A particularly high amount of AGE is created when heating food over 120 degrees, e.g. when grilling or frying something. Therefore, van der Walt advises to consume sausages, burgers, steaks and co. as well as fish and chips only in moderate amounts.

In addition to carbohydrates and antioxidants, our body needs the right amounts of fats and oils. They contain essential fatty acids that are needed to, for example, build up hormones or cell walls. Fat also gives us access to fat-soluble vitamins and protects sensitive organs through cushioning against injuries, even though we do not always find that visually pleasing.

But fat is not just fat, it depends on the fatty acids it contains. Typically, the following fatty acids get distinguished:

- **Saturated fatty acids:** They are included in e.g. butter, lard, cream, bacon, cheese, sausage and meat.
- **Monounsaturated fatty acids:** You will find these in e.g. olive and rapeseed oil.
- **Polyunsaturated fatty acids:** Omega-6 fatty acids are included in e.g. sunflower, maize germ and soybean oil. Omega-3 fatty acids are found in e.g. herring, mackerel, salmon and linseed oil.

Saturated fatty acids are mainly found in animal foods. Most of us eat more than enough of them. Too much, however, is not good for our blood vessels. They make our heart work unnecessarily hard. In addition, regular intake of saturated fat has been shown to reduce cognitive brain performance.

Van der Walt therefore advises strongly to reduce the intake of saturated fatty acids and to pay more attention to the intake of unsaturated fatty acids. Since our body needs both monounsaturated and polyunsaturated fatty acids, a varied use of various oils in the preparation of food is advisable. Two tablespoons a day of it are quite sufficient. Also, fish should be regularly on the menu.

While our body consists of about 50% water, it makes for about 80% in the human brain, which is why it relies on regular replenishment. In fact, the functioning of the brain is impaired as soon as the fluid loss is around 3%. This not only leads to a measurable shrinkage of the brain, but also impairs mental capacity. Headaches, tiredness and lack of concentration can be the consequences. At a normal activity level, the human body loses around 2–3 litres of fluid per day. This fluid loss depends on numerous factors.

For example, one calculates about 35 ml of daily fluid requirements per kilogram of body weight. When exposed to heat, exercise or fever, the required amount is even higher. About one litre is compensated for by the food intake, so that about 1.5–2 litres must be compensated for by drinking. This corresponds to about 6–7 glasses of liquid per day. The body can absorb only a maximum of 0.5 litres – about two glasses of liquid – at once. More is excreted by the body unused. It is therefore not advisable to drink in advance. Drinking units should be distributed throughout the day. In terms of glycaemic load, mineral water and unsweetened teas are to be preferred. Sweetened drinks such as cola and sodas should be avoided.

Since caffeine has a low dehydrating effect, coffee or black tea should be drunk at most at the ratio of 1:2 to the water. Hence, a cup of coffee should be followed by about two cups of water. If this is the case, the amount of coffee or tea can normally be included in the calculation of the supplied amount of drink.

Alcoholic drinks are unsuitable thirst quenchers. They should not play a role in the supply of fluids. This is partly due to their high glycaemic load and partly because the alcohol actually removes liquid and minerals from the body. This is also the reason why the consumption of alcohol leads to an increase in thirst.

Silencing the mind

The fourth and final foundational driver is allowing one's own mind to settle down through meditation techniques – a practice that many executives still use too little today. The connections between meditation and cognitive ability are meanwhile well-documented.

EXAMPLE

As early as 2007, psychologist Richard Davidson of the University of Wisconsin-Madison was able to demonstrate that a three-month meditation training course increases awareness and vigilance.

Also, positive effects on one's emotionality are proven today.

EXAMPLE

Psychologist Sara Lazar of the Boston Massachusetts General Hospital has been able to demonstrate that regular meditation shrinks the amygdala, a structure which is also known to be part of the anxiety centre. At the same time, neural structures associated with compassion experienced neuronal growth.

Even in the case of depression, meditation is proven to have positive effects, and even without side effects.

EXAMPLE

Zindel Segal, a professor of psychology at the University of Toronto, is considered to be one of the founders of MBCT, a method of psychotherapy that focuses heavily on mindfulness and meditation practices. In one study with patients who had successfully overcome depression, he was able to prove that meditation is just as effective protection against a new outbreak of this disease as the administration of antidepressants.

In Buddhism roughly three different forms of meditation are distinguished, even though the separation is sometimes a bit blurred:

- In concentration meditation, the practitioner should focus all of his attention on one object.
- In a second form, the objective is to develop the greatest possible compassion for other beings.
- The most scientifically studied form, however, is the so-called mindfulness meditation. Its goal is for the practitioner to become inwardly clear

and to arrive in the here and now, in which one directs his attention very intensively to the present moment, without any judgements or evaluations. Emerging thoughts are normal, but the meditator should break away from them, watching them without intention, like clouds passing by. Being at the moment seems like a trivial matter at first sight, but it's harder than you think. Many meditation teachers recommend, therefore, to focus only on the breath when getting started. Inhale. Exhale. Feel the diaphragm rising and the air as it passes along the nostril.

One of the pioneers of the concept of mindfulness in the Western world is the American retired professor of medicine, Jon Kabat-Zinn. In the late 1970s he participated in a retreat of the Vietnamese Buddhist monk, author and spiritual teacher, Thich Nhat Hanh, in the USA. There he discovered how this method works and its benefits for people who have to deal with a lot of pressure, such as executives. Kabat-Zinn adopted Hanh's key concepts, stripped them of all the purely religious elements and structured the exercises in the form of a reproducible eight-week programme, which since then has been gaining increasing popularity as Mindfulness Based Stress Reduction (MBSR). MBSR offers a pragmatic roadmap to learn meditation techniques, consisting of a two-and-a-half-hour group sitting per week and a day of mindfulness. The daily practice time should be 45 minutes. So, it certainly requires some energy and perseverance on the part of the participants, but it is certainly worthwhile. The essence of MBSR is that by consciously training non-judgemental perception, the automatic link between external stress and one's inner stress response is dissolved. The MBSR programme has been standardised worldwide and incorporates the following training elements:

- Practising mindful body awareness
- Choice of simple body exercises (yoga)
- Becoming acquainted with and practising silent sitting (sitting meditation)
- Carrying out mindful, slow movements (walking meditation)
- Special breathing exercises.

The aim of the method is to create an inner space and distance from the problems of the external world. In 1979, Kabat-Zinn founded the Stress Reduction Clinic, which was eventually converted into the Center for Mindfulness in Medicine, Health Care and Society at MIT in 1995, and has come to be seen as the bastion of the MBSR method. Since then, the concept has been tested in a number of different scientific studies. It is regarded as having been approved and, via global corporations, has now at least reached employee level even in Germany. Companies such as ABB, BMW, Bosch, SAP and Siemens offer their employees MBSR courses and some of them even provide their own meditation rooms. However, the first pioneers, as is so often the case, were American companies, such as General Mills, Target and Google, who have already been offering their employees the opportunity to practise meditation since the middle of the last decade, indeed with much success. In fact, more than 1000 employees and executives have already participated in Google's MBSR programme, which goes by the very fitting name "Search inside yourself". And it is, of course, very beneficial when top managers, such as media tycoon Rupert Murdoch and Ford CEO Bill Ford, publicly state that mindfulness has helped them to accomplish their tasks.

This technique can help executives to understand their own thinking patterns better in order to avoid stereotyped reactions such as reflexes and prejudices. It helps with taking decisions more independently. This competence of self-reflection is helpful not only in decisions, but also when a person is confronted with external changes. Many managers reported that they feel calmer, clearer and more resourceful through regular mindfulness exercises. Psychologists consider mindfulness as an ability that every person carries within themselves. However, in order to bring it to light and apply it in everyday life, it must be systematically trained.

So, it is about time for executives in Germany to get to grips with this concept as well. The daily practice of mindfulness begins with just a few small steps. With all these exercises, the focus is on the non-judgemental perception of what is happening in the present moment. There may be physical sensations, sensory perceptions, thoughts or emotions. With more practice, MBSR enables even daily work to be carried out with more conscious awareness and mindfulness. One principle of mindfulness is to give your full and undivided attention to whatever you are doing in this present moment, in other words not to read emails while you are eating and not to allow phone calls to interrupt your meal, for instance. It is the exact opposite of multitasking. The MBSR method is highly effective, just like many other kinds of bodywork. Why not give it a try yourself? You will find corresponding courses by searching on the internet for an "MBSR course" in your area.

Meanwhile, various meditation apps also enjoy a growing popularity. The advantages of these programmes are obvious: they offer the possibility to use almost any situation for a meditation. They meet the needs of all those who travel a lot and have a rather irregular way of life, as is the case with many executives. They can serve as a very good complement to mindfulness programmes like MBSR.

While there are many such apps on the market we recommend only one English app to our clients, simply because it fits very well to our target group as it largely refrains from any form of esotericism.

Headspace offers meditations for almost every situation. The sessions are led by the British voice of Andy Puddicombe, one of the co-founders of Headspace, who became a Buddhist monk at a relatively young age. There is a choice of several hundred meditations on various topics in the subscription model. Meditations can also be downloaded for later offline listening.

The app is simple, but with an appealing design. The design is restrained, the colours are tinted, everything corresponds to the serene mood that the meditations also want to convey. New users will first be introduced to the app through a ten-day free programme.

7.11 Authentic relationships: your personal supervisory board

Do you have friends? And I do not mean Facebook, Rotarian or business friends, but real friends whom you can completely trust. The Americans also call these real friends "friends with a capital F". What about esteemed business partners? Do you know how that person really is? Do they know how you are? How often do you speak to one another? People are social beings and, as such, are embedded in many systems of relationships such as the family, the circle of friends or the department in the company. These relationships can either be perceived positively as energy giving or negatively as energy consuming, e.g. when conflicts or other problems prevail. Relationships that are perceived as authentic represent a special kind of resource that has a strong impact on individual resilience. In these relationships a person can present herself as she really is without making an effort of pretending. Such relationships do not necessarily have to be tension and conflict free. More important are mutual trust, reliability and a strong emotional attachment. The more a manager is able to feel positively embedded in a handpicked group of peers, the better this will be for when the waves hit high again.

Being given someone's undivided attention with them showing a real interest in us is becoming more and more of a luxury in the fast-moving and increasingly superficial world we live in. Yet authentic, trusting relationships are fundamental for the consolidation and enhancement of mental resilience. This is particularly the case with people who are affected by the proclaimed "loneliness at the top", namely managers. Due to their role and responsibility, they do not have many people in their environment they can speak to in confidence, without there being a conflict of roles. Inspiring talks with people who are well-meaning and whom you can trust are rare and a real gift.

Who else around you would otherwise dare to give you open and honest feedback or even just a piece of advice? Most of the managers with whom we work in our workshops do really benefit greatly from being able to have a trust-based exchange with their peers. Once they have gotten to know this, they assign great importance to such relationships. In the field of research, these reciprocal relationships between managers are also known as Critical Leader Relationships (CLRs). A CLR can be described as a stable, enduring and trust-based relationship with another person (usually another executive) with the aim of obtaining support and advice in management-related issues. This should not be confused with friendships or the usual networking among colleagues. Together with a colleague from the London School of Economics, Åsa Bjoernberg, Nigel Nicholson – a professor for organisational development at the London Business School – conducted a study on the CLRs of 2700 international executives, including 400 women, who took part in various programmes of the London Business School. They wanted to find out whether and to what extent managers maintained CLRs and what benefits they saw in these relationships. The first striking discovery was that 92% of the executives questioned did actually maintain trusting relationships with other executives, within the meaning of a CLR – and even more so if they considered their working environment as problematic. This illustrates how important these relationships are for the development of individual resilience. So what concrete benefits can managers draw from these relationships? The following beneficial factors for CLRs were identified in a survey conducted with 2700 executives:

- Feedback: open and honest feedback with regard to the impact of one's own behaviour.
- Emotional support: friendliness, sympathy, encouragement, confirmation and praise, which strengthen the partner's self-confidence.
- Concrete help: practical support in resolving concrete problems.
- Advice: sharing one's own personal insights, which could be useful for the partner's strategies.
- Questioning: taking another standpoint, that is assuming the role of devil's advocate in order to question the other one's opinion and thus to broaden their perspective.
- Insight: conveying one's perspective of the world and associated topics, in order to help the partner to broaden his understanding.

CLRs generally do not just happen spontaneously, but must be maintained and that costs time and energy. CLRs work best between equals, and if both participants appreciate informal talks on a regular basis and both are equally able to benefit from this relationship. Then a slot for a joint dinner is sure to be found in an overfull schedule. But these kinds of relationships do not just work between managers of equal rank. Mentor-and-mentee-based CLRs, in which both sides benefit too, can also work well. The mentor can pass his experience on, which triggers a process of self-reflection in him and also strokes his ego. The mentee has an experienced sparring partner at his side, who – both as a well-meaning companion and as devil's advocate – asks thought-provoking questions.

However, many mentors are often too absorbed by themselves and too biased about their own experience, ask too few questions and are not good listeners. We therefore frequently try to help top managers to initially learn the technique of asking open questions and actively listening, to then encourage them to strike up a conversation and have an exchange among colleagues.

What is important is that the chemistry is right and they are on the same wavelength, and that no superficial and opportunistic relationships develop, but rather ones that are trusting and authentic. The aim is for both sides to value the exchange as an opportunity to show themselves as they are. This is no simple endeavour, but a very worthwhile one.

Who is on your personal supervisory board?

What about your personal supervisory board? Who enjoys your unrestricted trust and understands the world in which you live?

In our workshops we invite the participants to follow these reflection steps:

*   Create an overview that lists all the people that are important in your life.
*   Note for each of these people to which degree they can understand your professional and private world. Use a scale from 0 (not at all) to 10 (fully and completely).
*   Also note for each of them how much they enjoy your full trust. Again, use a scale from 0 (not at all) to 10 (fully and completely).
*   In the last step, note for each of these particularly important people, to what extent you are satisfied with the quantity and the quality of the interaction. Again, use the scale from 0 (not at all) to 10 (fully and completely).

Now you have all the data together to present your personal supervisory board, i.e. your most important authentic relationships. In our workshops we suggest using a format like in Figure 7.11.1.

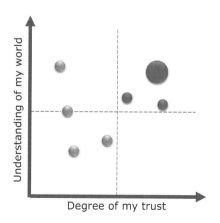

Figure 7.11.1 Your personal supervisory board.

What managers can learn from professional coaches

Not every close confidant who understands us is also a good listener. Executives, in particular, see it as their task to exude optimism and solve problems with well-intentioned advice. That does not have to be the right thing in every situation. In our experience it often is more helpful for a person if someone asks her good questions and then listens attentively. And that is exactly the core competence of coaches. As you may know, a key part of coaching is asking powerful questions. What you may not know yet is that a coaching conversation typically follows an intrinsic structure and logic. In our company we have developed our own coaching model over the years. It is called *Leadership Choices* and is shown in Figure 7.11.2.

Let's have a look at the model in more detail. As you can see it is made up of various elements which all represent a dedicated intention and approach during a coaching process.

Professionalism

This element forms the basis of the model and makes a statement about the professional ethos of the coach working with this model. These include e.g. the discretion of the coach regarding the content of coaching, the loyalty to the client and the client's company as well as complete transparency and authenticity in his behaviour.

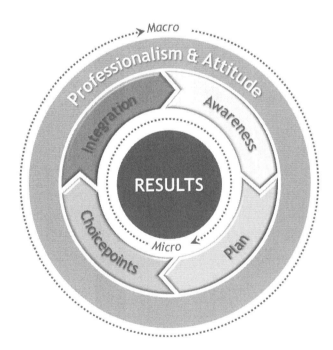

Figure 7.11.2 The coaching model "Leadership Choices".

Attitude

This describes the basic attitude from which a coach interacts with his client. This includes the coach's beliefs about factors that promote human growth, as well as his image of the world and man. It includes also to see the client as an expert on his life and his difficulties. Likewise, the focus is on the competencies and resources of the client, as well as the coach's ambition to promote authentic client behaviour.

The five different elements of this coaching model can be traversed at the "micro" and "macro" levels, that is they are valid for the entire coaching process as well as for each individual coaching session. Here is a brief overview of the meaning of the different phases in "macro mode", i.e. in terms of the entire coaching process.

Awareness

In this phase, it is about a comprehensive understanding of the initial situation of the client. This includes an understanding about his environment and background, his biography as well as his personality structure and his behavioural preferences. It may also include reviewing existing performance assessments and 360° feedback. Also, often strengths and weaknesses of a client are elicited and documented by the means of confidential stakeholder interviews.

Plan

Together with determining the initial situation of the client, a working alliance is formed between the coach and the client. Part of this alliance is the clarification of the assignment the client gives to the coach. Since the entity paying for the coaching is usually not the client himself, but his supervisor as a representative of the company, this is also about clarifying the expectations that the company has as one important stakeholder in the coaching process. Also included are the expectations of the coach for the client, e.g. with regards to time commitment and motivation to change. All this together forms the coaching mandate. Another aspect in this phase is the determination of the target scenario to be achieved with the help of the coaching process. This is usually a target behaviour, e.g. "more empathy in dealing with my employees", or a target state, e.g. "can relax on the weekend despite conflicts in the board". But it can also be about support in achieving a concrete external goal like "appointment to the board".

Choicepoints

This step is about identifying client behaviours to be optimised. Of particular interest here are situations in which the client feels he is flying with autopilot, i.e. where he perceives no possible choices in his behaviour. One central conviction in coaching is that it is better for a client to be able to access a wide range of alternative behaviour patterns rather than having only few or no options. The aim of the collaboration in this phase is the creation of new perspectives and behavioural variants that are in line with the value system of the client and can therefore be perceived as authentic.

Integration

In this phase the gained insights are transferred into the field of action of the client. Between the coaching sessions, the client explores new forms of communication and interaction with the environment and then reflects on the experiences with his coach in the next session.

Results

The ultimate goal of the cooperation between coach and client is to achieve the goals of the client. This element therefore marks the checkpoint to validate that the process was successful.

The methodology described above forms the guideline for the design of a coaching process according to the "Leadership Choices" model. In addition to the described "macro mode", the model is also used during each individual coaching session in a so-called "micro-mode". This is done by means of guiding questions, which are outlined in the following overview.

Awareness

- In what condition does the client appear at the meeting today?
- What has happened in the client's environment since the last session?
- What experiences has the client had in testing new behaviours?
- Which resistances or kickbacks did the client have to deal with?

Plan

- What does the client want to accomplish in today's coaching session?
- What should be different at the end of the coaching session?
- How is this guiding question related to the overall coaching mandate?
- Where does the client see his current level of goal achievement?

Choicepoints

- What observations can the coach offer to the client by means of feedback?
- What decisions does the client have to make today to enable new perspectives or behaviours?
- How can the experience the client has gained in testing new behaviours help him to finetune the approach?
- What alternative perspectives on the current situation of the client are possible?

Integration

- Which insights did the client gain during the coaching session?
- What new or different behaviours will the client be testing after the session?
- What type of homework would be a good support structure for the client to take another step towards their intended goal?

Results

- How will the coach know that the client has done his homework?
- What insights did the client gain during the coaching session and his subsequent reflections?

Authentic consultations

You don't necessarily need to be a coach to have a powerful conversation but it is a bit trickier than one would initially think. Therefore, we have started to focus on improving the quality of communication amongst managers. In our workshops we invite our participants to have special conversations, which we call "authentic consultations". These conversations are based on ready-made scripts, which contain a series of coaching questions. The flow and structure are based on the phases of our coaching model "Leadership Choices" which I have described before.

I know this sounds odd at first and indeed it feels the same for the participants in our workshops. However, once you get involved in this process, the benefit quickly becomes apparent. The questions in the scripts achieve the desired effect, even if both parties are fully aware that the other party is "only" working through a list of coaching questions. Trying to answer the questions inevitably leads to new insights, different perspectives and unexpected options for action. The pleasant side effect of this exercise is that the participating managers can then incorporate these very effective questions into their "normal" conversation toolbox as well. Below you can find such a script as an example.

SCRIPT: DEALING WITH A DIFFICULT SITUATION

The purpose of this script is to help others, let us call them clients, to deal with a difficult situation. In advance, the client has already described to his sparring partner the difficult situation. The partner then takes on the role of the coach and asks the following questions as literally as possible. After each question he watches his counterpart and listens attentively. It is important for the coach to resist his natural longing to step out of his role and help the client with tips and personal experiences.

Phase "Awareness"

- What makes the situation so difficult for you?
- How difficult is the situation on a scale of 0 (not difficult) to 10 (unbearable)?
- What feelings does this situation trigger in you?
- What is the worst thing that could happen out of the difficult situation?
- What have you already tried to improve the situation?
- How would a successful person with a completely different personality than you evaluate this situation?
- What would he / she do differently?
- Which of your typical behaviours are the least helpful in this situation?

Phase "Plan"

- What would have to happen to improve the severity of the situation by 1 to 2 points on the previously mentioned scale?
- How could you influence that?
- Assuming that this conversation will be helpful for you, what should be different afterwards?

Phase "Choicepoints"

- How could this difficult situation be a chance for you?
- What could you learn from this situation?
- If one of your colleagues / friends were going through a similar situation, what would you advise him / her to do?
- Where would you have to leave your comfort zone to improve the situation?
- What fundamental decisions do you have to make to improve the situation?
- What old behaviour patterns will you have to give up to avoid worsening the situation?
- What new behaviour patterns will you need to develop?
- Despite all your difficulties, what are you deeply grateful for?
- Suppose you look back to today in ten years. What advice would you give to your self today?

Phase "Integration"

- What exactly will you do now?
- What can prevent you from working on your goals?
- How will I see that you are working on your goals?

Phase "Results"

- How will you recognise that you have overcome the difficult situation?
- How will that feel?
- What will you achieve by doing this?

7.12 Meaning: gaining in strength by answering the question "Why?"

The Austrian psychiatrist and neurologist, Viktor Frankl, lost nearly his entire Jewish family in Hitler's concentration camps. He himself was held captive for three years at various concentration camps, including Auschwitz. Unlike many others, he survived. Frankl was the founder of logotherapy (Greek *logos* = meaning). Through his work, the component "meaning" was identified as being essential for inner resilience in the face of difficult circumstances. His form of therapy is intended to help people to make decisions that give their lives meaning and purpose again. For him it was important that meaning can be found in every situation, no matter how desperate. Meaning creates an inner realm with which one can counter external adversities.

In his book *Man's Search for Meaning*, he describes a key situation in the concentration camp which, in hindsight, was crucial for developing logotherapy: Frankl was on his way to a work assignment and contemplated trading his last cigarette for a bowl of soup. He also thought about how he would behave towards a new warden who had the reputation of being particularly sadistic. Suddenly, he realised how meaningless his life had become and felt disgusted with himself. He wanted to find a higher purpose in his life again. So, he imagined how, after his release from the concentration camp, he would hold lectures on the psychology of concentration camps, so that other people could understand what the prisoners had had to go through. Even though he could by no means assume that he would survive, he forged concrete plans which occupied him both intellectually and emotionally. This helped him to overcome the hopelessness of his situation.

What is the meaning of your life? Many managers we are presently working with have no clear idea of the meaning their lives have or could have. Even just mentioning the topic is quite unpleasant for many. And yet perceived meaning is the ultimate source of resilience. The reverse argument is also true: a lack of meaning poses a great risk to a person's own resilience, health and ultimately also to their life. The key question here is: Does what I do, do my decisions, my career, my life as a whole mean something?

Apart from external factors, such as a person's profession, and their actions and omissions, the experience of meaning has above all to do with internal factors such as a person's attitude towards life. This also includes belief in what is good, in things being in balance or in a higher entity. A person's values and their motives also play a role. The experience of meaning imbues your conduct with a purpose and a direction, as well as with a sense of belonging and harmony. Meaning does not place the individual and his sole well-being centre stage, but rather something that feels right and meaningful, and is larger than the individual. So, meaning is also related to spirituality in the broader sense of the term. Meaning is something each person can only find for themselves, even if it is further reinforced by our environment, be it through other people who are close to us or through a job where we feel needed. Since, in the broadest sense, meaning involves conviction, this component of resilience may vary in the same way as a belief or conviction can change.

The island of centenarians

The American Dan Buettner is an extreme athlete, adventurer and author for National Geographic. On his expeditions into different parts of the world he came across a phenomenon on which he first reported in 2005: the so-called Blue Zones. These are regions that have a significantly higher life expectancy than the rest of the world. One of these Blue Zones is the Okinawa archipelago, which is now part of Japan. Japan's southernmost prefecture consists of 363 islands, home to a total of 1.3 million people. 900 of these inhabitants are 100 years and older, which is an unusually high life expectancy even for Japanese conditions. The average life expectancy for Japanese men is 84 years, while UK men on average reach 82 years. In contrast the life expectancy for a US man is only 79 years. Anthropologists studied the life of people on Okinawa in detail and identified three essential factors for the extraordinary longevity of the inhabitants there:

- **Diet.** The diet is rich in fibre, low in calories and in fat and almost completely vegetarian. In addition, it adheres to the motto "hara hachi bu", which means "stop eating when your stomach is 80 percent full".
- **No retirement.** Before the annexation of Okinawa by Japan in 1879, this group of islands belonged to the kingdom Ryukyu. In the local language there is no word for "retirement". Even today, the elderly on Okinawa do not stop working but continue to fish or keep their fields in order.
- **Ikigai.** This word translates into meaning of life or colloquially "having the feeling of having something worth getting up for in the morning". In the Japanese culture the search for one's own Ikigai has an important meaning. Once a man has found his Ikigai, he feels a sense of joy and inner contentment.

What is your Ikigai?

So, what is your meaning? What difference will you have made when you leave this earth? Will your career and the price you have paid for it have been worthwhile? What legacy do you want to leave behind? What should people remember when they think of you? Many executives with whom we have worked initially have no answer to these questions. Often, they are already quite uncomfortable even talking about it. In light of the fact that all of our lives are finite, having a perceived sense of meaning can be the ultimate source of inner strength and self-guidance. The central question is, "Does what I do, do my decisions, does my career, my life as a whole have meaning?"

Managers are used to directing, influencing and maintaining control. And yet our lives all end with complete loss of control – with death. The benefit that this perspective brings with it is that it addresses the human need for meaning. When facing death, people often get a much clearer picture of the things that still mean something to them in their last remaining weeks and months, even if these things are actually quite trivial.

The experience of meaning gives orientation to one's own actions as well as the feeling of belonging and coherence. Meaning does not put the individual and his or her sole well-being at the centre of action, but rather something that feels right and meaningful to the individual, and greater than they are, with which they can align themselves.

Insights from the dying

This was also found to be true by Bronnie Ware, an Australian nurse who worked in palliative care for more than eight years, accompanying people in the last weeks and months of their life. During this time, Ware lived with these people and listened to them. Some were without regrets and had come to terms with their approaching demise; others were bitter and in denial until the very end. The issues that concerned the dying were similar. There were often regrets about not having lived the life of one's dreams. They blamed themselves for decisions they had made or not made. And there was regret about mistakes and the things that had not been done. Many were angry with themselves that they had only had these insights when it was too late. Ware incorporated these findings into a book called *The Top Five Regrets of the Dying* which became an international bestseller. The insights of the dying are listed in Table 7.12.1.

Table 7.12.1 Insights of the dying

I wish I had had the courage to live a life true to myself.	Many regretted that they had led the life that others expected of them, rather than the life they wanted.
I wish I had not worked so hard.	Men, in particular, regret having invested too much time in their careers, time they could have spent with the people they love.
I wish I had had the courage to express my feelings.	Many state that, even to their closest companions, they never showed their true self and feelings. They kept this to themselves for fear of rejection or conflict. Many had preferred to put up with a safe, but mediocre existence, instead of taking the risk of becoming what they could have become.
I wish I had stayed in touch with my friends.	All those facing death missed old friends whom they had lost track of in the course of their life. They regretted not having put more effort into these relationships, which meant that their day-to-day business had taken over and made even the closest of friendships fade over time.
I wish I had allowed myself to be happier.	Until the end, many were stuck in old habits and behaviour patterns. They realised too late that they had always had a choice to leave their comfort zone. They regretted having lost people that were important to them, because they had not been willing to leave their comfort zone.

What gives a life meaning?

Tatjana Schnell, Professor of Personality Psychology at Innsbruck University, has contributed pioneering work on the scientific, i.e. verifiable, exploration of the phenomenon of meaning. With her work, she refuted an important hypothesis by Victor Frankl. Frankl had identified meaning as the key resource for an individual's ability to cope, even under inhumane conditions. Frankl, who worked with many suicidal patients, described the lack of meaning as a disease of reason or as noogenic neurosis. The Greek word *noētós* contained therein means "mentally perceptible". According to Frankl, a person has either found a meaning in their life or they suffer from a perceived meaninglessness in their life.

The psychologist Schnell examined this hypothesis in a study with more than 600 participants and came to the remarkable conclusion that, other than the two groups postulated by Frankl, there exist a third, quite significant group, which she called "existentially indifferent". While nearly two-thirds of those questioned saw their lives as being meaningful, only 4% declared that their lives had no meaning and that they were experiencing a crisis of meaning. The group of "existentially indifferent" people, by contrast, did not see a greater meaning in life, but they also did not feel more suffering because of this. Schnell developed an inventory of 5 essential meanings in life and 26 sources of meaning in order to make the individual expression of meaning measurable:

Focus on afterlife

- Religion
- Spirituality

Focus on present life

- Social commitment
- Connectedness with nature
- Self-awareness
- Health
- Creating lasting values

We-feeling

- Community
- Joy
- Love
- Comfort
- Care
- Mindfulness
- Harmony

Self-realisation

- Overcoming challenges
- Living out one's full potential
- Power, creation
- Development, ambition
- Performance, achieving goals
- Freedom, independence
- Knowledge, learning
- Creativity

Order

- Tradition
- Earthiness
- Morals, values
- Reason, rationality.

People tend to feel fulfilled when what they are doing corresponds with what they consider to be meaningful. How can you bring your life more into line with what is meaningful to you? What measures do you want to take in order to achieve this?

What difference do you make?

Will your career and the price which you undoubtedly pay for it be worth it at the end? What do you want to leave behind as your heritage? What should people think about when they remember you?

The expression "to make a difference" literally means that a person's actions will change the world compared to what the world would have been without this person – ideally for the better.

It is particularly the case with top managers that meaning is often derived from the things they have created and for which they will be remembered. Steve Jobs was known for his memorable quote of wanting to "make a dent in the universe" with his invention of the Macintosh. Others are happier with less and instead committed, for instance, to helping their fellow human beings.

In Section 2.8, *The role or your IQ*, I described the work of Lewis M. Terman, a Stanford professor of psychology. His longitudinal study of 1500 pupils eventually provided crucial insights regarding the importance of meaning for a person's resilience. One of the many issues to be analysed by the study was the extent to which there is a connection between religious faith and longevity. The researchers found no correlation. However, it did show that people who were engaged in community service tended to be happier and live longer. An individual's personal happiness was merely a side-product and not the actual goal of their social commitment. However, many of the study subjects did not realise at first that being engaged in helping others was gratifying and meaningful.

In our workshops we ask participants to reflect on what difference they think they have made on different levels. This would certainly be an interesting question for you too.

What difference do you want to make with regard to the following spheres of influence?

- Your self
  This sphere includes your beliefs, convictions and attitudes.
  Example: I will be a better version of myself.
- Your inner circle
  This sphere includes your family and closest friends.
  Example: I am a shining example and a support for my partner/children.
- Your outer circle
  This sphere includes e.g. your friends and colleagues.
  Example: I inspire my colleagues and support my employees in their ongoing development.
- The world
  This sphere includes your company, your community or literally the world.
  Example: I build up a company/develop a company further.

You may want to use Figure 7.12.1 to capture your thoughts.

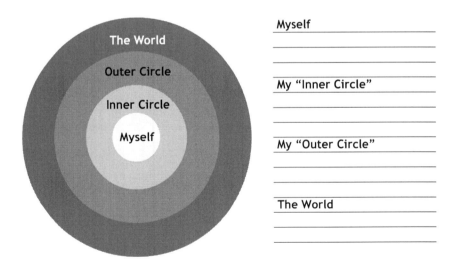

Figure 7.12.1 What difference do you want to make?

Figure 7.12.2 Images reach the subconscious parts of our brain.

Sources: Row 1 from left to right: Fotolia; psdesign1 & lucato / Fotolia; olly / Fotolia; Fotolia Premium. Row 2 from left to right: Fotolia; Andreas P / Fotolia, Sashkin / Fotolia; Angelo Giampiccolo. Row 3 from left to right: Fotolia; Sergey Furtaev / Fotolia, Simon Kraus / Fotolia; Hans und Christa Ede / gettyimages; valentinrussanov.

Let images speak

Often, unconsciously, we have a pretty clear idea of what makes sense in our lives. However, it is often difficult for us to articulate this and to give it a clear name. In our experience, the use of images often helps here because they communicate directly with the unconscious parts of our brain. We find certain images appealing, beautiful, fascinating, funny, boring, irritating, provocative or even repulsive. When we have a strong reaction to a picture, it often says something important about what we want in life or do not want at all. This can be a crucial trail in trying to articulate one's own meaning. Which of the pictures shown in Figure 7.12.2 are you talking about? What is the important aspect of this picture? Which important aspect of your life does it represent?

7.13 How everything fits together

In the previous chapters I showed how working on your own inner strength can be done on different levels. The FiRE model of resilience can be helpful for identifying approaches that reflect your own preferences. However, it

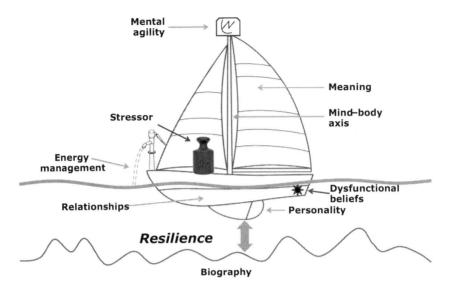

Figure 7.13.1 How the eight spheres of resilience are interrelated.

can and should also be used to identify new approaches that you have so far, either consciously or subconsciously, chosen to ignore or avoid. The various spheres are, of course, not separate from but interact closely with one another. One metaphor, which I think succinctly captures this interconnectedness very well, is the analogy of a sailing boat (see Figure 7.13.1).

A sailing boat has a hull, which carries it through the water. This can serve as an allegory to symbolise the relationships which "carry" a person. The boat also has a keel which stabilises it and keeps it on course. This represents that individual's personality with all its strengths and weaknesses. The biography of a person is the seabed, which is sometimes even and sometimes full of shallows. Obstructive beliefs are like small holes in the hull, which let water into the boat, so that it is lower in the water. Resources, on the other hand, are like fenders or buoyancy devices that lift the boat further out of the water. The sail stands for meaning. The ship radar represents the mental agility, as it constantly checks if the course needs to be adjusted to avoid potential obstacles. The mast is the brain–body axis which transmits the power of the wind onto the hull. The "sailing boat" as a complex system is constantly in motion. The wind and waves are continuously changing. If an additional load then comes – in the form of crises, conflicts and insecurity – then the boat is pushed further under the water, which can cause the remaining amount of resilience to be used up, so that the boat sinks deeper and the keel scrapes along the seabed. This produces unpleasant noises and scratches (emotional turbulence) and makes the boat run less smoothly (loss of performance). Occasionally it might even happen that the keel touches down and the boat runs aground (emotional crisis). Then one has to wait for the tide to come in again for the boat to come free. If the resilience field, which can also be described as the business climate, is favourable, then a strong wind fills the sail, representing meaning, and makes it big. This way the boat might perhaps come free beforehand.

Like every metaphor, this image also has its limits but it is a good memory aid and can shed light on some of the mutual dependencies. How is your sailing boat currently doing?

Bibliography

Blaszczak-Boxe, Agata; How Long You Sleep May Be in Your Genes; LiveScience.com, USA, 2014.

Campbell, Don; Mindfulness Therapy from University of Toronto Prof Helps Prevent Recurrence of Depression, Major Study Finds; www.utoronto.ca, Toronto, Canada, April 2016.

Davidson, Richard J.; Differential Effects on Pain Intensity and Unpleasantness of Two Meditation Practices; brainimaging.waisman.wisc.edu, Madison, USA, 2007.

Dotinga, Randy; How Well You Sleep May Depend on Your Genes, Study Suggests; consumer.healthday.com, USA, December 2014.

Drath, Karsten; Coaching und seine Wurzeln: Erfolgreiche Interventionen und ihre Urspruenge; Haufe, Freiburg, Germany, 2012.

Drath, Karsten; Resilient Leadership: Beyond Myths and Misunderstandings; Taylor & Francis, Abingdon-on-Thames, UK, 2016.

Fitzgerald, Margaret D. et al.; Age-Related Declines in Maximal Aerobic Capacity in Regularly Exercising vs. Sedentary Women: A Meta-Analysis; Journal of Applied Physiology American Physiological Society, Bethesda, USA, 1997.

Frankl, Victor E.; Man's Search for Meaning; Beacon Press, Boston, USA, 2006.

Lester, Paul B. et al.; The Comprehensive Soldier and Family Fitness Program Evaluation, Report #4: Evaluation of Resilience Training and Mental and Behavioral Health Outcomes; US Army, Monterey, USA, 2013.

Levy, Becca R. et al.; A Chapter a Day: Association of Book Reading with Longevity; Elsevier, www.sciencedirect.com, September 2016.

Nicholson, Nigel; Critical Leader Relationships; bsr.london.edu, London Business School, London, UK, 2011.

Schaeppi, Werner; Braucht das Leben einen Sinn?, Empirische Untersuchung zu Natur, Funktion und Bedeutung Subjektiver Sinntheorien; Rueegger, Zuerich, Switzerland, 2004.

Schnell, Tatjana; Deutsche in der Sinnkrise?, Ein Einblick in die Sinnforschung mit Daten einer repraesentativen Stichprobe; Journal fuer Psychologie, Berlin, Germany, 2008.

Schnell, Tatjana; Existential Indifference: Another Quality of Meaning in Life; Universitaet Innsbruck, Innsbruck, Austria, 2012.

Schnell, Tatjana; Beim Sinn geht es nicht um Glueck, sondern um das Richtige und Wertvolle, Tatjana Schnell im Gespraech; Psychologie Heute, Weinheim, Germany, 2014.

Schulte, Brigid; Harvard Neuroscientist: Meditation Not Only Reduces Stress, Here's How It Changes Your Brain; The Washington Post, Washington, DC, USA, May 2015.

Trentmann, Nina; Fuenf Dinge, die Sterbende am meisten bedauern, Was bereuen wir, wenn unser Leben zu End geht?; Axel Springer: Die Welt, Hamburg, Germany, 2012.

Ware, Bronnie; The Top Five Regrets of the Dying: A Life Transformed by the Dearly Departing; Hay House, Carlsbad, USA, 2011.

Weise, Elizabeth; Gene Found That Lets People Get by on 6 Hours of Sleep; abc-News, USA, 2017.

8 Epilogue

8.1 Research is "Me-Search"

The link between professional success and resilience has fascinated me for a long time. When I grew up many things were fine in my family and some things were not, just like for many others. As a child, I had always somehow felt that I was wanted and loved. However, for many years there was just too much alcohol and other drugs like tranquillisers being used at home. This created an environment of addiction and co-addiction of which I became a part. It created a secret behind the facade which we were displaying to the outside world as a family. It also created an environment where the really important things like emotions were not spoken about. As a child, you adjust to your environment and since you hardly have any means of comparison you just plod along; at least this is what I did. When everything at home is somehow fragile you are probably not very likely to become a rebel because you feel that your parents just have no capacity left to cope with any sort of trouble. Some weeks were worse than others. I recall that my mum was hospitalised at least three times because of acute intoxication. Once even during the exam period when I was finishing high school. Even when you get somehow used to it, events like these stick with you. Any attempts to talk about addiction and find an ally in my dad led nowhere.

Not surprisingly, this climate of silence in the face of traumatic events had a lasting impact on me. I was depressed and fatalistic. It probably would have been easy for me to take some wrong turns in life. However, there were a couple of important events that helped me to find a good course. Although, one often only realises this in hindsight. One key event happened at school during my 11th grade. Through a school friend I had been told about *zis*, a non-profit organisation founded more than 60 years ago, which gives study grants to young people. The idea was that once you were accepted, along with a topic which you wanted to do research on, you were given the equivalent of about €400 as a scholarship. You were not allowed to take your own money with you and you had to travel internationally. Also, you had to do your trip alone and stay abroad for at least four weeks. Furthermore, you were expected to write a thesis on your subject and keep a diary to capture your thoughts and emotions. The entire idea dates back to the French architect Jean Walter. In 1899 he cycled 6000 km from Paris to Istanbul and back just because he wanted to see the Hagia Sophia. Since he did not have much money he earned his living by playing the trumpet in the streets. He had experienced this as a very difficult but also utterly exciting endeavour which had changed his perspective on life. About 40 years later, after he had become successful and wealthy, Walter founded an organisation which would give study grants to young people to give them the opportunity to experience similar autonomy and that would promote their success both in their profession but also in life overall. He gave this organisation the name *Zellidja*, in reference to the lead and zinc mines which he had discovered in 1924 and which his company exploited in the village of Zellidja Sidi Boubker in Morocco. About ten years after the end of World War II the idea of Zellidja inspired the foundation of what is now called *zis* in Castle Salem, Germany. The organisation still exists today. The only difference being that a study grant today is worth the luxurious amount of €600.

About 30 years ago, two study grants from *zis* helped me to widen my horizon, stretch my understanding of what was possible and develop way more self-confidence. In hindsight, the experiences I underwent on these trips to Scotland and Iceland were priceless for my development. I learned that I could cycle 1700 km alone and stand to get wet every single day without giving up. I learned that you can live on very little money and still have a good time. I learned how it is to be threatened with deportation and how you can turn this around into getting an interview with the state president of Iceland. Today the word we use for demonstrating qualities such as these is resilience – and I have made it my profession to help leaders all over the world to develop more of this inner strength.

After an apprenticeship to become a cabinet maker and my engineering studies, I first joined the world of management consulting, which was very instructive and exhausting at the same time. Then I joined the mechanical engineering industry. As a manager of a large organisation I learned what it means to experience your own limits. I was responsible for a large international IT programme with around 200 employees in various locations around the world. During this time, there were many changes in top management, but I remained in the saddle. I was in shape, did a lot of sports, regularly ran marathons and triathlons and even completed the prestigious Ironman competition. And I was proud of myself and wanted others to appreciate my performance – but actually I wanted them to accept me because I had always felt that I constantly needed to prove myself in order to be good enough. But there was rumbling in the corporate headquarters. I had critics who thought the programme was badly managed and too expensive. I ignored them and instead worked harder to improve the numbers and please the critics. Moreover, my marriage was in crisis mode. After about four years under immense pressure one of my ears had stopped working properly. I woke up in the morning and could not hear properly on the right side. The feeling of not being able to control my own body was extremely scary for me. After too short a break, during which I received regular infusions,

I came back again. But I was weakened and a part of me did not want to do this anymore. In the meantime, my critics had continued their work and after almost a year, I was out. A good measure of this was my email inbox, which went from 200 mails per day to almost 0 within a few days. The feeling of not being used or wanted anymore was very strong and made for many sleepless nights. I felt a great urge to immediately take on the next best job so that I would not feel that feeling anymore. Being persuaded by my wife at the time, I did not do so and withstood the pain and the period of uncertainty. I took half a year for myself and processed the experiences in my first book which is written entirely out of my then martyr mode (so, please don't read it). After completing this sabbatical, I received a very interesting and lucrative offer for an international management position that I could not refuse. In retrospect, this painful episode had been one of the best lessons in my life.

While I emerged stronger from this crisis and progressed to become an entrepreneur and executive coach after further career advances in the consulting industry, my then boss, who had always been an icon of energy and diligence, suffered a severe burnout shortly after I had left. He never fully recovered. The question "why?" has kept me busy for a long time.

When I first heard about the concept of resilience and the associated research results about ten years ago, I was immediately fascinated. What enables people not only to cope with severe crises but also to emerge stronger from them? What quality enables people not only to survive life-threatening environments such as the concentration camps of the Third Reich, but to leave them mentally healthy and life-affirming? What do these people have in common, and what can managers learn from them today?

In recent years, the urgency of this topic has greatly increased for me. This had to do on the one hand with the fact that in my training as an executive coach I wanted to acquire solid basics in psychology. As an engineer and manager, I was naturally lacking them which is why I completed a several-month internship in a prestigious psychosomatic private clinic. There I got to know a lot of managers as patients who, as I learned from conversations with them, were sometimes just a shadow of their former selves. That touched me a lot. On the other hand, the explosive nature of the topic was aggravated by the decreasing predictability of the social and professional environment. In recent years this has been accompanied by an increase in unpredictable violence all over the world but also by a wave of burnouts and suicides, also in my circle of acquaintances. Understanding the concept of resilience is probably more important than ever in such times.

Today I am one of three managing partners of Leadership Choices and I have learned that I actually love being an entrepreneur. I am very grateful for the way my life has turned out. Together, my wife and I have four children and a big dog which keep us busy. They teach me what is really important in life. I don't always listen but I am getting better. While I still have the tendency to prove myself and work too hard, I can say that today I am able to connect what I do almost exclusively to what I believe is truly meaningful in life. This is a great gift. Being able to make a good living from what you love doing and what gives your life meaning is for me the greatest possible success in life!

8.2 Want to make young people more resilient? Here is how!

As I have mentioned, a study grant from *zis* (Figure 8.2.1) allowed me to travel to Iceland to study the scientific whaling programme there – a very political and emotional topic at that time. However, there was one little problem: there was no official way to get to Iceland with a scholarship of just €400, not even 30 years ago. The only thing that was making this endeavour look less like just another foolish idea of a premature teenager was a recommendation letter from *zis* and *UNESCO* stating that I was in fact on a mission and that it was OK.

So, I started contacting the Icelandic embassy and asked for their help to get me to Iceland for free. I was turned down of course. So, I started calling them and again was sent away. However, I kept on calling. Eventually they called me back and told me that I could go aboard a fishing trawler that would be leaving Bremerhaven in two days with a course set to Reykjavik. They did not forget to add that I should please never call them again. So, two days later I headed north to meet the trawler. Once we set off, the weather got really nasty and I was seasick for a full three days until we reached the capital of Iceland.

Once we had arrived I continued to live on the trawler for a couple of days in the harbour of Reykjavik. That was partly due to the cold weather – as it was still snowing in May. But mostly it was because of the immigration authority who wanted to deport me since I did not have enough funds with me to pay for my trip home. Also, at that time I looked like a stereotypical activist from Greenpeace or even Sea Shepherd, a militant offshoot of the eco-activists. The year before, they had sunk two whaling ships in Reykjavik harbour and sabotaged the central whaling station, causing millions in financial damages to the whaling industry. To make everything even worse, the pope was coming to Iceland while I was there and I was seen as a potential risk to his health. The only thing that could save me from being deported at that time was an invitation letter which the ministry of fishery had sent to me during the preparation for this trip. Obviously, this letter was at home, 3000

Figure 8.2.1 www.zis-reisen.de.

km away. And, for the benefit of younger readers, this was in the time before email and mobile phones. And even fax machines were nothing one would have at home. You had to go to the post office to send a fax. It was quite a big thing. Imagine the upheaval my situation caused at home. My parents were probably petrified from their worrying about their only son. By the time the invitation letter finally arrived I had developed a good relationship with a nice lady at the German embassy whom I had contacted in my dire straits.

Once I was allowed by the immigration authorities into the country, I went back to the embassy to ask her a favour. In a magazine, I had read an interview with Iceland's then state president Vigdís Finnbogadóttir (the name means "daughter of Finnboga") about the scientific whaling programme. So, I asked the lady at the embassy if she thought it was possible for me to have a chat with the state president of Iceland with regards to this interview. I still recall how she looked at me with a mix of irritation and amusement in her face. Long story short, a couple of days later I had my meeting with the head of state including me signing into the golden book of Iceland. It might be worth mentioning that none of my clothes even remotely resembled a suit or anything formal. I was really sitting with her in my hiking boots. However, the meeting went well and it even opened the door for me to work on Iceland's central whaling station, which had been sabotaged the year before (see Figure 8.2.2).

Figure 8.2.2 On the whaling station.

In retrospect, the experiences I had gained on this trip at 19 years of age were invaluable for my development and my later successes. There were numerous crises to cope with and it was necessary to be creative and to improvise – skills that are very helpful in this world. Today we would call this inner strength "resilience" – and I have made it my profession to help business leaders around the world to develop more of this.

Having had a childhood with some challenges, I learned for myself that limitations are only constructs in my head and these insights I would like to make available to as many young people as possible.

Therefore, I have decided to support *zis* financially by my own donations and also by raising money for them. In June 2017 I went by bike from Heidelberg, Germany to Verona, Italy on my first fundraising trip. It took me ten days to cycle 1000 km across six countries and climb a total of 10,000 metres of altitude across the Alps. I was able to raise just over €15,000 with this trip and started even to get some media attention for *zis*. In June 2018, I will have gone by bike from Heidelberg to Montpellier which will be about 2300 km and involve climbing about 20,000 meters in altitude. One single study grant costs only €900 including applied overhead costs. My goal is to raise funds for at least 40 scholarships with my next project; that is €36,000 in total.

You can find out more about my fundraising projects here: fb.me/ FundraisingForZis

You can find out more about *zis* here: www.zis-reisen.de

Please feel free to support. Or, in case you have children between 16 and 20 years of age and you want to help them gain more resilience in order for them to feel happy and successful in life, you might want to tell them about *zis*.

Index